CW00495955

MALAULA!

JULIUS BUCKLER:

MALAULA!

The Battle Cry of Jasta 17

Edited by Norman Franks

From a Translation by Adam M Wait

GRUB STREET · LONDON

Published by
Grub Street
4 Rainham Close
London
SW11 6SS

British Library Cataloguing in Publication Data
Buckler, Julius
Malaula!: the battle cry of Jasta 17
1. Buckler, Julius 2. Germany. Luftwaffe. Jagdstaffel 17
3. Fighter pilots – Germany - Biography 4. World War,
1914-1918 – Personal narratives, German 5. World War,
1914-1918 – Aerial operations, German
I. Title II. Franks, Norman L. R.
940.4′4943′092

ISBN-13: 9781904943808

Cover design by Lizzie B design

Typeset by Pearl Graphics, Hemel Hempstead

Printed and bound by MPG Ltd, Bodmin, Cornwall

Grub Street Publishing only uses
FSC (Forest Stewardship Council) paper for its books.

Contents

Acknowledgements

Several people have assisted us with this project and deserve our special thanks. Our mutual friend Greg VanWyngarden has been especially helpful in comments, photographs and advice on aircraft colours and markings. Dan-San Abbott gave freely of his time to draw the four colour side-views that appear on the back cover of the dust jacket, and of course thanks to Barry Weekley for his front cover artwork. Frank (Bill) Bailey and Christophe Cony gave information on French airmen and casualties. Jörg Mückler helped with Buckler's life chronology. Some photographs were also received from Neal O'Connor before his untimely death, and Stewart Taylor. Thanks too go to John Davies of Grub Street Publishing for his enthusiastic response to this project.

Malaula!

'Malaula!' sounded when the order to take off burst in amidst the bustling crowd in the officers' mess of the Jagdfliegerstaffel; 'Malaula!' when we were still busy pulling on our leather jackets and wrapping around our woollen scarves as we dived into the trucks driving up in order to race to the airfield; and 'Malaula!' echoed after us when we had revved the engines and roared away over the frost-covered earth of the wintry Flanders soil.

'Malaula!' – The battle cry of the Staffel.

In a furious dogfight when the enemy placed us in deadly peril by suddenly pulling up and turning his machine with lightning speed; when the certain prey of our machine guns eluded pursuit at the last second through a rescuing dive over enemy territory, or the trailing plume of smoke of the aircraft attacked finally proclaimed the hotly contested victory, then 'Malaula' was on our lips – quick prayer, curse, or triumph.

And 'Malaula!' often still echoed in my ears when in later years life's struggle forced me into swift action or hard decisions.

'Malaula!' – The battle cry of my Staffel!

Introduction

To this new Edition

In the 1930s, former German air ace Julius Buckler wrote, or perhaps dictated, an account of his war years in a book that was published in 1939 (*Malaula! Der Kampfruf meiner Staffel*), by Verlag Ernst Steiniger, Berlin, with an introduction by Peter Supf. Quite a few years ago a pal of mine in America sent me an English translation of this book which I read with interest, and have, from time to time, referred to. It is a good read, made all the more interesting because Buckler was a high-scoring WW1 fighter ace, and also because few books of this nature have been translated into English. Despite twenty years between the action and his telling of it, the book provides a wonderful insight into the world of a WW1 German fighter pilot.

Every once in a while I have given some thought to having the translation published and to editing it. That is to say, comment on Buckler's words and introduce where appropriate, factual happenings about his Staffel and his combat victories. When I finally asked my publisher, John Davies of Grub Street Publishing, whether this would find favour with him, I was pleased when he said yes.

Two things needed to be done initially, firstly try to see if the original publisher was still in being, and to contact the translator, Adam Wait. The first proved difficult and do date Ernst Steiniger & Co, have not been located, but I did find Adam, and he not only enthused over the project, but offered to make a far better translation, as his German had improved immensely over the years. All it needed now was to await the revised translation, and to do some research of my own on what Buckler achieved and whom he had met in combat above the Western Front between 1916-18.

Much is known about Julius Buckler and a lot more can be gleaned from his book, although it has to be said that it is not so much a chronological biography but more a collection of his time in the army, followed by flying tales. Two of my friends commented on his book. First was the late Neal O'Connor, a great collector of WW1 flying items especially medals of the German Air Service. In his last volume of aviation awards to Imperial German airmen he recorded: 'As a story, it makes for exciting reading. As history, it is to be taken with the proverbial grain of salt.' Then

Greg VanWyngarden, another renowned air historian, especially on the German Air Service of WW1, said: I think *Malaula!* is largely oral history, a collection of an old pilot's yarns loosely dictated with little reference to official records.'

As an air historian of long standing (too long some might say!) with a number of published works to my name, I find it somewhat refreshing to read a book where the author – Buckler – does not stick closely to the correct time, whether it is events that happened or aircraft he shot down. So to me it seemed an even better quest to try and put his various anecdotes and adventures into perspective. This does not mean that the original words of Buckler have been changed, merely that as the reader progresses though the book, he will find annotations by me, which will put more meat on the bones.

One certainly gets the impression of and can almost see, Buckler sitting at a desk jotting down his recollections without really worrying about the order in which events took place. Or one can equally imagine him sitting in an armchair, talking over his adventures while someone made notes which in turn became the narrative of the book. It would have been nice if, whatever route was actually taken, things had appeared in a more correct order, but perhaps the book was not meant to be written in this way. It is only today that we historians imagine all things should be written down in a more historically and chronologically correct form.

Many of the great German fighter aces of WW1, being little more than boys or very young men, fought with zeal and fervour, but sometimes the eye saw what the heart wanted to see, so many pilots had victories that did not, in fact, fall, or made the odd dubious claim. All can be explained in some way. With death a constant companion, perhaps it did not matter that the preciseness of an action was a little off centre. They themselves might be dead the next day, so that while we latter-day armchair historians and aviation detectives may from time to time like to prove that something or other did or did not happen, I hope we mostly comprehend the reasons behind certain statements and continue to hold most of our heroes in a good light.

Some of what I have written above will, I hope, become clear as you progress through the pages of a book almost seventy years old, covering events some ninety years ago. WW1 was a period of great conflict, great challenge, and a war fought by people very very different from those who fought in the Second World War, or indeed, people like us today. In fact there is almost no comparison. Aviation itself was new and every day men flew into the unknown. And I don't suppose any of the aviators of ninety years ago thought that long in the future people would make a study of their timorous activities in a war too horrible to really understand.

Today many countries mourn the loss of a soldier doing his duty in a foreign country. Two or three such losses fill the headlines. Each loss, of course, is a heartbreak for family and loved ones. Yet on some days in

WW1, the dead could be numbered in thousands. On the first day of the Somme, 1 July 1916, over 20,000 British soldiers died in the first hour of battle alone. We accept the history of those numbers, but cannot begin to think of the cost to these men's parents, wives, brothers, comrades, sweethearts, children, friends. Generations are different, aren't they?

So, enjoy Buckler's war story*, for what it is, and hopefully the comments I've made will make it an even better read.

Norman Franks, East Sussex, England

* Although we have not changed Buckler's words, there did need to be some slight changes in presentation (especially less use of italicisation) and perhaps, in a few instances, a better word used. Buckler's style of the day meant many short, sharp sentences. The book reads better if some are joined together to make a longer sentence. However, nothing has been changed of his original story and one hopes the reader can pick his way through the errors in chronology without it spoiling what is essentially, an excellent story.

Original Introduction

By Peter Supf

Only now, after more than twenty years, has Julius Buckler been able to decide, at the urging of his friends, to record his wartime experiences, which are astonishing in every respect. Inhibitions of a particular sort had restrained him from doing so. The reader detects this between the lines. With the words: 'From Roofer's Apprentice to *Pour le Mérite Officer*' [the book's original subtitle – Ed.], a purely superficial attempt has been made to describe the arc leading from the unknown working lad to the celebrated war hero and which in the figure of fighter pilot Julius Buckler encompasses a human destiny surprisingly rich in amazing events and unusual experiences. A destiny which is not based on extraordinary attributes, unusual talents, or especially fortuitous circumstances, but rather entirely on his own diligence!

Therein lies the exemplary nature of such a life for many thousands of young people. His successes are based on hard work, ability, sense of duty, patriotism, ambition, and a good measure of youthful audacity. So no superman stands before us in the person of this young German fighter pilot, whose mighty deeds remain eternally unobtainable by other mortals. But through the ardour of his heart, the strength of his courage, and a repeated inner struggle he accomplishes feats worthy of a Hercules.

The time of the 'Knights of the Air' who alone or with a band of likewise fearless comrades scoured the sky for the enemy in order to measure themselves against them in duels to the death, is over. Flying in close attacking formations, as present air warfare requires, demands a new nameless heroism which is yet greater in external discipline and inner willingness to sacrifice. However, the great heroes of the World War remain as models and admonishers! To them also belongs the labourer's son Julius Buckler, who was promoted to officer and decorated with the *Pour le Mérite* for bravery in the face of the enemy.

His father was certain that his son would become a roofer like himself even as he lay in the cradle. As a twelve-year-old he used his school vacations to carry roof tiles up the steep ladders to his father and the journeymen. Whilst doing so he carried not a tile less than the professional carriers. At the beginning of his actual apprenticeship he mastered the roofer's trade as well as an apprentice after two years of training. After one-and-a-half years of apprenticeship his father entrusted tasks to him which usually only a journeyman with three to five years of experience is capable of undertaking.

During his travels the roofer's apprentice Julius Buckler [at this time he had completed his apprenticeship and had become a journeyman – Ed.] was given the job of re-covering an entire roof from the peak to the eaves on a church tower in a small town. For a seventeen-year-old this was a great and honourable task, and not just from a roofer's standpoint. The inhabitants of the Swabian village felt this as well when they called him a *mordskerrle* ['a hell of a guy'], bought him evening drinks in the tavern and prophesied a great future for him.

With thirty-five confirmed aerial victories Julius Buckler ranks as seventeenth amongst all of the *Pour le Mérite* fighter pilots and sixth amongst those still living today [1939]. Because for a soldier from the ranks being promoted to officer for bravery in the face of the enemy is considered the highest distinction, it is as though Buckler received the *Pour le Mérite* twice – as has often been recorded in the newspapers. 'But how wonderful it must be for youth to receive such an order entirely for their own accomplishments,' said General von der Marwitz, on 3 December 1917, as he lay the *Pour le Mérite* on the twenty-three-year-old fighter pilot Julius Buckler in his sick-bed, who had just been promoted to Leutnant due to bravery in the face of the enemy.

Personal achievement was really everything for the young officer, who gazed upon the blue cross for a long time with reverence before smiling and touching it with his fingers. At that time he already had thirty aerial victories behind him, of which he obtained the 27th, 28th and 29th in a single day, and he was lying wounded in a military hospital for the fourth time. Of all the victories of Jagdstaffel 17, to which he belonged, he had achieved more than half.

For a long time, before command of the Staffel was transferred to him in August 1918 – after returning barely healed from his fifth wounding to the front and his comrades – he had been its leader in the air. Their commander constantly turned command over to him as soon as the Staffel flew against the enemy. This special and prominent position in the Staffel, Buckler owed solely to his outstanding bravery and his great flying ability.

Julius Buckler is one of the five German flyers [awarded the Blue Max] who came from a working-class background and were promoted to officer. And oddly enough – or perhaps it is not so odd – two of the others were also roofers. They were similar to him in their unflagging desire to engage in battle boldly and aggressively. Both of them fell in battle. One of them, Fritz Rumey, perished while pursuing a foe.[1] Overstrained by the furious speed of the dive, the wings of both aircraft came off almost simultaneously and their fuselages bored into the earth next to each other.

The other, Max Müller – 'Müller-Max!' – called the 'Flyer of Rottenburg' after his home town in Bavaria – suffered the same fate as that which Buckler prepared for his thirteenth opponent, of which he writes that he would be willing to experience everything again except this.[2]

In his war memoirs Buckler does not at all draw a picture of himself as a 'knight beyond fear and reproach'. He recognises his mistakes and knows his shortcomings. Fear is also no stranger to him. His honest battle with the 'inner *Schweinehund*' allows us to experience more intensely than otherwise the dangerous circumstances of individual flights. The way sympathy for his fallen foe as a living being and fellow man becomes for him an eternal problem of war only deepens the spiritual attitude of the combatant. His report ends with the final 'Malaula' of the Staffel.

Like so many old flyers, Buckler cannot entirely separate himself from the aviation world. Again and again he returns to it, often only in indirect contact. When he climbed into an aircraft for the first time in seven years, sitting at the controls was his old patron from the field, Major Keller, who in the meantime had taken over a civilian flying school and could use him as an instructor. But soon the aerobatic flying enticed him into again giving up this position in order to lead the gypsy's life of a stunt pilot moving from air display to air display.

At this time he met up with Udet[3] and Fieseler[4], who were likewise making an effort through their performances to awaken the will to fly again in the German people. But since maintaining an aircraft costs a lot and the aerial exhibitions brought in little money, he was reduced to a pauper by his love of flying. A chance encounter with an acquaintance brought him back to the building trade. Here once again due to his perseverance and ability, within a few years he held a leading position.

Buckler could not forget aviation, though. In 1932 he joined a flying unit of the SA. In the following year he obtained his new pilot's licence. As a regimental commander of the National Socialist Flying Corps he flew successfully in the great *Deutschlandflüge* [annual competitive long-distance flights] in 1937 and 1938. But none of this satisfied him!

---

[1] Fritz Rumey flew with Jasta 5 and achieved forty-five victories. On 27 September, flying a Fokker DVII, he collided with a British SE5a fighter, and although he took to his parachute, the apparatus failed to deploy and he fell to his death.

[2] Max Müller scored thirty-six victories and was also the recipient of the *Pour le Mérite*, flying with Jasta 2 and Jasta 28. He was shot down in combat with an RE8 observation machine on 9 January 1918. With his Albatros ablaze he took the final leap to Valhalla.

[3] Ernst Udet was credited with sixty-two victories in WW1 and was another winner of the coveted *Pour le Mérite*. He was also the highest scoring pilot to survive WW1. A sporting aerobatic pilot in the inter-war years he was cajoled into joining the new Luftwaffe, but could not cope with the political intrigue and in-fighting as well as a heavy work load, so committed suicide on 17 November 1941.

[4] Gerhard Fieseler flew with Jasta 25 on the Eastern front in WW1, gaining nineteen air combat victories. After the war he became both an aerobatic pilot and managed his own aeroplane company. He died on 1 September 1987, at the age of ninety-one.

Today he is still a soldier in body and soul and so he reports voluntarily for military training. Only in May of this year when he also flew the latest fighter planes was he satisfied. Now the old wartime pilot and *Pour le Mérite* hero stands tall next to his young comrades of the new Luftwaffe created by Generalfeldmarshall Göring. And when the Poles provoked us and forced us into battle, promoted to Major d.R. [Major in the Reserve], he took over the leadership of a Schutzstaffel.

Peter Supf

Translator's Preface

Adam M Wait

Considering the actual number of memoirs produced by German airmen of the First World War, one might say it is surprising how very few have been translated into English and published. Those of Germany's most famous flyer, Manfred von Richthofen, and the high-scoring air ace and pioneer of fighter tactics Oswald Boelcke, actually became available in English even before the war ended. An improved translation of Richthofen's *Der rote Kampflieger* was written by Peter Kilduff and published as The Red Baron in 1969. The original manuscript of *Hauptmann Boelcke's Feldberiche* by Robert Reynold Hirsch – *An Aviator's Field Book* – was reprinted by the Battery Press in 1991. Germany's second highest scoring ace of that conflict, Ernst Udet, also dictated an account of his flying experiences before the guns fell silent, but this book has never appeared in any language other than German. It was his second memoir, *Mein Fliegerleben* (1935), covering his flying career from WW1 to the early thirties, which was selected for publication in English two years after the original German edition was released. This was re-translated as well, by Richard K Riehn, with the title *Ace of the Iron Cross* in 1970.

A first-hand account of the most famous flying unit of World War 1, Richthofen's Jagdgeschwader I (colloquially known as the 'Flying Circus'), was written by the unit's adjutant, Karl Bodenschatz, under the title *Jagd in Flanders Himmel*. Though he was not a pilot, his book does present an insider's view of the personnel and operations of this legendary fighter unit. First printed in 1935, it was not until 1996 that it appeared in English, translated by Jan Hayzlett, as *Hunting with Richthofen*, published by Grub Street.

In the early to mid-thirties the memoirs of some lesser-known German aviators of the Great War were rendered into English by Claud W Sykes and published by the London firm of John Hamilton, Ltd. These included *Wings of War* (German title *Jagdstaffel-unsere Heimat*) by eleven-victory ace Rudolf Stark, and a trilogy of lively reminiscences by Hauptmann Georg Heydemarck, who served in a reconnaissance unit on the Western Front and in Macedonia The former was printed once more by Arms and Armour Press (London) in 1973, while more of this valuable series of books were re-issued in paperback by London's Greenhill Press in the 1980s. Two books that seem never to be out of print are *Knight of Germany* by Professor Johannes Werner, first published in English in 1933, and *Immelmann, Eagle of Lille* by Franz Immelmann in 1935. Both were translated by Claud Sykes and told the stories of the first German fighter pilots to win the 'Blue Max', Oswald Boelcke and Max Immelmann, and both were from Hamilton Publishing.

While Hamilton was supplying the British public with exciting tales of aerial adventures both from the war and more recent events in the Golden Era of aviation, there was a sizeable stream of First World War flyers' memoirs flowing from the presses in Germany. The sudden upsurge in the publication of such books in 1933 coincided with Hitler's rise to power and the number of *Kreigserinnerungen* of German ace fighter pilots, reconnaissance flight crews, and members of bombing units, multiplied steadily, not tapering off until after the beginning of the Second World War. Amongst the last of these was a book by fighter ace Julius Buckler with an eye-catching title *Malaula! Der Kampfruf meiner Staffel.* The author was a *Pour le Mérite* ace with thirty-five victories and also qualified as a 'balloon buster' with seven of these inflated observation platforms in his score. Buckler was in every respect the leading light of one of the less famous fighter units, Jagdstaffel 17. He scored more than a third of the Jasta's 110 confirmed victories and led it in the air until being promoted to become its Staffelführer in August 1918. Buckler's receipt of Germany's highest military honour also lent a touch of prestige to the unit. Moreover, he was the only member of Jasta 17 to serve from the first to last day of its operations. During this period, he was absent from the Staffel for about eight months as a result of being repeatedly wounded in action. His memoirs provide highlights of his service on the ground and in the air which, coupled with anecdotes, are all conveyed with a liveliness, modesty, compassion and touch of humour.

The decision to write his wartime experiences, as Peter Supf states in the original introduction to the book (reproduced here), did not originate with Buckler himself. The 'friends' who urged him to do so were no doubt in part located in official quarters. In the years leading up to the outbreak of WW2, there was an apparent drive initiated by the Nazi German government to produce memoirs of former combat flyers which could serve both as general propaganda for the broader public as well as a means of inspiring the nation's young men to join Hitler's newly-constituted Luftwaffe. This intention is clearly evident in the forewords and conclusions to works of German aviation literature published at the time. A succinct example is to be found in a few words of introduction to Jasta 6 pilot Carl Holler's *Als Sänger-Flieger im Weltkriege* (1934). They were written by naval ace and recipient of the *Pour le Mérite*, Friedrich Christiansen and read: 'Youth should recognise from the deeds of our war heroes, conveyed by a qualified authority, what manly courage, coupled with discipline and idealism are capable of accomplishing. Only those who have a firm goal in mind can accomplish great things! It is our task and foremost duty to instil this into our rising generation of flyers!'

At the outset of his introduction to *Malaula!* Peter Supf holds up the figure of Julius Buckler as an example worthy of emulation by German youth. He stresses the personal qualities which underlie all his accomplishments. It is clearly indicated that Buckler's memoirs are not just to serve the purpose of entertaining the readers and informing them about a famous flyer, but rather are intended to help shape their character and prepare them to be useful citizens of a nation bent on a war of conquest.

This is apparent already in the opening pages of the narrative. Buckler's father is presented as a model of soldierly virtue. The former infantryman turned roofer chose his profession in part because '(t)he continual proximity of danger suited his soldierly nature.' He educates his son in military principles such as 'He who wants to command must learn to obey.' The young Julius Buckler also learns of military strategy while at play, organising with his friends ambushes and pitched battles against other groups of boys. These exercises are described as helpful in building the necessary character for future soldiers. Buckler states that 'we lost the fear of looking the enemy in the eye and giving battle at an early age.' He learned in addition the value of loyalty and comradeship. Furthermore, the 'little tricks' devised later proved useful in actual warfare.

Though blatantly propagandistic elements of Buckler's memoirs – which may well have been inserted by an editor – might be of value for students of the Third Reich, this annotated translation is intended for those historians and hobbyists whose specific interest lies in discovering more about the history of aviation during the First World War. For this reason, some of the propaganda has been left out. The decision to do so was based on its lack of relevance to the primary subject matter, its dubious authenticity, and additionally in order to create a more palatable narrative.

A flagrant example of National Socialist propaganda is found in an anti-Semitic episode which is no doubt entirely apocryphal. This was inserted into the section titled 'Childhood' at a point when the Buckler family fortunes were beginning to look up. For some reason Buckler's father borrows money from a Jew and is able to repay all of it except the high usurer's interest. The Jew shouts angrily at him and refuses to listen to an offer to pay the sum in instalments. When the father is absent at work, this Shylockian character harasses the family. The seven-year-old Julius, who is enraged by 'this repulsive, filthy person with the greedy flickering look in his black eyes,' being the only male of the family present, defends his mother and sisters against this fiend. The stout-hearted lad, wielding a slat, drives the Jew away screaming in an abject cowardly fashion. Anti-Semitic episodes or statements were a token part of almost every war memoir produced in Germany during this period.

This is a fact which should not be concealed, yet the translator felt it was best to leave this part of the memoir out of the translation. It was considered preferable to deal with the matter in a preface, rather than disrupting the main narrative with such an offensive passage.

There is another troublesome character, equally (assumed) fictitious, who is not included in the translation. He is described as 'a shady fellow with glaring green eyes, bristly hair [and] dangling limbs.' So he appeared in a dream recounted by Buckler in a section titled 'The Inner *Schweinehund*'. This German expression refers to one's baser self which is governed by fear or sluggishness in doing the right thing. The nature of the 'inner *Schweinehund*' is spelled out quite specifically in this section. He is a 'scoundrel who creeps up on you when you are all alone, who whispers to you that your own little self is so important that you can avoid your great obligation to serve the whole and can shirk your responsibility towards your nation [*Volk*] in a cowardly fashion. Buckler struggles with him in the dream and achieves a temporary victory. However, the 'inner *Schweinehund*' accompanies Buckler on his subsequent flights as a sort of fear-mongering gremlin trying to dissuade him from performing his duty.

Peter Supf states that the occasional presence of the 'inner *Schweinehund*' brings the perilous circumstances of Buckler's flights closer to the reader. However, one might question how the introduction of a sort of fairy tale figure into the narrative is supposed to make it seem more real. It is clear from the description of this menacing kobold that he is not simply a literary device used to evoke an emotional response. Rather, the dark spirit serves another, quite odious purpose – that of programmatic indoctrination. The fear Germany's youth would feel when first encountering the horrors of war was naturally anticipated by those working in the Ministry of Public Enlightenment and Propaganda. It was a problem which needed to be addressed and neutralised as much as possible. In this instance, the natural desire to flee as a response arising from imminent danger is embodied in a sub-human creature which, if it cannot be permanently destroyed, must at least be forcibly driven away – that is, suppressed.

Though this curious personification of the 'inner *Schweinehund*' might be considered by some to be a necessary part of Buckler's memoir, as it reflects some whimsical aspect of his nature or expresses a facet of his imagination, it was decided to leave out all references to this mischievous hobgoblin. As previously stated, the purpose of this volume is not to reproduce ancient National Socialist propaganda. Furthermore, from a literary standpoint, the text is much better served without the odd creature, which in the end may have been intended to appeal to the juvenile members of the readership.

One final brief episode was omitted from the translation. It was titled 'Leave With a Face-Slapping' and appeared directly after the 'Solo Flight Festivities and Pilot's Test'. This section was devoted entirely to the description of a small incident at the beginning of Buckler's period of furlough after the completion of his initial flight training. Buckler visits his former regiment in Mainz and is insulted by an old, corpulent Unteroffizier who doubts his claim that he completed his pilot's training in such a short span of time. Buckler reacts with rage and slaps him soundly. The surly Unteroffizier, instead of retaliating, meekly submits with a stammered, 'It's all the same to me.' Buckler explains to the reader that his reaction was not one of offended conceit, but rather involved a matter of honour which was part of 'inner cleanliness'. Something of this sort may well have occurred, but the pointedly moral message intent of the described incident and the utterly contrived manner of its presentation provide some reason for doubt. Since this section contained no worthwhile information beyond the fact that Buckler visited his former regiment, it was left out.

Also in his introduction, Peter Supf states that 'the great heroes of the World War remain as models and admonishers' [*'Vorbid und Mahner aber bleiben die grossen Helden des Weltkrieges!'*] This is a theme that is built upon throughout the entire narrative. Buckler's first model of comportment is his father, from whom he inherits soldierly ideals. His father is a master roofer who teaches his craft to young Julius and instructs him in a proper work ethic. Then the tide of world events sweeps Buckler into a second trade, that of a combat pilot.

In his new field of endeavour Buckler is educated in various ways by an assortment of people. The gatekeeper he encounters shortly after his arrival in Grossenhain gives him a thorough initiation into 'the life and goings-on at the flying school'. There he discovered a Leutnant Walter Höfig, a true master pilot who flew 'like a god' and whom Buckler credits with 'the whole great transformation of my life'. Not only does Höfig provide very thorough and practical flight instruction, but he also dispenses sage advice, as when Buckler has problems with his landings.

Buckler's fellow pilot Hübner, with whom he shared his quarters at Frescaty, becomes a mentor of a different sort. He introduces Buckler to a whole new world of culinary culture and refined manners, which will later prove to be of special benefit when he becomes an officer. This training for new social surroundings is continued by his observer in Flieger Abteilung (A) 209. Oberleutnant Hubertus von Rudno-Rudzinsky.

Buckler expresses appreciation to all those who assist him in reaching his goals, but his ultimate inspiration comes from model figures – celebrated war heroes such as Hauptmann Oswald Boelcke. Buckler and 'Rudno' encounter the great Boelcke in the air and subsequently meet him on their own airfield, afterwards enjoying his presence as a guest in their mess. In the memoir this early air ace and pioneer of fighter tactics is portrayed as a man with an aura of transcendence, having been transfigured by a sacred cause, not unlike a figure of sainthood touched by the Divinity:

> An almost solemn gravity emanated from Boelcke and a great inner refinement was expressed in all his movements. One distinctly perceived the high sense of duty which filled him. He had dedicated himself to the Fatherland with every last thread of his being. From his eyes radiated the freedom of serenity of a person who stood above all things and who was every moment prepared to gladly sacrifice his life for that which to him was the most lofty ideal on Earth.

Boelcke is thus the tacit 'Admonisher', whose example bids others to dedicate themselves with equal fervour to the cause of the Fatherland. The image of Boelcke is conjured once more in the section titled 'The Thirteenth'. In a pensive moment, gazing out of the window of the mess at a brewing thunderstorm, Buckler reflects on Germany's great air heroes and how their accomplishments make his own pale in comparison. Above all he is haunted by the memory of Boelcke's 'serious countenance', remarking that '(t)here was but a single goal to be seen in his face, that of victory'. Buckler states that Boelcke 'was a model for us and a reminder'.

These reflections are dramatically underscored by distant thunder and lightning flashes on the horizon, with a theatricality reminiscent of Wagnerian opera. It is as though nature is mingling with voices from beyond to exhort Buckler to great deeds. On perfect cue, the roar of anti-aircraft fire interrupts his internal monologue and signals the call to action. Buckler swiftly responds, roaring off into the angry skies to a fateful encounter with an enemy flyer above the clouds. The foe is vanquished in a terrible climactic scene which Buckler recalls with an expression of horror.

The events described have basis in fact. The exact date of this aerial combat – 14 July, 1917 – is left unmentioned in the original memoir. However, the time, place and Allied airman involved have been established. It is also quite likely that there was inclement weather that day. That too could be corroborated with available documents. In any case, it is important for the reader to bear in mind that the ultimate importance of Buckler's memoirs to those who published them was not the recording of historical events *per se*, but rather the purpose they served. They were intended to promote the ideals of National Socialism in Germany and support Hitler's preparations for war. Accordingly, one might expect the description of events occasionally to be tailored to this end.

A good example of this is Buckler's farewell speech to the Staffel. It is not unlikely that the members of Jagdstaffel 17 would have fallen in for the final address by their commanding officer. However, such a speech would probably have borne little resemblance to that quoted, which is filled with themes typical of Nazi propaganda. The overall theme is that of loyalty. The whole issue of loyalty bears a special meaning within the context of National Socialist ideology, which incorporated a pre-Christian

Germanic warrior ethos in which *treue* (loyalty) and *ehre* (honour) were the supreme values. It also contains the myth so popular in Nazi propaganda that Germany was not beaten militarily, but rather owed its defeat to betrayal on the home front. Perhaps the most important line in this speech is the statement that, 'if the Fatherland should need us again, we will all be prepared to serve once more as far as it lies in our power.' The message to the reader, whose nation was just entering a new world war, is abundantly clear. This speech forms a necessary part of the conclusion to that sub-chapter and no thought was given to deleting any of it from the translation. It was however, considered inappropriate to reprint the speech without comment.

As a final note, it should be mentioned that there has been a slight reorganisation of contents in this translation of *Malaula!* The original German memoir was divided into fifty sections, which are too short to be considered chapters in their own right. The forty-eight sections in the English edition have been retained as sub-chapters with their original headings. These have been grouped into larger chapters supplied with new titles. This was done in order to bring greater clarity to the text as a whole.

Adam M Wait,
California, USA

Chapter One

A Roofer's Son

Childhood

My father was a roofer. When the frost came and brought construction work to a halt, his income dried up and our troubles began. Our meagre savings were quickly used up, and other work could not always be found. For this reason my parents looked forward with even more concern than usual to the winter of 1893-4, in which I came into the world.

Older people in Mainz, the 'Golden City on the Rhine', still remember this winter to this day. It was the coldest in many years, yet this also had its good side. Something occurred which worked like a miracle and rescued my parents from all their troubles. The Rhine froze over. Broad expanses were swept smooth into sparkling rinks, ice games were organised, booths were set up, sleds were rented, and little sausages and chestnuts were sold. Heavy wooden discs bounced dully off one another in games of ice skittles. Bands played marches and dance tunes. Banners fluttered and colourful Chinese lanterns swayed in the breeze of an early winter twilight. It was like one big public festival. There was enough work to go round and my father made good money. Using his savings, he had leased one of the many ice rinks.

On the 28th of March, the day I was born, the festival on ice was still in full swing, and it lasted on into the spring. I was hardly a few weeks old when my mother wrapped me in warm clothes and took me out onto the Rhine. While she helped my father, my sister, who was but a few years older, looked after me. In later years my mother spoke so vividly about the whole thing, the surging crowds and sounds of merriment upon the ice, that I feel like I really experienced it first-hand. Even today at sixty-nine years old she can recall every detail of this happy winter. In the spring, when it began to thaw, the ice started to split and crack, sounding just like cannon fire.

My mother was nineteen years old when she married. People called her 'beautiful Mina'. My father was a large imposing man whom no one would have taken as a roofer when he went out in his dark coat and perfectly white upturned collar for a Sunday stroll with his pretty young wife. His father had actually wanted to make a goldsmith out of him, but he decided on his own to take up the roofing profession. This was a dangerous trade! That may have been the very thing which attracted him to it, for he was not one to settle for a comfortable, mundane life.

He worked at a dizzying height, gazing upon the wide blue sky and looking down upon the city's maze of roofs, from which the many towers projected, as well as the sparkling Rhine with its barges and steamships. This was more than just a job to him, it was his heart's delight and an inner necessity. Up there he felt free and liberated from all restrictions. The continual proximity of danger and the hardships of his duty suited his soldierly nature.

Because of his great skill and conscientiousness he was hired for all the difficult jobs in the city. While repairing the roof on the high peaked tower of the St Boniface Church he was pulled up by way of a primitive hoist operated by an apprentice as he sat freely on a wooden board. Even the roofing work on the mighty cupola of St Stephen's Church was carried out by my father. He never demanded a special bonus for such dangerous jobs. As good a worker as my father was, one thing he was not – a good businessman. So it is no wonder that for a long time he did not succeed in becoming independent and that again and again poverty came knocking at our door.

Other winters arrived in which the Rhine did not freeze over, so my mother and father had to work hard to earn their daily bread. My father helped out wherever there was an opportunity, while my mother washed and mended clothes for strangers. We children, my two sisters and I, stayed home and played in the kitchen and the bedroom, which were the only two rooms in our apartment on the fifth floor of an old Mainz tenement building. We did not notice much of all the misery. However, it must have often been very difficult for my parents at that time not seeing any way out. Otherwise an event from my childhood which impressed itself upon me indelibly could not be understood.

I was six at the time, and yet another small sister was added to the family. One winter's day my mother picked her up in one arm, wrapped her securely, and told the rest of the family to dress warmly. She then left the house with us children and for a long time we wandered through the streets. When it began to get dark you went down to the Rhine, mother. As young as we were, we could still sense what was going on inside you. We could see it in your dismayed expression. In my fear I attempted to console you. 'Never mind, mother. When I'm big I'll help you.' 'Yes, my little boy,' you replied softly. 'God will not forsake us.'

But as you said this you gazed upon the Rhine searchingly and continued walking with us helplessly. I know, mother, that you never could have brought yourself to take our lives along with your own. But I do not know what would have become of us that evening if we had not in fact been helped by someone, as though he were sent by God. A man approached you who looked like an old ship's captain. He had probably been following us for quite some time. After a couple of warm words he pressed your hand and disappeared again. But you stared almost helplessly as before at the Rhine and at the coin in your hand. I also know, mother, that you would have rushed after the man and given him the money back, were it not for us children.

There followed an evening the likes of which can only really be understood by someone who has had a similar experience. We were quite beside ourselves with joy and gratitude. A winning lottery ticket could not have made us any happier. Our first trip was to a baker. Then we bought milk for my little sister, eggs, some marmalade, lard, and malt coffee. Loaded up with these delicacies, we headed home.

My father probably sensed that something was wrong when he came home from work and found the kitchen unheated and his wife and children missing. He must have waited in great anxiety, for when the door opened and we came in, he rushed towards us, took my mother in his arms, and kissed her. He stood there with some misgivings as we triumphantly unpacked the delicacies, but there was a questioning, almost alarmed, expression in his eyes.

'Jule,' my mother said, 'we have no coal or wood in the house. Go get some.'

'We'll have some money by tomorrow,' my father answered in a worried tone. Then my mother laid a one mark piece on the table. A hundredweight of coal cost 80 pfennig and the wood cost 20. My father stared at the coin in shock and his countenance darkened.

'Jule, go on now!' my mother urged. 'The children still haven't eaten anything and they're frozen through. Later, when they're in bed, I'll tell you what happened.'

Then, after a long meal, as we lay warm beneath the covers, my older sisters and I in a bed and the youngest one in the cradle, the fire crackling in the next room, we heard our parents speaking with one another in urgent tones for a long time. We knew how much our father loved our mother and that he would understand everything she did and not be angry with her. We of course had no idea how much this experience hurt his pride, how horribly it upset him, and brought home to him the entire untenable circumstances of our existence. Reassured, full, and satisfied, we fell asleep.

Soon spring arrived and construction started up again. My father found work and seemed to be earning more than usual. In any event, there was never again an instance in which we were without money and had to borrow from merchants in the neighbourhood.

* * *

At six years of age I entered primary school. Learning was very easy for me. In the evening my father would listen to me recite my lessons. First came one's duty, then play; I never knew anything different. When I was through with my homework I would then have to do some shopping, take care of some business orders, or run small errands for strangers. There was often no time left for play. And so it went on from year to year.

My youngest sister, who was named Elisabeth and was everyone's darling, died when she was three quarters of a year old. Malnutrition and the gnawing effects of my mother's anxiety at the very time she was carrying the child may have contributed to her early death. This occurrence had a remarkably profound and heavy effect upon me. My mind could not grasp it and yet it occupied my imagination to a great extent, especially in the evening before I said my prayers. My little dead sister had become a sort of guardian angel to me who was secretly looking after all of us in heaven and who, so I fancied, watched over me with quite special affection.

When left to my own devices, I ran down to the alley. For a boy – in the meantime I had turned ten years old – there was opportunity enough to let off steam. As in all other smaller and larger towns, we primary school students were in a constant feud, an ancient feud so to speak, with the students of higher schools. The assembly point of the enemy camp was the Big Sand. This was the Mainz parade ground where the annual Kaiser Parade took place. Nine years later I was a participant in it as an infantryman. We set up our camp in a sand pit, while look-outs safeguarded it against the enemy. Here campaign plans were drawn up, stratagems devised, and ambushes prepared down to the last detail.

Because I helped with all the household chores and in addition – in order to earn a few groschen – chopped wood, hauled ice, and set up ninepins in a nearby pub, I was superior in strength and dexterity to most of the boys my age. In addition, I had inherited an air of practicality. So I was always automatically chosen as the leader of important wartime operations, ambushes, daring flanking movements, or sneak patrols. When it came to battle we first advanced throwing rocks and attempted with well-aimed throws and loud war cries to send our opponent fleeing. If he stood his ground we attacked him with our fists and self-fashioned wooden weapons such as swords and spears. Then it came to a regular battle which finally ended in wrestling and boxing matches.

The model for these battles were the knife fights of the infamous Rentengasse gangs – members of the Mainz underworld – in the harbour district. These were often quite bloody and we heard about them, but never saw them take place. I was in the fifth class at school, which was well-known for its gutsiness. Wherever trouble was brewing and a reliable assault party was needed, we of the 'fifth' were on hand.

However wild and disorderly our battles may have appeared to non-participants, they never got out of hand. There were unwritten laws to which we strictly adhered. We maintained our sense of honour no less than officers and members of student fraternities. The younger boys had nothing to fear from us. Conscious of our superiority, we merely chased them away from the battlefield with threatening words.

If this playful kind of warfare only arose from our bravado and desire for adventure, it still had its benefits in that it sharpened our senses and gave us a first taste of military thinking. Later, in the war, when it became a matter of life or death, I sometimes profited from the little tricks we learned at the time. In addition to that, we lost the fear of looking the enemy in the eye and giving battle at an early age. We learned to trust in our own strength and to value comradeship. Everyone knew what to expect from the others, and everyone appreciated the respect he enjoyed amongst his comrades and because of this felt himself doubly obligated to stand his ground.

Another opportunity to put one's courage and agility to the test was offered by joyrides on steam trains and horse-drawn trollies. There it was a matter of jumping off at full speed just before the conductor came to collect fares. We did not intend to be dishonest and most of the time we had to run back along the stretch we had ridden for free. For us boys it was a sport like any other. We brought about our own punishment in that often enough while jumping off we sprained our ankles or hit our heads on the pavement. Of course, one proudly tried to hide it. One time I fell so badly that I had to be taken to the doctor and have my head bandaged. This resulted in me receiving a sound thrashing at home.

Also very popular with us boys in Mainz were feats of climbing. The Rhine bridge with its pillars and arches offered a perfect invitation. In the summer it was not especially dangerous and if one made a false step or could no longer hang on, then one merely fell into the depths of the river. We could all swim like fish and the sun quickly dried our clothes. One day in March when it was still cool I absolutely had to risk another climb. Whilst doing so I slipped and fell into the icy water below. Due to the high water at this time of year the current was pretty strong, so I was only able to make it to shore with great effort and became thoroughly exhausted. Out of fear of punishment I ran around in the cold March wind until not only were my things dry, but I had also caught a bad cold. On my sick-bed I had to promise my mother never again to make the Rhine bridge the object of my stunts. I stayed true to this promise in the sense it was meant at the time, but twelve years later I flew an aeroplane beneath that very same bridge, which was a daring stunt not only by the standards of that time.

The worst punishment for a boy in Mainz was to be prevented from going to the Mainz fair. This happened to me when I was twelve. For days I had been busy at the fairground setting up booths, carousels, swing-boats and shooting ranges. All of Mainz was looking forward to the day on which the hustle and bustle would begin, and no one was looking forward to it more than we boys.

Since the fairgrounds were taken, we had to move our sling games to the 'Brand,' a spot in front of the post office. For these games we used a wooden ball of considerable size which was thrown with the aid of a length of twine. The higher and farther it flew, the greater was our pride and the respect of our playmates. Ambitious as I already was then, no throw could be high or far enough for me. In my enthusiasm I let all caution go to the wind and misfortune struck! The ball duly soared with full force into the shop window of a clockmaker. A few seconds later the furious store owner grabbed me by the collar and, without listening to my stammered apologies, dragged me before my paternal judge.

To my surprise, for the first time I did not receive a thrashing. My father, who had a definite and well-considered way of bringing up his children, now probably thought me too old for that. But the punishment which I received instead was in my view much, much worse. For every mark my father paid for the broken window pane – it would cost five marks – I would have to remain at home for a full day. To my sorrow they were the very same days that the fair was taking place. While my friends were riding the carousel, swinging, or in some other way enjoying themselves, I stood at the window like a prisoner and stared miserably over the rooftops. Nonetheless, the punishment seemed just to me. From early on I knew the value of money and realised how hard it was on my father to have to pay such a large amount for my stupid stunt.

* * *

Many people are pursued by a run of bad luck and it was the case with me that year. Amongst my many daily obligations was also the duty of a non religious novice. That meant being at church punctually every morning, and since I was on good terms with the bell-ringer, I was allowed to take part in ringing the bell before mass. What appealed to me most was the dizzying climb to the belfry. I was up above in the tower more than I was down below in the sacristy.

On the day before Whitsuntide I received a new suit. This was a big event for the whole family. Early in the morning I went proudly with my new suit to the church. On Whitsuntide morning High Mass was sounded, whereby all the bells were rung, This was not so simple as it was especially difficult to bring 'Grandmother', as we boys called the largest bell, into motion. Each time the ringing ceased there was a scuffle because everyone wanted to hang on the rope of this big bell, which due to its mighty inertia took the most time to stop swinging. I was already hanging on the rope when two rowdies grabbed me by the lappet [a small hanging flap] of my jacket. That threw the rope off course and it swung sideways, carrying me up against one of the belfry's beams. This had a nail in it which, to my horror, made its presence known by snagging onto my new jacket and slitting it open. When I inspected the damage, I found, to my great sorrow, that there was a tear of about fifteen centimetres gaping open on the back of my suit. After the mass was finished I ran to one of my aunts who was a tailoress. She sewed up the tear for me with skill and compassion. However, you could still see it and the beautiful suit was marred forever. What would my mother and father have to say about that?

As a foretaste of what I could expect to come, I received a stern reprimand from my father for showing up late to eat. During the meal I pressed my shoulder as closely as possible against the back of the chair, and luckily, because of the recent reprimand, nobody paid any particular attention to my posture. Before the usual Whitsuntide stroll I eagerly helped do the dishes and tidy up and while doing so turned so adeptly that no one got a chance to see my back. But I could not endure the agony until it was discovered and so voluntarily confessed my horrible bad luck to my father. He turned pale and became very serious. After a long discussion with my mother his wise sentence was pronounced: 'You shall no longer go to the bell-ringing!'

In my contrition I found this judgement to be especially mild and I accepted it gratefully, almost shamefully. My shame was yet greater when I was not even excluded from our afternoon stroll and when we entered a sunny tea garden there was even coffee and cakes. For us children this was an event of world-wide importance! Even when we were on a trip somewhere, all we ever had was army bread with plum jam which my mother wrapped up and brought along from home. It was the only kind of bread we knew and we were happy to eat it. The soldiers generously distributed it in front of the local barracks. Even today I am grateful to them for that. Food is the chief concern among poor people and every member of the family was especially interested in this important matter.

While working as a messenger I had won the favour of a butcher shop girl who stood behind her counter with chubby red cheeks. For ten pfennig I received from her a greasy bag of sausage ends in which the skewers had been stuck and which for the most part were never sold. Especially on Saturdays the contents of my bag held enough sliced meat for a family of ten. We always made a feast of it and afterwards my father lit his weekly cigar which cost six pfennig. At that moment there was no family happier than ours!

Roofer's apprentice

The year 1906 brought an unexpected upswing in our fortunes. In Bad Nauheim, the management of the public baths had large new buildings constructed. My father was entrusted with the roofing work and with what he earned from this job he was later able to become independent.

At exactly the same time came my school vacation, so I was able to accompany him to Bad Nauheim, and for the first time, my family experienced separation. The fact that it was so difficult showed how devoted we were to one another and how satisfactory our life together was in spite of all our sorrows.

After I had looked around the building for three days and had climbed around everywhere, I got bored and began to hand tiles to the journeymen. Soon I was strapping loads of heavy tiles onto my back and climbing the steep ladders. Even though it was difficult at first, I did not haul a single tile less than the professional carriers. The building contractor must have observed my diligent efforts to keep up with them. In any event, for the three weeks of my vacation I received free room and board and in addition, thirty marks. That was a fortune in my eyes. A day before school was to begin again my father took me back to Mainz. It never occurred to him to let me travel alone. At that time children still did not travel around in the world the way they do today!

My initial period of independent work in which the journeymen and my father as well treated me as one of them and took me seriously, so to speak, had a profound effect on my subsequent development. I had ceased to be a stupid boy, now regarded myself to be a young man, and made my plans for the future. No work, no pay! From now on I used up all my holidays to work with my father, who in the meantime had become independent. By doing so, I first of all earned money and secondly, I learned something in the process. I was through with playing forever. The struggle for survival had begun.

My father did not make the work easy for me. In his conscientiousness he checked my work even more closely than the journeymen. 'Lad, that can't stay like that. As your master I would be ashamed.' He took it for granted that I would then take everything apart and start the work anew. The extra time was not charged to the customer, but rather was deducted from my pay. So it came about that by the beginning of my actual period of apprenticeship I could do as much as someone who had been an apprentice for two years. After a year and a half my father entrusted me with work which normally only a journeyman with three to five years of experience is capable of handling.

Even as I lay in the cradle, my father was certain that I would become a roofer. I, however, had had another plan for a long time and did not want to become a roofer, but rather an engineer or architect. My talent for drawing seemed to qualify me for such work. I spent every free minute on some sort of handicraft, but of course, for both of those professions one needed more than a primary education and above all one had to have money. That was missing, so my father found a compromise. He made it clear to me that in any case it is a good thing to learn one profession well, and as a roofer I would rise high, so to speak, in the building trade. I could then later work my way up or, in my case, I would in a sense work my way down.

Therefore when I was finished with school I went into my father's business as an apprentice. There was a lot to do. A large factory had assigned my father the continual maintenance of the roofs of the factory building and living quarters, so we actually lived for the first time without financial worries. Two evenings a week I attended courses at the trade school and I pursued sports in two other courses, i.e., I performed gymnastics in a volunteer gym squad. People did not know of many other sports at the time. My day's work began at sunrise and ended shortly after the evening's instruction or gym lesson, after which I fell dead tired into my bed. But this period from March 1908 to February 1910 was the happiest time of my youth. My fingers and the palms of my hands were almost always sore and the skin on my face was scorched by glowing tar-sprayers. But how wonderful were my eight hours of sleep and how happy was I to get up again and proceed with satisfaction to my job! My father was a strict but fair master. 'He who wants to command must learn to obey.' This military principle lay at the root of all his training.

Towards the end of 1909 we were entrusted with the roofing work on a new building which by all means had to be finished before the frost set in. It was a mild winter so we were able to work from early morning to late in the evening. While doing so my father must have over-exerted himself and caught a cold. Up to that point he had never been seriously ill. By 6 February, when the Shrovetide festivities were close at hand, he could no longer get up. The doctors diagnosed pneumonia and his fever got worse from day to day. My mother and I kept watch alternately at his bedside. We only left him alone for a few minutes when we hastily ate meals in the kitchen. My father used the opportunity to open a window. The heat of the fever had probably become unbearable for him. The consequences became apparent that evening as his temperature reached an alarming level. We spent the night sleeplessly and in great anxiety.

The next morning, the 10th, as I sat beside his bed, my father began to speak in a strange soft voice. He gave me advice for everything, for my mother, my sisters, the business, and my future life. I listened to him with a sense of depression and was close to crying. Then he said, 'Get your mother, my boy.' When my mother approached him he looked at her for a long time and then softly said, 'Mina, take care of the children for me,' then fell asleep forever.

For the first time I saw my mother in a state of helplessness. She sat bent over in the kitchen and sobbed to herself. I had to arrange for the burial, order a coffin and wreaths, inform the clergyman, and take care of all the formalities. It was good for me as it kept me occupied. Only when my father's fellow tradesmen lowered the flag and struck up the song: *Ich hatt' einen Kameraden*, did my pain release itself in liberating tears. The worst moment for all of us was when we came home to the apartment with my father no longer there.

* * *

Except for his good name, my father had left nothing behind with which we might have continued the business. An application to the Chamber of Handicrafts to make me a journeyman with two years' apprenticeship was refused, so I had to complete my third year with another master.

Our salvation was a small tavern which my father had leased in order never again, as in previous years, to be entirely without income in the winter when construction came to a standstill. My mother now took over this inn and continued to run it on her own. In my free time I helped her and served the guests. In this way I learned how to deal with people and by doing so my knowledge of human nature was in many ways enriched.

'There is no dishonour in work.' How often did I hear my father say these words. And there was one other lesson which he imparted to me often enough. 'Before you pass judgement, always put yourself in the position of the accused, not the judge.' I have followed this teaching right up to the present day. I have always tried to put myself in the other person's shoes and tried to understand the reasons for his behaviour. This has kept me from making many unjust or overly harsh decisions.

Above all I had to get my third year of apprenticeship behind me. After completion of my journeyman's exam I wanted then to continue my father's business, but things came out differently. During this third year, I received more blows than in the sixteen years I lived in my parent's house. My new master's son was a brutal fellow. When he came into the workshop drunk, and that was the case most days, he took his cruel mood out on me. He beat me for no reason and made my life difficult whenever and wherever he could. I put up with it for a long time and consoled myself with the fact that in a year it would be all over. But one day I lost my patience and when he was about to beat me once again I took hold of a spirit level and struck him so mightily about the skull that he took to his heels. From that day on this fellow never came back to the shop. He totally disappeared from Mainz. Later I discovered he also had no qualms about hitting his own parents, who were glad to be rid of him in this way.

Two months after finishing my apprenticeship I took my examination. I passed it with a rating of 'very good'. I also received a good report from the trade school, so equipped with these references and a journeyman's diploma, the world now stood open for me. Travelling to Bad Nauheim and occasional rafting trips on the Rhine awakened within me the desire to see more of the world. I had sat around in the workshop far too long for my restless blood. I therefore decided to go travelling, and I have never regretted it.

On the road

With a tied-up bundle attached to a stick on my back, the journeyman's diploma and a couple of groschen in my pocket, and a heart filled with wanderlust, I set out. As with every proper German lad since time immemorial, the South called out to me. For me, from the mid-Rhine area, this meant Hesse, Baden and Swabia. Then I wanted to see the beautiful old Franconian cities which had been talked about so much in my history class: Nuremberg, Bamberg and Bayreuth.

My first goal was Darmstadt, so I marched along the highway in the direction of Gross-Gerau, the same road along which I would often enough have to walk later on as an infantryman. My homesickness grew with every step deeper into unfamiliar territory. Why did I have to go out amongst strangers when I had it so good at home, anyway? Did my mother not anticipate my every wish? And here no one cared about me. I would have preferred to turn around, had I not feared being laughed at by my sisters and friends.

In the evening I came across a farmer who was just about to start chopping wood. Because this was one of my favourite occupations and I could expect to earn myself a good dinner, I offered to take over the work and did such a conscientious job that one piece of wood had almost the same length and width as the other. In two hours I was done and received a hearty meal and a warm straw bed in the barn. On the following morning I was given a good breakfast and even a mark for the road. 'What more can one want?' I thought as I marched onwards. One could live quite nicely chopping wood for two hours a day.

My master in Mainz had given me a letter of recommendation for [work in] Darmstadt, and the result of this was that they kept me there and would have preferred for me not to leave. Ten days after my departure I could already send a gold piece home to my mother. Since I did not smoke and did not drink much either, and my master's people took care of everything else, I was able to save almost all of my earnings. After ten weeks though, in spite of all the tempting offers and promises, I continued on my travels.

I followed the mountain road and late in the evening arrived dead-tired at Fehlheim, near Bensheim. Here I lived with my aunt, my father's sister, and with the best of intentions I could not eat as much as was demanded of me. Any sort of resistance was futile. I had to fit in a day of rest and submit my appetite to further tests. In between I had just enough time to climb up the Melikobus and have a look at Auerbach Castle. With the blessings of my aunt and enough food for at least two days in my bundle, I continued on my way.

It became more and more difficult for me to understand the people 'down under'. Via Heppenheim, Weinheim and Mannheim, I finally reached Heidelberg. Oh, you dear beautiful city of Heidelberg! Whenever I think of you I must voluntarily hum the popular melody *I Lost my Heart in Heidelberg*. I fell in love with my master's young, pretty, and lively daughter, and I might have ended my travels there in Heidelberg. Who knows how differently things might have turned out? In this case she was definitely not the shy one, but I, with my seventeen years, was still too young and inexperienced to allow myself to be lured onto dangerous terrain with passionate glances, affectionate chatter, and a sudden lack of self-assurance. So this first experience of love lost none of its purity. When I left after twelve weeks it took a long time for my heart to follow. Today I am glad that everything has turned out the way it has. The love I felt at that time has long since been transferred to you, you dear, beautiful city of Heidelberg!

After a few days of travel with a heavy heart, I came to Jagstfeld, on the River Kocher. Here I was entrusted with such a difficult and dangerous job that my love-sickness, without my really noticing it, soon began to lose its passion and slowly ebbed away. The church tower of Jagstfeld, a pointed tower of small circumference but considerable height, was to receive a completely new roof. The old master to whom I had introduced myself assigned me this honourable task. As my father once did, I now sat every day on a narrow board at a dizzying height and let my feet dangle in space. Even more difficult than carrying out this job was trying to understand the local workers, who understood me as little as I did them. This sometimes led to ticklish situations.

Almost a quarter of a year passed before the tower roof was newly covered from the high peak to the eaves. I may say without exaggeration that at this time I was the hero of Jagstfeld. Not just boys and girls looked up at me admiringly or waved to me from their windows. Old people as well watched me in amazement and shook their heads. Evenings in the tavern I often heard in the most beautiful Swabian dialect what a 'hell of a guy' I was and how I was certainly destined for great things someday. Wherever I went, people invited me to dine with them and that certainly was of benefit with regards to the amount of money I was able to send home to my mother each week. Indeed, during this period I did not even use up a third of my earnings.

Then one day I wandered further on to Heilbronn, and from there to Ulm and Ingolstadt. Bavarian mannerisms suited me better than those of the Swabians. I warmed to the people here far more quickly. I worked for fourteen days in Heilbronn and six weeks in Ulm. Using earnings I had saved, I treated myself to the luxury of some time off. I travelled via Nuremberg, where I stayed for two days, to Bayreuth, the town sacred to all admirers of Wagner. I counted myself amongst them even though I had not seen a single Wagnerian opera. I had only heard a march now and then from *Tannhäuser* or *Lohengrin*, as played by some beer-garden band. But this music had inspired me greatly and so it came about that a journeyman from the Rhineland stood before the Villa Wanfried and the festival hall with a pounding heart.

Finally I headed home via Bamberg, Würzburg, Miltenberg and Worms. I hardly need mention that, as in Nuremberg, I had to look at all the sites, monuments and antiquities of these cities. My thirst for knowledge was always great. I preserve in my memory many a beautiful gable, wrought-iron portal, and picturesque alleyway. These are the sort of things one sees if one also roams around where no guide shows one the way.

After two years of travelling I came home again in a brand-new carpenter's suit. Great was the joy of my mother and sisters, and I had brought something for all of them. There was no end to my storytelling. All the while I felt like the hero of a novel and only now did I become properly conscious of a lot of things I had experienced along the way.

Chapter Two

The Call to Arms

With body and soul a soldier

My period of military service was approaching. I looked forward to it, since because of my father I had a soldier's nature in my blood. First I tried to get into the cavalry, then the artillery, and finally the engineers, but in all three branches of the service I had no luck, so all that was left was the infantry.

I wanted to at least try to get into a telephone unit or a machine-gun company. It was remarkable that I could never get anything I wanted in life right away. There was always some sort of detour, but in the end, though never without a struggle and often in a manner which was mysterious and surprising to me, it did finally lead to my goal.

In the meantime my mother had married again. Because there were still four months until my conscription date, I helped out in the tavern. My step-father had brought a small land holding and fishery into the marriage.

When on Sundays the locals came to a dance, I served one half of the hall and three waiters were busy in the other half. But my tips were always much larger than those of the three professional waiters combined. Why? Because I knew the people and accepted them as they were. On weekdays I worked in a sawmill. I began as a wood carrier, and after a month became a foreman. And soon I, who up to this point had no knowledge about the various kinds of wood, was in charge of sorting wood and knew my way around oak, beech, ash, and pitchpine.

From eight o'clock in the evening until well past midnight I set up pins in our bowling alley, just as I had done as a boy. Those were hard-earned groschen. Besides that there were all sorts of things to do, like chopping ice, woodcutting, harvesting asparagus, and above all, fishing. One time I succeeded in catching an unusually large pike in my net. It was 1.8 metres long and 27 centimetres thick, and became the prize of a bowling tournament fetching a total of 127 marks. Everything I earned went into the common [family] coffer. The needs of the tavern could be covered to a considerable extent by our own farming and fishery. With the savings I wanted to open my father's business again, but that was still a long way off; first I became a soldier.

In October 1912 I joined the 8th Company of the 117th Infantry Regiment. That a citizen of Mainz actually performed his military service in Mainz was in and of itself a rarity which caught people's imagination. Unfortunately, on the very first day I drew attention to myself in a somewhat different, and in fact quite unpleasant, way. Even before I tried on my boots, I ventured a remark to the quartermaster corporal that they would not fit. At that, he threw myself and the boots out of the quartermaster's store. After three days of greasing them with might and main, they fitted as though they were moulded onto my feet.

In the first weeks of my service we had an Unteroffizier [corporal] with whom everything went like clockwork. There was no squad more satisfied or eager to serve. After the strenuous duty our meals were eaten with a hearty appetite and we slept like logs. During the day we busted our tails and gave our best, but unfortunately those good days did not last long.

Our Unteroffizier was transferred and his place was taken by a loathsome fellow from Detmold. His silver stripes went to his head. He only allowed himself to be addressed in the third person and hounded, humiliated, and tormented us in every possible way. However repugnant he was to us, and however much we had to suffer under his megalomania, we still remained good soldiers.

However, we were no boot lickers! One of the 'old hands' from Room 107 came to us recruits in Room 108 and bellowed: 'Here, you idiots, polish these boots!' He received a prompt reply: 'Polish your big fat boots yourself!' Then we got our hands on him and tossed him out the door. Our new Unteroffizier found this sort of behaviour towards one of the 'old hands' utterly shocking. He watched us and treated us like revolutionaries and anarchists. This highly offended our sense of honour, so we decided to teach him a lesson and soon found a good opportunity to do so.

One of the dirty tricks he used to play in rainy weather was to have us constantly come to a halt before one of the many puddles in the barrack square. Then came the order: 'Lie down!' We splashed down into the water with our entire bodies so that afterwards we looked as though we had all been dragged through the mud. We now arranged it so that when we heard the order: 'Halt!', we would make one more giant step into the puddle. Upon the command: 'Lie down!', we wound up lying on the far side of the puddle. In this way the mud splashed about his ears and he suffered the additional annoyance of seeing us lying on dry ground. Furious, he repeated the experiment, but on the second attempt he still failed to make us lie down in the water. Nonetheless, he still had to wipe the mud off his own face.

'Muskatier Buckler!'
'Present, Herr Unteroffizier!'
'You devised this!'
'Yes, sir, Herr Unteroffizier!'

'Do you know you are going to "Father Hoffmann"?'
'No, Herr Unteroffizier!'

['Father Hoffmann' was apparently the name of the 'clink.'] The result of this brief conversation was an hour of additional drill. We endured it and he became sick with rage. So we were rid of him for at least a short while. When he returned, during our leisure hour, he avenged himself. Most of us already had on the trousers we wore when on leave. He used a flimsy excuse to make us repeatedly lie down and stand up in the room to the point of exhaustion. We finally got fed up with it and at a sign from me we all dropped to the floor with such force that the boards cracked. We did this intentionally because the room of the Feldwebel [sergeant] was below us. What we hoped for happened. The Feldwebel charged up the stairs and yelled at the Unteroffizier, demanding to know what the hell he was playing at. So that put an end to his authority forever.

Enough of this. This man was a barrack square phenomenon, the sort produced by pride of place and utter subordination. Fortunately one did not come across them too often. We knew quite well that drill was necessary in order to turn a bunch of men into an effective fighting force. But we had a fine sense of when this drill turned into harassment. We were certainly not afraid of mud and water! It was just the mean and malicious nature of this person that vexed us.

* * *

This period too passed. Soon I had the marksman's braid, had become a Gefreiter [lance corporal] and on 27 January 1914 was promoted to Unteroffizier. At that point I had had enough of the silver-striped oppressor. In order to free my comrades from him, I convinced him that the agitation from training troops was bad for his health and that it was in his best interests to seek out a more comfortable post in administration. He followed this advice. When war broke out, he was to be found in the rear echelon. That was typical of this sort of braggart.

I owed my quick promotion to Unteroffizier after one and a quarter years to the following incident. Generalleutnant von Plüskow, who was well known in peacetime, was attending a field exercise. During a charge by my company, von Plüskow called out to us: 'All the officers and non-commissioned officers of the 8th Company have been shot dead.'

Immediately my order rang out: 'Attention! The 8th Company follows my command. 8th Company up! March! March!' After the discussion, I had to step forward and the general expressed to me his appreciation for my swift thinking and action.

It comes to war

As I had wished, I was finally trained as the leader of a telephone section. As such, I went to war. The war itself came as a great surprise to us, who lived in barracks, read few newspapers, and did not talk at all about politics. We marched out as though we were headed for a manoeuvre and without any concept of what war meant in reality. Even the farewell from my mother did not move me too much. I could hardly understand her deep anxiety.

On 2 August 1914 we lowered the flags as music played. On the barrack square the regimental commander gave a speech which was attended by the Grand Duke of Hesse, Ernst Ludwig, and the Grand Duchess Eleonore. Our thirst for action was stirred. We felt like warriors and already a little bit like heroes as we marched to the railway station. Every man in the 8th Company fancied himself greater than a member of the 1st Company, so much did courage swell within our hearts.

Yet there was a moment when my manly self-confidence faded away and I felt like a child, which I actually was with my nineteen years. A woman unexpectedly slipped through our ranks and kissed me. It was my mother. All of this happened as if in a dream. Then we marched onwards. For a few more steps I still felt a lump in my throat, then the marching music tore me back into the great stream in which individual fate was immersed.

Loading the troops into the train went off without the slightest delay, as though following a precise programme. The train began to move as we waved, shouted, laughed, and cracked jokes. Where we were going, nobody knew. All we could tell was that we were heading westwards.

It was a merry journey! We were well provided for at every station we stopped at. Young girls handed us cigarettes, chocolate, and beverages. The August heat made us mightily thirsty. We heard so many nice words and noticed so many affectionate glances that we considered ourselves to be awfully dashing fellows. It was just a shame that now, of all times, we had to go to war when things could have been so nice at home.

In Königsmachern, on the Luxembourg border, we detrained and set up our first wartime bivouac. Our company did not post any sentries, so we all stayed close together. The days passed quickly with gathering supplies, cooking, washing utensils, and lounging about. The wildest rumours began circulating; horror stories were told. We got each other all worked up, while our restlessness increased. The idleness and loafing around became unbearable, so we breathed a sigh of relief when on 11 August the order to march came.

The sun radiated in a cloudless sky and soon we were darkly tanned. The march led us through the Ardennes and the beautiful valleys of the Meuse. On the 19th we arrived on Belgian territory. Many of us were tormented by thirst, though oddly enough I did not feel any. For some it was fateful; they became sick and died. It was believed that the water had been poisoned.

When the wind blew in our direction we could hear artillery fire, but it was coming from quite far away. So it did not surprise us when once again the order came to stop and set up camp. But we had hardly begun to erect our tents when a counter-order came for immediate departure. I do not know whether it was the same for others, but an unknown nervousness came over me. Was it the fear of the unknown, of things I had never experienced? It was not connected with any definite idea and I believe it would have vanished entirely if only the goal of our march was evident. The sound of gunfire became more distinct. What was going on up there? What was that really? A battle? I would soon find out.

* * *

From the unusual pace of our march, which more and more resembled a real forced march, we could see that we were going to face some action. Perhaps it was a matter of coming to the aid of our comrades who lay somewhere in heavy battle. Suddenly we were all dominated by the thought that comrades up front could perhaps be killed or taken prisoner if we did not arrive on time. Every trace of fatigue disappeared; no order was necessary to spur us on. We ran more than we marched until we finally reached the village of Glaireuse. It was still inhabited and it had not been long since French cavalry had left it. To our great disappointment there was no sign of the enemy.

The attitude of the French inhabitants was hostile. It was written all over their faces. Hidden weapons were found and men seized and interrogated. Distant machine-gun fire, with the roar of artillery fire in between, heightened the sense of menace, of the proximity of danger.

In a small church a field service was held. A clergyman delivered a sermon, the likes of which I have never since heard. It was simple and human, and moved me deeply. Yes, it freed me from all my fear and raised me so far above my little self that I felt like a new man when I stepped out of the dim interior into broad daylight.

Baptism of fire

On 21 August I received my baptism of fire. The French occupied the village of Maissin and the surrounding heights. It was about noon. Then we received the order to attack.

We advanced in a ravine as a heavy thunderstorm broke above us. The roar of thunder was mixed with the howls of the first shells, the sky above and earth below were illuminated by flashes of light. Screams pierced the air and horses reared in fright. Earth sprayed in all directions while iron splinters hissed through the air. Horrified, we stumbled in this direction and that, and threw ourselves down.

Then the steaming field kitchen received a direct hit. As the smoke cleared I saw men and animals lying mutilated in a bloody tangle on the ground. My heart almost stopped at the sight of it. I was afraid to breathe. This ceaseless din, the screaming, and the moaning of the wounded robbed me of my senses for moments at a time, as I lay clutching at the earth. When would it strike me?

Lying still, having to wait, not being able to help anyone, not being able to defend myself – that was the most agonising thing during this first experience of war.

The trumpets blared: Attack! In an extended skirmish line we advanced towards the village, living targets for the enemy lying under cover. My comrades fell to the right and left of me, dead or wounded. The old soldier's saying came to mind: *Not every bullet finds its mark.* Suddenly I was running and still breathing so it was true enough. But our losses were too heavy, and the order came to retreat. I would have much preferred to keep running forward rather than to be shot in the back.

Now the protective curtain of darkness began to fall and finally we once more reached the village from which we had set out some hours before. Many men were missing. The hostility of the populace now took on more threatening forms. Shots were fired in an ambush. Here was the first time I aimed a weapon at a person, a specific individual person. A *franc-tireur* – a sniper – fired upon me from the semi-darkness of a street. I whipped my rifle up to my cheek and fired. Today I am still glad I missed. Lightning quick a human being stepped between myself and the shadows of darkness with arms raised in supplication. It was a girl of about twelve years of age, the daughter of the *franc-tireur*, who wanted to shield her father with her own body. I approached her and spoke a few words with her. What else should I have done? The youngster burst into tears. The war was not her fault and the fact that she wanted to save her father was brave.

As chance would have it, when I returned to the same area four years later during the retreat, I saw the girl again. In the meantime she had developed into a real beauty. I also made the acquaintance of the father, a careworn old man, who could only poorly conceal his glee over our retreat.

That night after the repulsed attack, sleep was unthinkable. Although the houses were thoroughly searched and anyone who in any way seemed suspicious was arrested, there was no end to the shooting. A patrol entered my billet and wanted to take the owner of the house into custody. He was accused of having just fled into the house from the street, but I was able to clear up the facts of the matter and he was set free. His wife and children, who understood nothing of our conversation, cried pitifully. The man himself remained completely calm and stood there as though his mind were elsewhere.

The next day when we bivouacked out in the open and each of us received not one, but three portions from the field kitchen, it became clear to us that we had lost two-thirds of our comrades during the unsuccessful attack.

That same morning our artillery moved into position. After a short preparatory bombardment another infantry regiment had stormed the village which we had tried to take and sent the French into flight. While moving up we saw many, many dead who lay in the fields or ditches and we saw the carcasses of dead horses, those beautiful animals, with bloody foam in their mouths and with their legs stretched rigidly towards the sky.

After a forced march we entered the village of Bertriz. Here as well there was treacherous fire from the windows. Those caught in the act were put up against a wall. We moved into billets, posted guards, and sank into deep sleep. Yet even before night fell we were turned out and left this dangerous area, a little fortified by the short rest. We would have rather died in open battle rather than be killed in an underhand way in our sleep. We marched the whole night and while passing through a wood shots were fired and we soon found out that the sharpshooters were sitting up in the tree tops. We had no time to clear the woods of the malicious marksmen, and just marched and marched....

* * *

We proceeded through the Ardennes, uphill and downhill. Then we continued through the valley of the Semois [River]. On the morning of 25 August we trod upon French soil near the town of Matton. The enemy had withdrawn from the Thiers sector without a fight. Before their arrival, the French had blown up the iron bridge over the Semois, so we crossed it on one of the makeshift bridges constructed by the engineers.

In the meantime it had started raining. Soon it was coming down in buckets. In the evening we set up a bivouac in an open field. I have never slept better than on this night, lying soaking wet in pouring rain on an incline with my pack under my head. The following morning we did not need the shrill tone of the non-commissioned officers to rouse us from our sleep. We woke with a start at the mighty noise of a shell striking close-by. It was of huge calibre! Then everything was quiet. We got a quick gulp of hot coffee from the field kitchen and an apple served to clean one's teeth. Then we went on.

The corner between Thiers and the River Meuse, south-east of Sedan, had already played an important role in 1870 [Franco-Prussian War]. The enemy artillery, which had the range of every single point here, was suddenly put into action and brought this territory under heavy calibre fire. Forcing our way across the Meuse seemed impossible. The pontoon bridges, which the engineers had laid down despite the heavy rain of fire, were destroyed again and again. But then our own artillery was brought to bear and indeed with such force that one enemy battery after another was silenced.

We used the short pause in the fire to cross the river with the pontoons. As we did so there was a lot of laughter in spite of the seriousness of the situation. The bullet holes in the iron sides of the boats had been plugged in a makeshift fashion and we had to use our hands to keep them from leaking. This provided an amusing and exciting test of strength between water pressure and muscle power. The sudden switch from low spirits to a burst of merriment is one of the psychological experiences which probably everyone has had in war. The cause may lie deep within human nature, which always automatically strives for equilibrium and has a defence mechanism ready which assists both in the physical and mental healing process.

After we had crossed over, it was a matter of determining how far the enemy was from us and whether he occupied the Meuse heights and the woods to the east of us. For the first time there was a call for volunteers. Before I even properly considered what sort of dangers might be involved in such a patrol against an invisible enemy, I had already called out: 'Here!' Immediately after that I was on my way with two men. At last we crept and crawled towards the wood which was about six hundred metres from us. When one of us imprudently straightened up we were fired upon from the woods. A few minutes later artillery fire from the Meuse heights commenced, and with that the enemy himself revealed his position. Our regiment advanced in a charge and soon our comrades had caught up to us and oddly enough we stormed the wood and adjoining heights almost without any losses.

On 28 August the battle was reduced to little skirmishes on the western side of the Meuse heights. Nowhere did the French offer serious resistance and we chased them before us, giving them no chance to rest. After a heavy engagement in which there was a lot of shooting here, there, and everywhere, the order to halt finally came. Everyone was so deathly tired that he fell down wherever he happened to be standing. I was the contact between the first and second battalions, but the need for sleep overcame me in an open field.

It was pitch-dark when I awoke. I had no idea how long I had slept and all around me were death rattles and groans. With every step in the darkness I stumbled over a body, a helmet, or a rifle. This whole field in which I had peacefully slept was so covered with dead and wounded that I could make my way forward only very slowly, feeling ahead of me with my foot. How gladly I would have helped one or the other who lay there in pain and called out to me: 'Hey comrade! Water!', but my water bottle was empty. I did not have a torch on me and could not even see who was calling to me. Soon the medical orderlies would come and search the field thoroughly. For me there was but one goal – get to the battalion!

So I stumbled onwards across the nocturnal field of dead. What if I were to head in the wrong direction and fall into enemy hands? I continued on my way with clenched teeth, while every sound froze me in my tracks. I will confess that this night taught me what it really meant to get the 'creeps'. The sensation stabbed at me from the darkness, causing me to jerk as though I had been stuck with a needle. It grasped at me with shadowy grey hands, so that I leapt sideways with a shudder. It moaned and groaned in my ears and I had to clasp my hands over them in order to keep myself from going mad.

I would have preferred to throw myself down and remain lying between the dead until day came, but my sense of duty drove me on. If only I could know what orders my battalion had received while I slept. How could I have slept so soundly? My comrades probably thought I was dead. Where might they be? I had to find them this very night.

From a distance I heard the sound of rattling wagons and clopping horses so hurried towards it as swiftly as the darkness would allow. However, I did not approach too closely. Were they German or French? I lay in wait under the cover of night until I heard voices. Those were German words – thank God! I ran towards the moving column and called out to them. It turned out to be the baggage train of my regiment and I also found out that my battalion was billeted in the village ahead of us.

Nobody had missed me. The horror of this day was so overwhelming that nobody thought about anyone else. The dead were still lying around everywhere in the streets of the village. There was white bread and canned food, so along with the good food from the field kitchen there was also chicken, fresh eggs, bacon and ham. In addition, red wine was issued to us. In spite of that we could not work up a proper appetite and we silently ate as much as was necessary to still our hunger. Then we rolled ourselves up in our coats. Sleep! Forget! Sometimes we woke with a start and a gurgling sound escaped one's throat.

We were granted a few days of rest. We could have used them to write home, to read something once more, or at least to converse with one another. However, we preferred to sleep, continually sleep. Finally, after three or four days, we began to look at one another and speak with one another as usual. When someone laughed, we glanced up as though something unusual had just occurred. Only gradually did our old cheerfulness return. You can get used to war.

The retreat from the Champagne

On 2 September we broke camp. On the highway near a village we were surprised by well-directed heavy artillery fire that suddenly rained down upon us. We spread out across the nearby fields and dug in as well as we could. The enemy swept the entire area with shell-fire in a methodical fashion. It was not the sort of heavy bombardment we were to become acquainted with later, but to us it was a living hell.

We remained lying there like that for another sixty-three hours. It was a test of nerves which we younger chaps could withstand only by stretching our strength to the furthest limits. It was during these difficult hours that I became a man, for I know from that point on my face took on harder features. Even during the night the artillery fire did not cease. Again and again shells impacted here and there in a flash of bright flame, the shrapnel spraying through the dark air in a shower of sparks. In the quickly vanishing flashes of gunfire eerie threads of white smoke became visible which reached downwards like the arms of a polyp.

Around noon on the third day the fire ceased as suddenly as it had begun. In the church tower of the nearby village a priest was discovered who had directed the artillery fire by means of signals. He was arrested and false signals were used to direct the fire onto another target where it could not cause any damage. We tried to make up for lost time with forced marches but while doing so we suffered a lot in the great [late summer] heat. Many men were left lying on the roadside with swollen feet and swollen tongues, but finally we reached Massiges.

Now we were in the Champagne region. The *lousy Champagne*, and we were to become thoroughly acquainted with it. For days on end we marched onwards through the continual heat along its wretched roads caked in white chalk dust. After difficult battles we crossed the Rhine-Marne canal and now stood deep in the rear of Verdun. Verdun – the grave of so many brave soldiers. Later Verdun was often my destination on many dangerous flights. However tenaciously the enemy defended the arc south of the Rhine-Marne canal, we nonetheless advanced victoriously. In our minds we could already see ourselves entering Paris in triumph.

> [It would be at Verdun in early 1916 that the German 5th Army was given the task of taking this city that stood on the River Meuse. By then it was more than just a city, it was the Région Fortifée de Verdun (RFV – the Fortified Region of Verdun), a veritable citadel defended too by a number of forts on its eastern side. To lose Verdun would open the road to Paris, but it would also become a symbol. To lose Verdun meant that France would lose the war. The Germans knew this and in 1916 decided that the French would defend it to the last man. This is exactly what the Germans wanted and planned – to bleed the French army white. In the event, the Battle of Verdun, which lasted for most of 1916, cost the defenders 543,000 casualties, while the Germans suffered over 434,000. The city did not fall, and little was achieved during those many months. In itself Verdun had no major strategic value, other than its geographical position and that symbol of French nationalistic pride and resistance. By September 1914, when Buckler arrived at Verdun any plans to assault this city were put on hold, as Buckler now records.]

Then the inconceivable happened. The order to continue the chase did not come. We knew nothing of the fact that to the north of us in the region of the 1st and 2nd Armies a decision had been arrived at which determined not only the outcome of the strategic campaign plans in the west, but also those of the entire war, and beyond that assured long difficult years for the Fatherland.

The order to retreat, which arrived on 11 September, was incomprehensible to us. The fact that we were moving back seemed to be no less inconceivable to the enemy. At first he considered it to be a possible ruse, as he followed only with hesitation. Soon he came to regard it as a miracle – the great *Miracle of the Marne*. To us it remained a fateful mystery.

> [The fact was that the German advance had spent itself during its massive advances. German forces had crossed the Marne on 4 September 1914, but that was as far as it had gone. Once the French realised this the Battle of the Marne began on the 6th, General Joffre, the French commander, opening his counter-offensive, supported by the British on the French left. Within a few days the Germans began to dig-in, trenches appearing along the length of the Chemin-des-Dames, showing that they were determined to stand. The period of trench warfare was about to begin, and as winter approached, the trenches began to be dug from the North Sea coast to the Swiss border. The war of movement in France was at an end. The war of barbed wire and machine guns was about to start.]

Embittered and cursing, we began to retreat. If the French were now to follow in forced marches we, yesterday's victors, could be pursued in wild flight as tomorrow's defeated foe. So it was extremely important that the retreat be covered as well as possible and that the retiring army disengage itself from the enemy as quickly as possible. Once again there was a call for volunteers. Shortly before daybreak I set out with two men in order to determine how far the enemy had followed.

At first light we reached a barn, and were just about to advance further beyond it when we heard voices. This caused us to disappear into the interior of the barn as quickly as possible. Judging by the sound of their footsteps, the approaching enemy patrol likewise numbered but a few men. We held our breath and listened to see if they would pass on by, but the barn also appeared to the enemy patrol to be a suitable hiding place for a short time. The steps came closer and the voices became louder. We stood pressed up against the wall breathlessly silent until the members of the patrol – there were three of them, just like us – had entered the semi-dark space. Then, before their eyes could adjust to the dim light, we rushed them. They made hardly a sound and then the horrible deed was done. We hid their dead bodies in the hay. We had done our duty.

Soldiers must not speak of how much our hearts pounded, how much we were shaken by our actions, and how much sympathy for the poor men burned within us. If the circumstances were reversed, the others would have done the same thing to us. They would have had to. We were, one like the other, responsible for thousands of lives. We were just not ourselves, we were parts of a dangerous whole, destructive cogs of a murderous machinery known as war.

We went back over the rain-soaked roads to Massiges, from where we had set out on our victorious advance. Here we saw trenches being dug everywhere, so there was apparently no intention of advancing once again from here and preparations were being made for static warfare. That did not suit us at all. We had become used to the aggressive spirit of the first weeks of the war, and now we were supposed to hide in the ground? We had become moles!

We were yanked out of our foul mood on 14 September as the news arrived that we were to be withdrawn from the 4th Army and be re-deployed in another position. Hopefully it would be a position from which we would again advance. Because we marched, fought, sweated, and laid our lives on the line, we simple soldiers felt that we should have a say in how the war was conducted. What did we know about the grand operations of the armies and the reasons for our forced marches?

After the breakthrough on the Marne failed to succeed it was followed by the fateful retreat in the centre of the battle zone. Then the goal was to envelope the northern flank of the French. The enemy tried to prevent this flanking movement and the result was to race to the sea. All of this led to a consolidation of the front between the sea coast and the alps. It was only many years later that I read about all of this in a book about the war. At the time I did not dream of this happening, nor that I myself would fight for two full years on the fixed front – not on the ground, but in the air.

Assault

After two difficult days of marching we again come into contact with the enemy and got involved in heavy fighting. We were allowed no time to rest. On and on it went and that was fine with us. We believed in victory again and that gave us the necessary strength to endure calmly all the hardships. In spite of great losses we were in good spirits.

When on the 24th we arrived in the region between La Fère and Ham [points along the St Quentin Canal, which flows to the south of the town of St Quentin and connects with the Sambre Canal just to the west of La Fère. Just to the north of Ham, Péronne had been taken by German forces on this day.], we had to engage immediately in the battle which had broken out to the west of Ham. The French fell back through Roye and established their position there. We prepared for an assault.

Even the assaults we carried out at home in the form of an exercise were overwhelmed with tension. But this tension could not be compared with that which now filled us, when it was a matter of life and death, victory or defeat. We were to advance in four hours. In the whole area it was so quiet that one could hear every little sound, even one's own heartbeat.

Three hours and fifty minutes had passed, which for us was an eternity. Now bayonets were fixed. In the last ten minutes that remained to us we thought a lot about home. I remembered my first fighting exercises in which I was beaten black and blue until I went to the cellar and filled with fury, took my rifle and practised. After four weeks I had dealt with everyone in the company and I even succeeded in overcoming the recruiting officer, who was a feared bayonet fighter.

Three minutes more. I thought of my parents, especially my mother, of my sisters, and of our tavern. Would I ever again be a waiter on Sundays in an overflowing dance hall? I would really like to catch such a big pike once again. How long was it, anyway? That's right! One metre, 18 centimetres. How ridiculous it was to think about something like that right now.

One minute. My heart is beating at twice its normal rate. There: tatata! The signal to attack! Up! March, march! We proceed at double-time across the open terrain. All of this was not much different than on the parade ground. However, that quickly changed. Suddenly we were facing men who were equally determined to achieve victory or die. They did not yield, not a single step. The bayonets quickly disappeared as fists gripped barrels and the rifle butts did their work. We grimly hacked away at them, to the right and to the left, striking whomever we could. We had to get through, here and now, and at any price! Finally the enemy fell back and we took Fresnoy by storm.

While we were digging in, 'The Watch on the Rhine' resounded. At dawn we determined that the French had also made use of the night to entrench themselves. The regiment remained lying here and here it stayed until the spring of 1917, when it was ordered by the Supreme Army Command to leave the position and move into the Siegfried Line. The regiment – not I.

Wounding and home service

In the meantime I had received the Iron Cross 2nd Class. For what? Had I done something special? Was it for my voluntary patrols? [This medal is worn for just twenty-four hours following which just the ribbon is worn through a buttonhole on the front of the tunic.] Sometimes at night I dreamt of quite different undertakings, of a daring surprise attack which I led and which resulted in an active enemy battery or an enemy-occupied château or a whole regiment falling into our hands. But up to now there had been no opportunity for such a true deed of heroism.

Once again we advanced in an attack from our entrenched position. While doing so we were surprised and pinned down by the enemy artillery. For twenty-four hours we lay amidst the barrage, slightly dug in or crammed into shell holes, until our own artillery had silenced that of the enemy to the extent that we could continue the charge. In the hand-to-hand fighting I was stricken by a mighty blow to the left shoulder and another to my knee. I stumbled and collapsed in a state of unconsciousness.

When I awoke I was lying in a field hospital amongst screaming and groaning men. The artillery fire came closer. Quickly the field hospital was dismantled and we were transported to the rear. A hospital train took most of us and I was dropped off at Mainz, my garrison and home town. What a stroke of luck! My mother and sisters now visited me daily in the town's military hospital.

After eight weeks my broken shoulder joint and the haemorrhage in my knee had healed to the point that I could report back to my regiment as fit for duty. But my wish to go back to the front with one of the next transports was not fulfilled. Non-commissioned officers with combat experience were needed at home for the training of replacements and I was assigned – sentenced, it seemed to me – to stand day after day on the barrack square and drill young and old recruits until they were ready for the front.

However important that task might be, I felt like a slacker. And, unfortunately, there were some of those around back then. I witnessed how certain people again and again managed to secure a special posting and avoid being sent to the front. The war had been unable to do away with class or social distinction and Germany suffered because of it. This contributed quite substantially to its later collapse.

In my view of the service, there were no distinctions; everyone was a soldier. A higher degree of education merely obliged one to accomplish more. That is the attitude I maintained while training my home guard and territorial reservists. Most of them could have been my father, but my youth did not bother these fine fellows. Perhaps respect for my Iron Cross 2nd Class – which was not yet too common before the end of 1914 – and my wound contributed to the fact that they performed their duty for me with eagerness and affection. I think they would have run through fire for me. With me the period of duty was short and for that reason all the more strict. After they had performed their duty I left the men in peace. In this way I kept them willing, cheerful and ambitious. Admittedly, it sometimes seemed strange to me when such an old fellow stood before me, a young lad, and said: 'Yes sir, Herr Unteroffizier!' That my manner of treating people was the correct one was revealed during inspection, as my company performed the best in every respect and marched in such a smart way that they received special praise from the commander.

I had in addition an unpleasant duty. I had to take deserters, of whom there were fortunately only a few, and people who in some other way had violated the law, to the military prison. One of my delinquents remains unforgettable. He was a giant of a fellow and a dyed-in-the-wool social democrat. He arrived at a military hospital wounded, but after his release he did not return immediately to his regiment, as was his duty, but rather went home to his wife without permission. For this he received three days close confinement. When he found out about his punishment he lost his head and cleared off. I received the assignment of looking for him and turning him in. Because there was hardly a nook in Mainz that I did not know, I succeeded in tracking him down the next day. He was staying in a pub situated in an out of the way alley and in which there were often wild goings-on.

I had my mind set on helping the poor chap. Perhaps I could convince him in a man-to-man talk to come along voluntarily, so I left the two men who accompanied me behind in the vicinity of the pub. I arranged with them to come to my aid when signalled to do so, but otherwise they were to remain in the background.

Just like any other guest, I entered the dim, smoke-filled bar room without causing any fuss. As soon as the giant saw me, he wanted to force his way past me and take off. I did not draw my revolver nor did I shout at him, but rather held him firmly by the arm and gently, but urgently, informed him that the most sensible thing for him to do would be to remain calm and do everything I say.

'If it weren't for you I'd be gone by now!' he grumbled as he sat across from me gloomily. 'For all I care, they could have shot me as I fled.'

'Don't speak such nonsense,' I said. 'Think of your wife and children. Because of these three miserable days you want to make yourselves unhappy for the rest of your lives. Surely it isn't worth it? A decent fellow tries to make up for what he's botched up.'

'That's what I want to do,' he grated despairingly. 'Just send me to the front. I'll show you all that I'm no dishonourable scoundrel. But I won't go to jail! No, you won't bring me there. I'm no criminal.'

I gave him a good talking to and made it clear to him that no one can simply go on leave on his own accord, especially in wartime. I told him I knew quite well that he had been a good soldier at the front, and good soldiers were needed now. He should not do wrong against the greatest thing a person has, one's Fatherland.

I finally got him to promise to come along willingly and we proceeded peacefully side by side to the barracks as though returning from a stroll. My men followed in an inconspicuous manner so that he did not even see them. In the barracks I reported everything to the Hauptmann [captain]. With his intercession, the penalty was lifted and the man was sent to the front with the next transport.

Thirteen years later I saw him again. He came from Mainz to Mannheim for a flying exhibition when he heard that I was going to be flying there. He did not look much different and in the meantime he had become a well-to-do entrepreneur. During the war he had attained the rank of Vizefeldwebel [sergeant-major] and he proudly wore his Iron Cross 1st Class. For myself this reunion was a cause for great joy and I was happy to have prevented him from committing a blunder back in 1914.

Not every case of this sort ended so mildly. I delivered up a lot of nasty young fellows to 'Father Hoffmann' who because of their dishonourable or base conduct had quite justly earned their punishment. But I did not care much at all for this 'executioner's post'. Day by day I found the training of replacements less and less enjoyable. I wanted to get back to the front again.

Chapter Three

Fledgling Wings

Student pilot

Then came a letter which indeed, as they often say, had a decisive effect upon my whole life and directed it forever onto different paths. Hauptmann von Brandenstein, my commander from the 8th Company, advised me that if I desired to go into aviation, then I should report to Hauptmann von S.

Up to this point my only experience of aviation was now and then seeing an airman flying away above me, and before the war seeing the two flyers Gödecker and Fokker carrying out their hops on the 'Big Sand' in Mainz. Fokker was still very young, only a couple of years older than myself at that time, and I had occasionally helped him wash out benzine cans. For this he took me along on a test flight, which admittedly, was only a hop of about forty metres length and two metres high. But the prospect of escaping the boredom and inactivity of barracks life and finally getting back to the front, did not allow me a moment's hesitation in reporting to Hauptmann von S.

[Jacob Gödecker was a qualified engineer, and although he had a boat-building business, he was interested in aviation, and studied aerodynamics in 1902. Within a few years he had built his own monoplane, with others following. He soon met up with Anthony Fokker and they worked together at Gödecker's workshops for a while.

Anthony Fokker was the famous Dutch aircraft designer who, after offering his services to both Britain and France, was to be accepted by Germany, and his Fokker Company supplied the German Air Service with some of the most famous aeroplanes to fight on the German side in WW1. These were the Fokker Eindecker, Fokker D.I and D.II, Fokker Dr.I Triplane, Fokker DVII and DVIII. He was born in 1890, so was around four years older than Buckler. His early life was spent in Haarlem, Holland, but by 1908, when he went for military service, he had already started inventing things through engineering. His association with Mainz, and thereby with Buckler, must have occurred when he went to an engineering school at Zahlbach, where the pupils were working on aeroplane design.

He then went into partnership with fifty-year-old Oberleutnant von Daum in order to build a flying machine of his own design that he named 'Spinne' or 'Spider', which was completed in 1910. However, von Daum wrecked it when Fokker was away, so another was built the following year, the year in which Fokker also gained his flying licence (No.88). Von Daum wrecked the second machine, and the partnership was dissolved. Fokker began building a third machine at Gödecker's workshops, and afterwards used to fly as a test pilot and instructor for Gödecker. By 1912 Fokker had his own company at Charlottenburg, Berlin.]

Months of agonised waiting passed until one day the order arrived stating that I had been posted to Flieger-Ersatz-Abteilung 6 [FEA – flight replacement unit] at Grossenhain, although I had no idea where this place was. My farewell visits were carried out quickly and the only person I did not say good-bye to was my mother, in order to spare her renewed agitation. Later I wrote to tell her that I had suddenly received a new posting, at home in fact. For the time being I mentioned nothing about flying.

I was somewhat bewildered when I arrived in Grossenhain [on the Elbe, in Saxony, north-west of Dresden] and heard the people there speaking in a remarkable singing cadence. So that was Saxon! It took some time until I got used to it. It was probably the same for the others with my dialect, since I spoke an unadulterated *Meenzerisch*.

After some time an Oberleutnant from my regiment came to Grossenhain in order to be trained there as an observer. I owe it to him that I was soon detailed to become a pilot. I received a crash helmet and a leather jacket and was permitted to walk upon the airfield for the first time in order to see these dangerous machines close up. How peculiar and complicated did such an engine look. A six-cylinder, someone explained to me. In front was mounted a wonderfully fashioned wooden plank – a propeller, it was called. Igniters were stuck in the individual cylinders, which were called 'spark plugs'. Such a spark plug nearly brought my young flying career to an abrupt end, before I had properly begun it. One of the old ground crew swung a propeller in order to show me how by doing so the engine would be brought to life. When he tugged, the motor clattered frightfully and exploded like an old blunderbuss. The propeller whirred round in a circle several times and then stopped.

'Remove the spark plugs,' growled the mechanic. I had already told him that I could drive an auto, from which he may have concluded that I knew my way around an engine. 'Here is the spark plug wrench.'

Eager as I was, I sprang with a single bound upon the wing [Buckler's foot going through the fabric] and grabbed for the unfortunately still glowing muffler with my left hand. The result of my rash behaviour was a hole in the wing and a burned hand, the consequence of which was three weeks in the hospital.

After my hand had healed I was sent to the Deutsche Flugzeugwerke in Leipzig. The airfield here lay close to a wood, and right away upon my arrival I saw a burned and completely charred 'something' being brought out from between some trees. Disconcerted and with the feeling that this flying was really a damned dodgy business, I reported to the office of the flying school. In a flash the formalities were completed. I had my billet and stood among the student pilots, many of whom had already flown solo and considered themselves demi-gods. What these fellows dished up for the novices in terms of hair-raising stories could really give one the creeps. But I had already learned all about horror on that nocturnal field of dead at the front, so listened calmly to all the wild prattle. However, inwardly I was so stirred up by the frightful experiences of the demi-gods, described in such detail, that I could not sleep during the night. Besides, I was afraid of over-sleeping.

Flying duty was to begin at 04.30 the next morning. Punctually I set off on my way to the airfield. On the way some comrades came towards me, chatting merrily with their crash helmets in their arms. Were they already on the way home? I did not dare ask. I had heard something vaguely about night flights. At the corner of the wood I met Windisch, the only chap I knew by name, and I was never to meet him again. He became well known through a quite special feat of heroism which he carried out with his observer, Oberleutnant von Cossel, boldly landing to blow up a railway line far behind the Russian front. [Later], after twenty-two victories he was awarded the *Pour le Mérite* but did not live to see this supreme wartime decoration. He failed to return from a pursuit flight on 27 May 1918. Nothing was ever known about his fate. Outside of 'good morning', Windisch did not say a word and likewise walked past me. Something is not quite right here, I thought to myself.

> [Rudolf Friedrich Otto Windisch came from Dresden and like Buckler had served in the infantry, and had also been wounded before 1914 had ended. He had reported to the flying school at Leipzig in January 1915. In May 1916 he was flying with FFA62 (Feld Flieger Abteilung No.62) on the Russian front and the mission Buckler refers to was undertaken on the night of 2/3 October. Windisch flew Maximilian von Cossel there, landed to drop him off, and then flew home. Von Cossel blew up an important railway bridge near Rowno-Brody, and Windisch returned the next day and picked him up. Both men were decorated for their feat with the Honour Cross with

Swords from the Principality of Waldeck, and the St Henry Medal in Silver from Saxony. Later, Windisch served with Kampfgeschwader 2 in France and then with Jasta 32, and in 1918, as Staffelführer of Jasta 66. With a victory tally of twenty-two, he had received the Knight's Cross with Swords of the Royal Hohenzollern House Order, the Austro-Hungarian Bravery Medal in Silver, 2nd Class, and the Saxon St Henry Medal in Gold.

On the day of his last victory he was brought down and as his men saw him on the ground it was assumed he had survived. At this time the award of the *Pour le Mérite* generally came after a pilot had achieved twenty victories, although not if the pilot had been killed. Assuming he was a prisoner of the French, the award was made, but as Buckler related, Windisch was never heard from again. After the war it was suggested that Windisch had been shot whilst trying to evade capture and had tried to steal a French aircraft. Another theory is that French soldiers simply killed him.]

The entrances to the hangars were closed. On one of the hangar roofs, extending outwards from a pole, was an inflated tubular thing which resembled a trouser leg filled with air. This was a 'windsock', as I later learned and it was due to this sack, wildly tugging and flapping on the pole, that all was not right here. Because of this the flight cadets were heading home and the hangar entrance was closed, with not a single aeroplane in the open. Due to the windsock's excited behaviour it meant, for the initiated, 'flyer's weather' i.e. no weather for flying. Therefore the old 'aces,' apart from the conscientious Windisch, did not even go to the airfield, whilst the others immediately turned around again. However, they had let me, the novice, continue to walk oblivious of the problem. Everyone had to gain experience on his own, and this is the way it should have been.

* * *

For me it was of inestimable benefit. All alone like this on the airfield, I could look around undisturbed and thoroughly acquaint myself with the terrain and many other things. In front of the mess I met the gatekeeper, and was able to question him to my heart's content without exposing myself to ridicule. So from him I learned all sorts of things that are extremely important for a young student pilot. Our friendship was quickly established by the Iron Cross 2nd Class, which we both wore. After I told him something of assaults and night-time patrols, and also allowed him time to do the same, he became communicative. First he advised me not to be in a hurry when it was windy, otherwise I would be the first at the field and have taken the one hour to walk there in vain. If I allowed myself time I could already see the others coming back from far off and could quickly return and lie in bed again. I took this advice in the following days, then we were quartered in barracks. Indeed, we were so well accommodated and so sumptuously provided for that we did not regret it. Back to my gatekeeper….

'You must absolutely try to get to Höfig', he continued with his well-intended advice. 'This is an old pilot, a Flieger-Leutnant, and our best flyer. He does crazy things! When he takes his first flight with you, then dead certain there will be a corkscrew [manoeuvre] from two thousand metres, as though pulled down by a string. Stick with it without vomiting and he will definitely make a good pilot out of you.'

'Corkscrew?' I asked timidly. This was again a concept about which I knew absolutely nothing. My new friend just grinned. He was in his element.

'First he climbs with his machine until he has reached the height of two thousand metres. Then he tips the machine on its wing, tears round several times to the right and several times to the left. Then he dives down….' He stopped and asked anxiously, 'Are you alright? You look so pale.'

'I haven't eaten breakfast,' I stuttered in reply. In reality, the whole world was spinning around me. My gatekeeper and front-line comrade took me under the arm and dragged me into the canteen. Until breakfast came, he continued talking:

'After the dive he levels the machine out and goes around again a couple of times to the right.' He demonstrated to me on the chair how much one sat at an incline in the machine during such a corkscrew. 'Then around again to the left and finally he speeds towards the hangar. Just when you think you are about to go into the hangar roof with a mighty crash, he has already landed with you. And if you can then look him straight in the eye, don't stagger or look for something to hold onto, then yes, he'll be like a father to you.'

While I now ate breakfast and at the same time considered whether I should now desire or fear that this very dare-devil Höfig might become my instructor, my companion went on and on, from corkscrews to wheel chocks, from cracking up and wheels being lost during take-offs, to landings in the woods and from that to instruction, the instructors, and the 'demi-gods', to their whims and their tricks. In the course of four hours – in the meantime we had switched to whisky, with which I had not been acquainted until then – he initiated me so thoroughly into the life and goings-on at the flying school that I could not have learned it better in as many days. I also learned from him the names of the other instructors. There was 'dear Böhme', Steinbeck, Gasser, Schlerf, Rehse, and as chief pilot, 'old Oelerich'. The commander of the school was Hauptmann Willi Meyer, likewise an old peacetime pilot.

[Of these Willi Meyer had gained his flying licence in

November 1911 (Licence No.137); Heinrich Oelerich in October 1910 (No.37); Hans Steinbeck in February 1911 (No.68); Hermann Gasser in May 1912 (No.202); Walter Höfig in November 1913 (No.585); Kurt Rehse in April 1914 (No.735).]

The trial flight

After three days of calm air, flight activity began. There were continuous take-offs and landings, and I was so taken by it all that I almost missed it when they called out: 'Buckler, off in the machine!'

Helpful hands crammed a heavy helmet on my head, wrapped a scarf around my neck, and assisted me in clambering inside and buckling me in. Who was sitting behind me at the controls I did not know. The amused, somewhat maliciously gleeful looks from those standing around made me feel like I was a mere dummy on this flight. And I myself felt very odd and useless in this cumbersome mummery. Since I did not know anyone outside of Windisch and the gatekeeper I was not able to figure out who was working the controls of my machine even if I did look back. While climbing in I had only seen that the one sitting behind me had no shoulder tabs, so I thought in my naiveté it could not be a Leutnant. It was not Höfig, so thank God I would be spared the corkscrew.

Filled with courage by these thoughts, I nodded to those remaining behind and even thought how nice it would be if my school chums could see me like this. Then the aeroplane sped away. In my excitement I had not even noticed the propeller being swung. The machine jolted horribly [as we taxied out] and the motor clattered frightfully. I became somewhat uneasy and above all I was horrified at how trees and houses which stood at the edge of the airfield were in such a frantic rush to remain behind.

Hardly had we detached ourselves from the earth and gained some height when everything appeared to grow more peaceful. Trees and houses moved more slowly and the distance from them became greater. On the panel in front of me three gauges began working. From my friend on the airfield I had learned that one of them indicated the height and now I saw with creeping dread how the indicator on one of the gauges rose from one number to the next: 500… 1,000… 2,000. Remarkable! Two thousand metres above the earth and I did not feel the slightest bit dizzy when I looked down. My roofing trade had taught me to be free from vertigo and I was downright proud of that which I believed was responsible for this lack of dizziness. I had no idea that other people experienced no dizziness while flying. This conception confirmed for me at this moment that because of my trade I was obviously quite especially suited to become a flyer. Admittedly this perception was not to last very long.

I dared to turn my head somewhat. Frightful, this stony face behind me. What if it were Höfig after all? The altimeter showed just 2,000 metres above the earth when the right wing rose vertically. There was a howling in the wires and in my head. Involuntarily I looked up at the rising wing-tip, and when doing so I felt so strange that I quickly stared straight ahead once more and immediately the uncertain feeling went away. The machine came out of its steep attitude and appeared to want to fly straight ahead again. I rejoiced. So this was the dangerous corkscrew? Now if it continues to.... Goodness gracious! The thing began to go around to the right. Now the left wing rose steeply upwards. This time I refrained from looking upwards, closed my eyes, and held on tightly. It was a good thing the person sitting behind me could not see my face, otherwise he might have thought I was afraid.

Was I afraid? Suddenly I was even more afraid of being afraid, or in the event, showing it. If the person sitting behind me was indeed Höfig, it was dead certain that the dive would come now, and then I would know it was he. Hardly had I thought this when the aircraft stood on its nose and sped downwards, as it seemed to me, directly towards the roof of the hangar. With a jerk the nose of the machine rose again and it was pulled into a loop. The clattering of the engine ceased and before I had quite oriented myself again, the wheels touched the ground. The machine wobbled and my heart pounded heavily.

But the short distance which my pilot needed to taxi up to the front of the hangar sufficed to allow me to recover from this last fright to the extent that I climbed out calmly, did not stagger, did not look for any support, and when the man with the iron face stood before me and looked at me I could look him straight in the eye. This was, I knew, the decisive moment, because this man really was Leutnant Höfig, and I had passed the test.

It was a good thing that my future instructor did not see me ten minutes later! The reaction was violent, but it never happened again. Through the couple of minutes in which I overcame my fear and pulled myself together, I had earned myself the best flight instructor one could get and to whom, when I think about it, I owe the whole great transformation of my life. This was the fellow who loved to fly and he flew like a god! I can allow myself this judgement today after almost twenty-five years of flying.

First solo flight

On the following day I was stuck into a training machine for the first time. In front of me I had a steering wheel which did not look much different from those which our local skippers have on the Rhine. My feet rested on a rudder bar.

'Listen closely,' said Höfig, who took his seat behind me. 'During the first flight just feel along. During the second, place your feet on the rudder bar. If you push that to the left, the crate will go round to the left and when you push to the right, it will go around to the right. If you want to fly straight, then keep your feet still.' Just as brief and to the point were his instructions for elevator controls too. 'When you push, the crate goes down. When you pull, it goes up.'

How simple these explanations were and just as simple was the whole method of instruction. First climbing, then diving, then banking, then take-offs, then landings, and finally, everything together. It was astonishing how quickly he taught us this. There can only be one explanation for this – he was not only an excellent master teacher, but was also an awfully sharp pilot. He did not just allow us to fly on a leash, as it were, but rather he let us almost run into the ground and yet always found the right moment to prevent the worst from happening. He deliberately allowed us to plunge into danger and to undertake all manner of possible and impossible experiments in order to extract ourselves from them, until he did away with them by suddenly taking charge if the student himself did not succeed in this. Only in this way was it possible for us to be ready for the first solo flight after just a few training flights. In my case it was nothing short of record time, even according to the standards back then.

It was a calm day and Höfig had just undertaken a flight with me. After he climbed out, he said, 'So go up alone now.' I believe I turned as white as a sheet. If only I had a couple of more minutes to think things through properly once again. However, Höfig's order had already been followed. There were no longer any machines in the air, all the propellers were at rest. Just mine was turning. The motor did not stop once so that I might have gained a short delay. No, it hammered merrily and perfectly as though it could hardly wait to convince me of its reliability.

So, lever up; full throttle. Off! What the devil? What's wrong with the machine? First it swerves to the right, then to the left. Has it gone crazy? Close throttle. Bang! It is already upside down and I am hanging from the seat harness.

'Propeller and undercarriage gone,' the mechanic reported to the Leutnant. As I stood before Höfig, I stammered meekly. Everything was probably pointless now. I would probably never be able to fly solo. He took no notice of my stammering, but rather had another machine made ready for take-off.

'Okay, but now pull yourself together.' I grabbed the lever.

'Again, damn it!' I heard Höfig say. Yes, sir, again damn it, and pull myself together. I gasped for air, concentrated for a moment, and opened the throttle again. Then, as if it were the simplest thing in the world, the machine ran over the smooth turf, lifted off, and I was in the air. I was flying solo.

This thought was nice, was heartening, but unfortunately somewhat troubled by the memory of the broken machine in which I had just been hanging with my head pointed downwards. Just keep calm little Buckler, I encouraged myself, what others can do, you can do just as well.

Three kilometres straight, then briefly around and down again, just as in training flights. But before I was aware of it, my three kilometres became ten, and I was 200 metres high when I finally worked the rudder. I was in the air twelve full minutes. It seemed inconceivable to me, although it seemed more inconceivable that I was suddenly standing once more upon the earth with wheels intact. But in the end I had done everything as if in a dream and actually while doing so had only thought constantly of Höfig.

I was already looking forward to being able to report the smooth landing to him, but then came his order: 'Take off again immediately!' So the first solo flight was to be followed by three more on the same day. Only during the fourth solo flight was I properly convinced that I could now really fly and land solo. Höfig and all my comrades congratulated me and, confused and proud, I endured it.

Solo flight festivities and pilot's test

It occurred to me that the 'solo flight festivities' were supposed to be held today in Lindenthal, which is what Höfig had decided. Because with our meagre financial means not every pilot who completed his solo could conduct his own festivities and be the sole host, it was established that several pilots would always get together and celebrate and thus share the costs. I quickly shaved and got dressed.

On the street I met a pair of fellow solo pilots, who like myself were coming with a crash helmet and leather jacket. We were not just a little proud that the young girls were turning to look at us. We had the 'old hand' to thank for this ridiculous attire, who had convinced us that, beginning with the first solo flight, every pilot goes out only in aviator's garb. When we arrived at the pub where the celebration was to be held, we were then also received by the 'old hand' with the appropriate guffaws. So our pride again quickly dwindled to nothing.

A proper grand celebration was held, all entirely in pilots' style, with amusingly mimicked demonstrations of take-offs and landings, gliding flight and corkscrews, together with drinking and dancing. There were also young ladies present.

As dawn broke it was raining and the presiding 'weather god', i.e., the one to whom this role had fallen in the course of the proceedings, promised us with his divine authority a full day of rain. This meant a day of rest, of which we had urgent need because in the state in which we lined up before Hauptmann Meyer on the airfield in the morning, we would not have been surprised if he had closed the school and sent us all to the front as infantrymen. But it need not have been a rainy day at all, as the good Hauptmann Meyer knew all about the frame of mind of a young person who had his first solo flight behind him. He simply let us retire and we were grateful to him for that. We also never gave him an occasion to have us line up in such a condition again.

Of course we did sometimes assemble and unfortunately it was often in order to lay a comrade to rest. It was unsettling when just a few hours before one had been chatting with one another in a carefree manner and now the other person had already fulfilled his young destiny. These are things which make a deep impression, especially when one is as young as we were then.

There followed a period of solo flights. They consisted of short circling flights of about five to seven minutes. Then it was time for precision landings, which were carried out from a height of 500 metres with the engine switched off. When doing so, one had to land within a circle and bring the aircraft to a stop inside it. We constantly flew in figures of eight as preparation for doing banked turns. Training was concluded with a high-altitude flight up to 2,500 metres. Improbable as it may seem to young flyers today, it took almost an hour to reach this altitude with the aircraft we had back then.

Because I still did not know much about orientation and nothing at all about tail winds, when I had reached the prescribed height of 2,500 metres, I suddenly found myself over the Leipzig main railway station. To switch to a glide at such a height seemed extremely dubious to me, but I pulled back the throttle lever and went into a glide, somewhat too steeply, as the wires whistled [in the slipstream] and I came down precipitously. However, I succeeded, and even today I do not know how, in landing smoothly on the airfield. A few minutes later I stood before Höfig as a freshly trained military pilot with three weeks' leave in my pocket. My entire training had lasted a little less than four weeks.

Flight instructor

When my leave was at an end I returned to Lindenthal, again without saying farewell to my mother. Here I was surprised by the news that I was not going immediately to the front, as I had hoped, but rather I was assigned to be a flight instructor. With my youth and utter lack of experience – a flight instructor! I would have preferred first to earn my spurs flying at the front rather than act as teacher and role model for the mostly much older pupils without the necessary experience.

My secret fear of not being quite up to this job was unfortunately confirmed by my first landing [after returning], which could be forgiven a beginner, but was entirely unworthy of an instructor. I landed with such a badly bent axle that an archer would have only needed a string and an arrow to go hunting with it. It was shaped like a semi-circle. It was not to be the last bent axle either. After seven flights seven axles made their way to the repair shop. That I was not relieved of my duty remains a mystery to me.

I was annoyed by the ridicule of my colleagues, most of whom could fly better only with their mouths. I went to Höfig and poured out my troubles to him.

'Landing is part of flying,' he said, 'just as in riding when the horseman must bring his mount to a halt. Each flight is only completed after landing.

You're just afraid of putting the machine on the ground.'

However humiliating it may have seemed to the others, for me, an instructor, I asked Höfig to make another training flight with me. I would have thought that not doing so indicated an inappropriate sense of shame. Because here it was a matter of properly understanding the flying trade, just as my father had taught me to practice the roofing trade in a thorough fashion. Then behold, after the training flight I landed the machine intact. Höfig climbed out and I then made ten more flights around the airfield and each landing was better than the others. The curse was broken.

* * *

I was assigned six flight pupils and duty began at 04.15 in the morning, which meant getting up at 03.30 and going to bed very early. Amongst my pupils was one by the name of Jannak. He was a musician and, in fact, a good one. He was also a good student pilot, the first one I allowed to take off for a solo flight.

His first solo flight stirred me up inside almost more than had my own. He opened the throttle and the tail of the machine came up. Then he swerved to the right, got the machine back under control, raced straight ahead, and lifted off. Thank God, he was flying! He flew exactly as I myself had done at that time, much too long in the same direction. Why did he not finally go into a banking turn? Suddenly he turned and banked, but one couldn't call it a bank; he described a wide arc in the sky. That was fine as far as I was concerned, better than banking too sharply. Then he began to glide, much too late it seemed to me. Then everything went dark, as I closed my eyes in order not to have to see what horrible thing would now occur. So it came about that I did not witness the first landing of my first pupil, which was completed smoothly in every respect.

I was much more concerned about the lives and health of my pupils than the equipment. However, this degree of sensitivity disconcerted me and once more raised the question, this time for a different reason, whether I was suited to becoming a pilot and especially a flight instructor. Again it was Höfig, the good teacher and friend, who helped me, understood me, did not smile, did not scoff, but rather assured me based on his seasoned experience that my inhibition rose from a quite natural sense of duty and through familiarization would disappear on its own. And it did.

One solo flight followed the other. One after another my students passed the military pilot exam and the solo flight celebrations multiplied. Admittedly, it did not go off without a crash, but after all it was war. War! In the daily routine of school activity one could almost forget about it. I had been at the front and wanted to get back to it. The more time slipped by, the more burning was the desire in me to get serious with my flying career and to be able to show out there what I had learned. I therefore reported to the commander and asked for a transfer to the front. He listened to me kindly, but nothing happened.

New types of aircraft arrived. Höfig took me along for acceptance flights. They climbed better and higher than the old ones. With some of them we attained at that time – the end of 1915 – a height of 3,000 metres. Through the testing of every newer type Höfig acquired quite a tremendous amount of experience and was by far our best pilot.

When school activity ceased, I practised on a trumpet which Jannak, the musician, had given me as a souvenir of his first solo flight. Although I had all the necessary breath for blowing and a good musical ear, I had soon to give up trumpeting for the sake of my fellow man, who like Wilhelm Busch, found that this music involved too much noise. I have nevertheless preserved the trumpet in memory of Jannak. He suffered a terrible fate. After he had survived the entire war, since he could not find work as a musician, he got a job as a mechanic at an auto repair shop in Berlin. On a midsummer's day one of his fellow workers carelessly lit a cigarette while filling up a car with gasoline and Jannak went up in smoke with the others.

Since I did not have any other passion [after discarding the trumpet] I dedicated myself solely to flying duty. I received more and more new students and was also allowed to participate in test flying. This was the greatest thrill. One day a machine of the latest design arrived, a DFW, which was called *Puppchen.* Like a frivolous little lady, she capered and wagged her tail about in the air so lightly, elegantly, and flirtatiously. As can happen with such little ladies, she was almost my undoing.

Hauptmann Meyer's chauffeur absolutely wanted to fly once and he had in fact got it into his head that he only wanted to fly with me. On a cloudy day I took him along, after the Hauptmann had expressly authorised it. Instead of remaining below the clouds, which hung at about 300 metres, I sped with Puppchen into the 'soup' in the hope of quickly pushing through and being able to show my guest the beauty of a flight above the clouds. There the motor acquired a strange sound, like a kind of booming roar.

Puppchen began to dance and turn like mad. The chauffeur screamed and screeched like a hysterical woman. I saw the airfield approaching me at lightning speed but nothing I tried to do helped, we kept on spinning. So I left the machine alone and that, it turned out, was the right thing to do. Just four metres from the ground Puppchen lifted her nose, lowered her tail modestly and flew straight ahead in a well-behaved manner. Then she made such a soft and careful landing that eggs really could have lain beneath her wheels without breaking. After this miraculous escape the sissy chauffeur, who with trembling knees could hardly hold himself upright, hurled insults at me. I resolved to take along no more unnecessary ballast any time soon.

Only when I was in my quarters did I become conscious of the whole magnitude of the danger in which we had found ourselves. I began to wonder about how man's subconscious intervenes in his fate, because quite instinctively, without my being able to account for the reason why, I had left the machine to its own devices. In order to explore the matter further, I spoke with Höfig about it. In his calm, reflective manner he said: 'It is possible that what you did here was the correct thing. But otherwise, when things get precarious, don't close your eyes and wait for the crash. No, always steer towards the side in which the machine is spinning.' He was right and I would have occasion sometimes to follow his advice.

On the same day I was called into the office of the commander. Had the chauffeur told on me? Or did my involuntary dive also create an unpleasant sensation in other quarters? Would I receive a reprimand, or even punishment? I was not aware of any recklessness, for I had not made this wild dive on purpose.

'You have been ordered to the flying school at Metz,' said Hauptmann Meyer as I entered the room and walked up to him. A disciplinary transfer, I thought, and I dared to object timidly.

'But Metz isn't situated at the front, Herr Hauptmann.' Smiling, the good man consoled me with the fact that Metz was nevertheless only about 25 kilometres from the French border. So I had to get packing. I only had a rucksack, but a real flyer only travels with a little suitcase. So in all haste I purchased a small reed suitcase, packed up, and bid farewell to my comrades, with special sincerity and gratitude to my instructor Höfig.

Chapter Four

The Eyes of the Artillery

The more cultivated lifestyle

Did the train to Metz not pass through Mainz? Yes indeed, but I could not bring myself to get off it without permission. So I travelled through my hometown as a thoroughly trained military pilot wearing the spare uniform which I had purchased with my extra flight pay and student's bonuses and greeted my mother and sisters in spirit only. They would certainly have come to the railway station filled with joy, had I informed them in time by way of a telegram, but what would be the point of burdening my poor mother's heart with repeated partings?

There was a long stop at a station before Metz, where one noticed the greater proximity of the front. One saw soldiers sitting around covered in mud, just as they had come from the trenches. In my new uniform, which really smelled of the rear echelon, I felt like a refined jackass. Instead of going second class in the waiting room and eating roast as I had planned, I put on my worn-out service uniform in my compartment and ordered small sausages and potato salad in Waiting Room III. Full of deep respect I looked at the dirty men in whose features the horror of war had left its mark. While I had slept every night in a soft bed and eaten regularly three times a day, what privations had these poor men suffered at the same time? And for this I even received extra pay. Was a flyer not a soldier like any other? It seemed unfair to me.

I arrived in Metz in the afternoon. My father had served here as a soldier and I recalled a story from his days in the army at Metz that he had often related to us as children and which lived on in us as a sort of legend. Back then he was the orderly of a Hauptmann and one day this officer took him along as a beater on a boar hunt. During this a wounded boar charged my father, who was only able to escape his dangerous assailant by quickly fleeing up a tree. The enraged beast tore at the roots with its tusks so that the tree began swaying and my father tumbled down. A timely shot from the Hauptmann saved him from being gored.

Now I was in this legendary city. I took a streetcar out to the airfield at Frescaty and admired the new Zeppelin hangar, the big beautiful administration building, the aircraft hangars, the repair shops, and many other things there. Here as well there was a little wood in the vicinity. Small wooden areas near airfields have a particular force of attraction, especially for young flyers. It is as though the trees therein were magnetic.

> [Frescaty was the base for Armee Flug Park 5, an army aviation supply depot, and other units.]

I introduced myself to my new commander, Oberleutnant von Schmickaly. All old flyers know this name and mention it full of reverence. This outstanding flight officer was equally loveable as a superior and as a human being. From the first moment I had the impression that my luck could not have been any better. He asked me about my civilian occupation and when I told him that I was a roofer by trade, he nodded with no less friendliness and approval than if I had told him that I was a prince of noble blood.

> [Kurt Schmickaly came from Berlin and was twenty-eight years old. In 1916 he flew with Kek Metz (*Kampfeinsitzer Kommando* – a single-seat fighter detachment based at Metz flying Fokker Eindecker machines) and was severely wounded on 22 October over Malzeville, near Nancy, and died the next day. His death on the 23rd came the same day as Jagdstaffel (Jasta) 17 was officially formed at Metz and Schmickaly may well have commanded this new fighting unit had he not been killed. Buckler would later serve with Jasta 17.]

Schmickaly began to speak immediately of flying matters, the one thing close to his heart, and went on about LVGs, Aviatiks, AEGs, Albatrosses and Fokkers, till my head was spinning. I had not heard a single word about many of these types and he was very considerate not to reproach me for my ignorance, which he must have seen in my astonished eyes. Then he downright apologised when he dismissed me with the words: 'Unfortunately you must take up your quarters in corrugated tin barracks, as all the other buildings are occupied.' To please him I would have lain on a heap of dung.

I shared my quarters with a certain Hübner, who hailed from Bremen, and had been a language teacher. He tactfully made me aware of one instance of my poor German in that he described it as a dialectal peculiarity of Hessian character and in less than six weeks I had broken myself of this poor speech habit.

Hübner took upon himself not only the refinement of my speech, but also other aspects of my manners. On his birthday I was allowed to be his guest at Moitrier's. This was the finest restaurant in Metz, which is well-known to all gourmands. There were things there which I had never seen, let alone eaten: oysters, truffles, morels, lobster tails, omelette soufflé. For the first time it became clear to me that there were better things in the world than legumes, which I had eaten with great relish as an infantryman and also at my parent's house, especially when there was bacon in addition. How gladly would I have passed on some of these delicacies to my mother and sisters who were eating bread and marmalade at home and knew as little about these fine things as myself up till that moment. Hübner, you were a good comrade, a good teacher, and a good host, but an awful flyer. At least you were back then, and this was to your everlasting sorrow.

'Blue Mouse'

My comradeship with the good Hübner, which proved to be so profitable and pleasant for me, unfortunately came to an abrupt end. Once again my wild flying was to blame. I also test-flew machines at Metz and for a long time I had been accustomed to settling into each machine and speeding away fearlessly. I had so far been able to handle each and every one of them.

'So, Buckler, today you're flying the Blue Mouse,' Oberleutnant von Schmickaly said to me one day. 'Blue Mouse' sounded odd; it was an Aviatik machine. Blue Mouse, I will think of you for as long as I live. You were the most nimble, lively, cunning beast of an aircraft I have ever encountered. You were meant for an expert's touch. You were a delightful and dangerous pastime and one could not help being fond of you. Yet you bestowed your favour only on those who trusted in you completely, and devoted themselves to you entirely, and who controlled you totally – while keeping a tight rein on you. Woe to the poor soul who did not know how to treat you. Oh, how mean you could then be, how vile, how spiteful, how malicious. Then you were the merciless diva, a villain, a she-devil who dragged her unfortunate lover with her to hell. How many you have on your conscience!

You let me drive you hard and harass you. I could do whatever I wanted with you; you were into it. Be honest, Blue Mouse, wasn't it great? Even today I am enchanted by you. I must have abused you awfully, although in my ecstasy I hardly noticed. I suppose we probably played a much too wildly amorous game in the sky, for when I returned with you to the earth and to my senses I was then separated from you forever. Perhaps it was feared that I might do you some harm in my recklessness, as supposedly happens with possessed lovers who find release only in death.

Along with Oberleutnant von Schmickaly, Hauptmann Keller had witnessed my flight. His name as well has long since entered the annals of aviation history covered with glory. His bombing raids conducted against England with great daring and determination have earned him the nick-name 'Iron Keller' or *Bombenkeller*. Today he is the General der Flieger in the new German Luftwaffe.

[Alfred Keller came from Bochum, Westphalia, and was thirty-two years old when the war began. A former army cadet, he became an observer in the German Air Service before the war and in late 1914 commanded FFA27, and later AFP 5. He commanded FFA40 in 1916 and converted it into a night bombing unit, and in the spring of 1917 commanded Kampfgeschwader Nr.I. He had flown with this unit in Macedonia but the daylight sorties were too costly so he was ordered to Flanders to fly black-painted Friedrichshafen bombers. In late 1917 he was awarded the *Orden Pour le Mérite* (announced on the same day as Buckler's). In the Luftwaffe he commanded bomber units and in WW2 he won the Knight's Cross of the Iron Cross for his work during the Battle of France in 1940. He was still active in May 1945. He died in February 1974.]

'You flew brazenly!' Hauptmann Keller said when I landed. So I expected something bad was about to happen. 'You are coming with me immediately to the army aviation supply depot.'

He must have already arranged the matter with von Schmickaly, as he was standing right next to him with his unwavering expression and raised no sort of objection. So I was receiving a disciplinary transfer for a second time? Or maybe the Armee Flug Park needed a flyer who had some confidence in himself and enjoyed taking on awkward machines? Well, I would soon find out. First of all it meant get packing. I said farewell to Hübner, my teacher in matters of the more cultivated lifestyle.

Hauptmann Keller took me along immediately in his car. I had never driven in such a fast and heavy automobile. He raced down the highway at a speed that made me feel as though it were greater than that of an aeroplane in the sky. The trees flitted by so awfully fast that I thought all that was needed was a lost wheel or a stone lying in the way and I would end my flying career in a roadside ditch. In spite of these pessimistic observations by someone who had not often in his life travelled by car, we arrived safe and sound at the Armee Flug Park.

It was already late in the year, cold and rainy. I received first-rate quarters, and what astonished me, the 'disciplinary transferee', was that I was allowed to dine with the officers. How I benefited at that point from your improvement of my manners, down to the skilful handling of knife and fork, my dear Hübner!

Hauptmann Keller was a splendid fellow and a born leader. He did not need to protect his authority with artificial barriers. He had a natural and warm-hearted air about him. Of quite opposite nature was an officer candidate who was the chief pilot and a test pilot at the AFP. He also sat at the table and was a crude, thick-set fellow without any heart, including a heart for flying. I immediately noticed that he could not stand me, perhaps he feared the competition. It was all the same to me.

The airfield was flooded by constant downpours and for that reason we took off from a small elevated field in the vicinity. One day an Abteilung urgently needed a machine. There was one available which had just been made ready for take-off, but had not even been tested yet. Keller sent for me.

'Do you feel yourself capable of taking off in the machine from up here?'

'Yes, Herr Hauptmann.'

Without a second thought I jumped into the crate, made a test flight, and landed again smoothly on the field atop a small hill. Presumably, I had therewith finally proven my readiness for frontline service to Hauptmann Keller, who really knew something about flying and aircraft. A few days later he relinquished me to a Flieger Abteilung at the front. But whom did I basically have to thank for my good fortune in being sent to the front as a pilot? Only you, Blue Mouse.

Flieger Abteilung (A) 209. First flights at the front

Again I was brought to my new scene of operations by car. How nice we flyers had it in that respect! When switching from one sector of the front to another, a poor infantryman rumbled along all day by rail, crammed together with many others in a freight car, only to have then still to march many kilometres.

My new commander, Hauptmann Funck, received me like a comrade and immediately took me into the officers' mess. In his Abteilung the non-commissioned flyers sat together with the officers. A splendid breakfast was served up. There was no one else present at this time in the mess, just Funck and myself, and he gave me a thorough questioning. This was no superficial interrogation. In order to be able to size me up properly, he was interested in knowing who I was, what I had learned and what I had accomplished.

> [Werner Funck came from Posen, East Prussia. He was born in September 1885 and so was nearly ten years older than Buckler. Joining the army in 1904 – 33rd Fusilier Regiment – he was commissioned in August the following year and made Oberleutnant when war came and Hauptmann a year later. By then he had joined the Air Service, learning to fly in 1912, and just as the war started, was flying with Flieger-Bataillon Nr.2 on the Eastern Front, where he was decorated with the Prussian Crown Order 4th Class with Swords, and then sent to FA13 in 1915. Among his comrades with this unit was Oswald Boelcke and his brother Wilhelm. He moved to FA(A)209 in November 1915 as CO and was promoted to Hauptmann. He was further decorated with the Ducal Saxe-Ernestine House

Order, Knight 1st Class with Swords, in March 1916.

After leaving FA(A)209 in September 1916 to take command of FA55 and then FA(A)251, he remained CO till March 1917. He spent most of the rest of the war in charge of two army aviation depots, AFP 1 and AFP 4. Then after a short period as a liaison officer with the Austrians he took charge of AFP 17 in the first half of 1918. His other decorations included the Iron Cross 1st and 2nd Class for his war flying and later the Knight's Cross of the Royal Hohenzollern House Order, and Hindenburg Cross with Swords. Served again in WW2 in the Luftwaffe, which he had joined in 1935, mainly with various air equipment units. By 1945 he held the rank of generalmajor. He died in Bad Kissingen in October 1965.]

As always, the first question [Funck asked] concerned my civilian occupation. It was the one question I dreaded somewhat and which at the same time became for me a secret test for the one who put it to me. I was not ashamed of a trade which was also that of my father, having grown up experiencing his respect for it.

So why did this question nonetheless always cause my face to redden? I had learned there were people who had turned up their noses at the word 'roofer' and who from the moment they heard it no longer considered me socially acceptable and in whose eyes it degraded me. That touched a sore point with me for it affected my honour. At that time I was still too young to be able to judge properly the worth of such people who disapproved of an honourable labourer's profession. I still allowed myself to be overly impressed by them; today that has changed. Now I know what to think of such people, and there are still some of them around. I know them and could mention them by name, only they no longer impress me. Today I know that they are small-minded people who have never really learned about life, and who for this reason have remained spiritually immature. Because they cannot properly appreciate work they also have no respect for it. They are the drones of life, the caste-minded, and eternal philistines. I have no more respect for you. I have seen through you and found nothing hidden.

With Hauptmann Funck I could immediately see in his face, which did not wince with embarrassment or sympathy, that my honest answer did not meet with any narrow-minded estimation.

'To me a roofer who can fly well is preferable to a scholar who is frightened by the noise of the engine,' he said, pressing my hand warmly. 'You have been quite especially recommended to me by my friend Keller. Now let's show you to your quarters. By the way, your observer who's coming tomorrow, an Oberleutnant, was in his private profession a shoe-shiner over in America. A splendid fellow. You will get on fine with him.' All this sounded like how one spoke among comrades and I resolved to show myself worthy of his comradeship.

'I almost forgot the most important thing,' Funck called after me as I went to the door. 'Your machine is number seven.'

* * *

My first trip was not to my quarters but to my machine. To my great joy I met an old comrade on the airfield who was with an Abteilung which shared the airfield with us, and he insisted in taking me around, showing me the machines, and introducing me to my new comrades. I was especially thankful to him for that, as I always had a sort of stage-fright when it came to the usual introduction in the officers' mess. I saw my machine, a DFW, and made the acquaintance of the *Werkmeister* [or senior NCO mechanic], the ground crew and the dogs which are to be found at every airfield.

I had no more time to change for lunch. I found out that all the others appeared in their service uniforms and that at the rear I had been very falsely informed about the customs of a Feld-Flieger Abteilung. However, I still ran into a little bit of embarrassment when Hauptmann Funck indicated to me that I should take the seat to his right. I had in fact heard that in many an officer's mess it was the custom that every new arrival was the guest of the commander on the first day. That this custom also extended to non-commissioned officers surprised me. To be sure, it was war, and we were all fighting for our Fatherland.

Hardly had we sat down when immediately a lively discussion began which was especially instructive to me and revolved almost exclusively around flying matters, about ranging artillery, a new piece of wireless equipment, and the evaluation of photographs which had just been taken from an aircraft. This was all new territory to me, having not yet learned anything other than how to fly. The striking musical accompaniment to these discussions was provided by the ceaseless fire of the artillery, whose batteries were located less than six kilometres from our airfield.

The two comrades who were billeted in the same quarters with me, a nice big room with spanking clean camp-beds, lay down for a noon-time nap, but I felt like going out to the airfield again. I did not need to familiarize myself any further with my machine for I knew the type thoroughly. What interested me more was the layout of the airfield. While pacing it off I determined that the field was anything but good. It was very small, had poor soil conditions, with considerable variations in height, and a lot of ditches around. So that meant pay a hell of a lot of attention! In order to try it out, I settled into my machine and taxied away over the field. After a good take-off I climbed to a nice altitude in order to gain the best possible overview.

At 3,000 metres height, looking to the west, I saw how the sun was preparing to set with a reddish glow. So much beauty captivated me to the extent that I entirely forgot where I was. However, I was quickly made aware that I was here at the front. White and black cloudlets were suddenly hanging in the air around me and then there was a detonation in close proximity, so like an old warrior I quickly throttled back and dived. In my ignorance of the conditions of the front and the layout of the lines [front line trenches], and attracted by the glorious image of the peacefully sinking sun, I had flown much too far to the west and found myself over the enemy trenches.

In the landscape below me two sharply defined trapezoid-shaped structures caught my attention, which could only be forts. I had no idea that there were Forts Vaux and Douaumont, around which so much blood had been spilled and much more would yet be shed.

> [These two forts were perhaps the most well known in front of the city of Verdun, and had seen much fighting during 1916.]

I landed again after an hour. Because there was still enough light, though dusky, I went up a second time in order to impress upon my mind from a low altitude the way to the front and its layout in our sector. I did it at the same time in the interest of my future observer.

As I flew forth once more, peering sharply downwards and only anxious not to renew my acquaintance with enemy anti-aircraft fire, I immediately got to know a second, no less dangerous peril which threatened a novice flyer at the front who flew alone and suspected nothing menacing. There was a ‘tack-tack’ sound next to me and while I throttled down and tore the machine around I just managed to glimpse a shadowy lattice-fuselage aircraft with blue-white-red cockades speeding by me. This was the first enemy aircraft I had seen.

I only realised how lucky I was not to have been shot down right on the first day when after landing the mechanics asked me about the origin of the holes in my wings. I shrugged my shoulders. ‘Don’t know,’ I said. The mechanics laughed. They knew their stuff and were thoroughly familiar with their machine. Besides that, it had just come from the factory brand new. On the following morning the holes were neatly patched, circles were painted around them, and they were furnished with a date.

Rudno, my observer

Late in the evening of this first day with my new unit, Artillerie Flieger Abteilung 209, my observer arrived. His name was von Rudno-Rudzinsky, but soon everyone just called him Rudno. When you came in, dear Rudno, we all glanced up at you, the blonde giant. With your two metres height you towered above every one of us and your eyes radiated so much energy and self-confidence that we sensed you would be a good comrade and fellow soldier. To me you became more, much more than I can ever thank you for.

Now you have lain for twenty years in the calm depths of the ocean, but you live on in me and I am thinking of you and speaking to you as I write this down. These pages should provide testimony to your loyalty to me and my loyalty to you.

Your first question was: 'Who is my pilot?' Then you, a grand fellow of thirty years [*sic* – in reality, twenty-three], stood before me, a boy of hardly twenty, and you looked upon me like someone who was your brother and whom through one of life's coincidences you were seeing just now for the first time. I had observed how you previously regarded the others. Your gaze fastened upon me and I had the feeling you would never leave me.

You pulled me into a corner, ordered wine, did not ask anything, and began to talk. We were still sitting there when all the others had gone and I had learned as much about your fate as though you had confessed your entire life to me. You did not want to be a stranger to me, so I should not have to fly tomorrow, perhaps to my death, with an unknown pilot.

Because you had married the woman you loved against the will of your relatives, you were disinherited and outcast. Then you bravely accepted your fate, left the colours, travelled across the Big Pond, and began a new life there. You did not shun any form of work, sold newspapers, washed dishes, and shined shoes. You really experienced everything the way one sometimes reads in novels. As a coal trimmer you returned home at the outbreak of war and after serving in the cavalry and infantry you joined the air service. Here you felt you were in the right place.

Although we were the last to leave the officers' mess, on the following morning we were the first on the airfield, which was the way we always kept it. Our duty took precedence over everything else. Like my father, you were strictest with yourself and for that reason my friendship with you always remained mixed with respect. If in spite of that I caused you a lot of pain and sorrow, it was only because of a blind passion for something which attracted me with overwhelming force.

Soon after our first take-off the engine spluttered. Despite that we continued flying and cruised around the front for two hours. When we came back we knew that we got along just as well in the air as over a glass of wine. Neither of us was fussy and we both had a touch of frivolity, because we of course would never have been allowed to fly with a spluttering engine.

In the evening after our first flight together at the front you invited me to share a bottle of champagne and suggested that we should use the familiar form of address 'du'. When I hesitated for several reasons – you were an officer, much older, of the nobility, and I a non-commissioned officer – you then became infuriated and only calmed down again when I agreed to use this term (and how proud I was of that inwardly!), at least in non-official matters.

Though early on I became independent in my work and was outspoken with regards to professional and practical questions, when it came to emotional matters I was a bundle of inhibitions. One should not forget that for us boys, whether we came from the school bench or the roof trestle, the war was our first education in manhood. This was not only in regards to character, but also in terms of comradeship and in a social sense. The war came for us in a period of life in which other young people join student societies, journeyman's associations, dance circles, or sports clubs. During the war we were trained in self-confidence, poise, sociability, and manners by our comrades. For us, accordingly, they also became a model of social virtues or vices. You, my dear Rudno, continued to work on me where the good Hübner left off. How you did so, with so much sincerity, tact, and kindness! To be certain, manners in wartime were more coarse than in peacetime, as brought about by the 'rough business' of war. It depended upon the man and his make-up.

* * *

In the early days we received short orientation missions. We? You received them and then we both carried them out. We had to reconnoitre enemy battery emplacements, determine troop movements behind enemy lines, and sketch the layout of certain sections of trenches. Besides that, we still found some time to photograph on our own. Soon we discovered that our reconnaissances, sketches, and photographs were all similarly accurate. Although it was easier and less dangerous to take oblique photographs, it was our ambition to photograph the enemy trenches and positions as vertically as possible. Of course, in order to do that one had to fly directly over the enemy and that was seldom done without coming under heavy fire.

> [Due to there being no radio communication between the aircraft of either side in WW1, direct fighter support for such reconnaissance missions was difficult to provide. The best that could be achieved was for both sides to provide almost continual fighter patrols over the front in order to combat or at least ward off any hostile aircraft that came along, or had been ordered up, to engage the recce machines. It was, nevertheless, still a very dangerous occupation for the two-seater crews, as the observer needed to spend much of his time looking at the ground for signs of activity, batteries, or targets, rather than scan the sky for approaching hostile aircraft. The pilot could of course do this, but he was also preoccupied in flying and remaining over the area of interest and so could not give full attention to the sky about them either.
>
> The RFC, with their doctrine of always taking the war to the enemy, spent much more time over the German lines, and their back areas, than the Germans tended to do, but there was still considerable activity by the Feld Flieger Abteilung crews in

observing the British and French positions. Both sides, of course, used tethered balloons a couple of miles behind their respective trench systems, with trained observers dangling in wicker baskets below these gas-bags. Using binoculars and telescopes they could observe their respective enemies and also direct artillery fire. They were vulnerable to attack, but were heavily defended, so dangerous for opposing pilots to assail.]

After a short time we were also called upon to range the artillery. Back then, in the period from January to November 1916, this was still carried out in a very primitive fashion. The observer could indeed send wireless messages down below, but had no reception up above. Communication with the ranging aircraft took place by troops [or forward artillery observation posts] laying out cloths, the various arrangements indicating to the observer that his wireless signals were understood and whether the battery was ready to fire or not.

If the battery had indicated its readiness, the observer sent the order: 'Fire!' The observation aircraft flew in the direction of the target, the observer reported to the battery the position of the observed shell bursts, and returned back to it. If the target were bracketed, the observer ordered: 'Fire for effect.' Then the battery fired everything it had. The regular flying back and forth betrayed what was going on up there and usually swift villains rushed to disturb the game. The smartest thing to do then was to 'scram', because our heavy 'barges' were far inferior in speed and manoeuvrability to the light birds of prey.

When foggy days came we had a lot of free time, using it to bathe or swim. [One would assume Buckler meant during the summer months.] For this purpose we had a self-constructed pool of forty metres length, twelve metres breadth, and two metres depth. We got the water from a spring by way of a 250-metre long pipe. A drain was provided for so that we could always bathe in clear spring water. Alcohol also played a not inconsiderable role on such foggy and lazy days. And you, my dear Rudno, as an 'old American', were never opposed to a good whisky.

In this period of the war an event took place that exerted the greatest amount of influence on my flying career and drove it in a direction which up to then was unknown to me and from now on attracted me with a magnetic force. I must especially emphasize this, as otherwise certain lapses in discipline of which I was guilty would be entirely incomprehensible in the light of my otherwise strict sense of duty.

Two fighter pilots had come to our neighbouring Abteilung. They flew Fokker aircraft, which compared to other machines back then were awfully fast and manoeuvrable. Both of them were keen fellows, real go-getters. When I saw them race past me for the first time, like express locomotives past a slow train, I was pained by my heavy mount. From that moment on, all my plans and inspirations were aimed at one day being able to sit in such a marvellous aircraft. I was like someone who up to now had only known farm horses and then for the first time saw a thoroughbred. The effect the appearance of the two fighter pilots had on me was downright fateful for my good Rudno.

> [This was well into the period of the Fokker Eindecker's time of superiority at the front. Not that Anthony Fokker's monoplane was any great shakes as a fighting machine, but he had managed to fit a machine gun to the front of the monoplane, directly in front of the pilot, and with a series of gears and cams, had invented a way of letting all the bullets from the muzzle of said gun to pass through the whirling propeller blades without hitting them. This immediately changed the face of air combat, but as there were so few of these fighting machines available, and the Germans had not yet embraced the concept of single-seat fighting squadrons, the Eindeckers were spread around most of the two-seater units for protection and, if not engaged in such duty, taking off to engage hostile two-seaters over the front or on bombing missions to the German rear areas. Generally, the Fokker pilots came from within the Abteilung's men, those who felt they would like to fly these nimble monoplanes and engage the French or British machines that flew on their sector of the front. Although few in number, they created such an imbalance of air power that their activities during late 1915 to the autumn of 1916, wrested a good deal of the air dominance over these sectors away from the Allies. Yet because they were so few in number, and the secret of the interrupter gear was not to be divulged to the enemy, the Fokkers were engaged in a purely defensive capacity. This defensive stance remained for the rest of the war, even at the time when fighting squadrons – with better equipment were formed – after the Somme battles of 1916.]

* * *

We had finished ranging the artillery and you waved to me contentedly: 'Let's go home!' For the first time I did not obey your order. I put the Albatros on its nose and rushed downwards so that the wires made an eerie sound and you began to curse like crazy.

> [Although Buckler had said FA(A)209 flew DFW two-seaters, the unit was obviously using Albatros C-type two-seaters now, in addition to its other equipment.]

I could have let you know what was going on, but did not want to out of fear that I might arrive too late or you would hold me back. I wanted to completely surprise you with our first victory. We went lower and lower in corkscrew turns and then I dived vertically upon my – I mean 'our' – victim, a Farman. But before I could open fire I had to tear my machine around, for I did not want to collide with a Fokker which suddenly, out of the blue, threw itself between me and the Farman and shot it down right under my nose. It was a good thing for us, because I probably would have rammed it!

Furious with the Fokker pilot who robbed me of my prey, I flew home with you, who were fuming behind me. To our surprise, the Fokker landed a few seconds later next to us on the field. We approached it filled with curiosity, as the young officer climbed out. From the collar of his leather jacket hung a blue cross – the *Pour le Mérite*. Smiling, he introduced himself: 'Boelcke'. We accompanied him to the officers' mess and for a short time he was our guest.

The impression that Boelcke made on me was so deep that even today his memory stays within me as a vital force. An almost solemn gravity emanated from Boelcke and a great inner refinement was expressed in all his movements. One distinctly perceived the high sense of duty that filled him. He had dedicated himself to the service of the Fatherland with every last thread of his being. From his eyes radiated the freedom and serenity of a person who already stood above all things and who was every moment prepared to gladly sacrifice his life for that which to him was the most lofty ideal on earth.

[It is difficult to date some of Buckler's encounters, but this sortie which involved Oswald Boelcke was probably 21 March 1916. Boelcke, flying with FA62, and along with fellow Fokker pilot Max Immelmann had been the first fighter pilots to receive the *Orden Pour le Mérite* in January 1916. After January he was not in action again until March and on the 21st he describes a fight in which a German two-seater is involved: 'In the morning, at about 11 o'clock, I saw a German biplane in battle with a Farman west of Ornes [NE of Verdun]. I swooped down on the Farman from behind while another Fokker came to our aid from above. In the meantime, I had opened fire on the Farman (who had not seen me at all) at a range of 80 metres. As I had come from above, at a steep angle, I had soon overtaken him. In the very moment as I was passing over him he exploded. The cloud of black smoke blew around me. It was no battle at all; he had fallen in the shortest possible time.'

Although both Boelcke and Buckler identified the machine as a Farman, this particular victory was over a Voisin of VB109 which fell at Les Fossers Wood at 11.15 am. It was easy for

Farman and Voisin machines to be confused. It was Boelcke's thirteenth victory, and both Frenchmen died.

Boelcke would go on to score nineteen victories by June, at which time he was pulled away from the battle front. Immelmann had fallen a few days earlier and Germany did not want to lose both its air war heroes. Boelcke, of course, was the instigator of pooling fighter aircraft together into hunting units – Jagdstaffeln – while he was on leave, and returned to the front in August to command Jagdstaffel (Jasta) 2, one of the first twelve Jastas to be formed.]

From this day on I dreamt only of fighter planes and aerial victories. Gradually I also infected Rudno with my madness, who for a couple of days was seriously angry with me because of my undisciplined attack on the Farman. Now we both pondered how we could begin to become pursuit flyers. After a number of whiskies, sitting as the last remaining guests in the small garden in front of our officers' mess, our conversation once more revolved around aerial fighting and shooting down aircraft.

'What's the fastest way of accomplishing the goal?' you asked.

'In any case, not by sitting around here and drinking,' I answered excitedly.

'So let's go,' was all you said.

We did not at first go to sleep, but rather waited until the day dawned, then we rushed to the airfield. At six o'clock we found ourselves at 2,500 metres over the front, but we had bad luck. Not a tail was to be seen. We could hardly keep our eyes open due to fatigue. Then, once more quite the frivolous Rudno, you handed me a note which read: 'Off to Metz for breakfast.'

On the flight there I detected that something was wrong with the motor. I only realised that there was not another drop of coolant in the radiator when the motor seized up with an audible bang. Fortunately we saw the Metz airfield already there below us. From 1,500 metres we went down in a glide with a dead engine. There was a crackling sound and we could smell something burning. Heavens, if the crate began to burn! At the time we still had no knowledge of parachutes.

We crouched down like panthers before springing and listened intently to every sound as the aircraft glided gently to earth. I have never longed for the earth as much as I did during this descent. I should have liked to have grabbed her and held her tight, good old Mother Earth. Never have I so much felt like your child who had run away and now longingly sought your bosom. Bosom of the earth – eternal refuge!

We landed with three white-hot cylinders on the airfield at Metz. The final seconds were punishment enough for our frivolity, but what would the Hauptmann say about our hot-headed joyride into the fiery dawn which ended so glowingly?

Rudno, you now showed that you were a good diplomat. While you were on the telephone and I stood behind you with an anxious expression on my face, you presented the matter to Hauptmann Funck with such skill that two hours later he too appeared at the AFP, after we in the meantime had enjoyed an abundant breakfast at the kind invitation of Hauptmann Keller. As a replacement for our machine, Keller gave us the newest and best machine in the entire depot. It was a type that had not yet flown at the front. Just like a few months earlier, I once again had to take off on a test flight from the small hilltop field with a machine that was as yet untried.

The sleepless night spent carousing out of a thirst for action, the adventure with the crackling and glowing motor, the favourable outcome of our independent and unsuccessful undertaking, the warm welcome from Keller – my patron to whom I owed my whole presence at the front – all of this may have contributed to the fact that in an elevated and high-spirited mood I twisted about in the sky with the new machine in an acrobatic fashion quite contrary to regulations. In any event, after the landing I was chewed out by the flight director of the AFP to an extent I had never experienced before, not even as a recruit on the drill square. He did not leave me with a single redeeming feature.

However, he had not taken you into account, dear Rudno. You cast yourself into the fray on my behalf with a fire against which the white-hot glow of the motor seemed like a faint gleaming. With us it was just as in any proper marriage – one does not use the term ‘flyer’s marriage’ for nothing. We could both quarrel and be angry with each other, but if a third party got involved, then he had to deal with both of us. So it came about, to the secret annoyance of the other crews in our Abteilung, that for all our lack of discipline we returned to our airfield rewarded with a new machine.

We doubled our efforts in ranging the artillery and achieved good results. Admittedly, we tried attacking observation balloons without success, for however well the machine showed its mettle, it was by no means a fighter plane. Fighter plane! The dream of flying one would not leave me alone.

The end of a ‘flyer’s marriage’

It was a distinction for us to be entrusted with the ranging of a ‘Long Max’, a 42-centimetre gun, on Vaux and Douaumont. Every round cost a small fortune. At a high altitude, and yet still pursued by anti-aircraft fire, we cruised back and forth for two-and-a-half hours between the ‘Max’ and the front. It was incredible that a whole pack of enemy fighters was not loosed upon us. Our only support was four aircraft from a neighbouring Schutzstaffel [ground support unit, normally tasked with strafing and bombing front line troops and positions]. Tremendous black pillars of smoke, which were recognisable as such even from our height, marked the points of impact of the large calibre shells.

Then in our immediate vicinity we heard a report like that of an explosion and then a clattering sound as when a threshing machine is running. I closed the throttle and everything was quiet once more. When I then gave it full throttle it started clattering again. What could that be? With a very uncomfortable feeling we looked around us on all sides. Then we noticed, not exactly to our re-assurance, that the fabric of our wings had been so perforated by shrapnel that shreds of it were fluttering and snapping in the strong slipstream. What was much worse was that I found out that the fuel tank was completely empty, so it too had been holed by shrapnel.

I did not need to switch off the engine first, as it had ceased running on its own. With shredded wings and a dead motor we were hanging over Verdun at a height of about 4,000 metres. The only thing missing was enemy fighters.

Again we went downwards in a glide, and we only began to feel better as we saw Verdun fading away behind us more and more. We had never glided from such an altitude and, as strange as it may sound in this situation, we so much liked the smooth, almost soundless glide that we laughed between ourselves. Only from the ground did we hear gunfire and artillery rounds being fired and exploding on both sides of the trenches. Like two imagined princes in a flying trunk, we thoroughly enjoyed the silent trip to earth. After the war, gliding became for me a pleasant sport that I often pursued.

As we saw the row of trees that bordered our airfield coming towards us, we were forcibly reminded that our aerial sojourn for all its beauty was no fairytale excursion, but rather gravity and its forces were subjecting us to very earthly laws. With all the flying skills at my disposal I barely succeeded in clearing the tops of the trees to set the machine down on the airfield. In the next instant we were sitting in a heap of wreckage. We did not need to clamber down from our cockpit seats, we could just step onto level ground. Rudno cursed. Like every observer he knew more about landing than the pilot and railed at the 'lousy landing' until the mechanics revealed that the undercarriage had been riddled with shrapnel and would not have withstood the gentlest of landings. Besides that, a piece of our propeller was missing, so for better or worse he had to realise that he had done me an injustice. In the evening we celebrated our reconciliation.

Our marriage had been subjected to many blows, but it held. Because it was built upon the best foundation that there can be for a marriage, namely, mutual trust. But even in the best marriage it can come to a point where one partner can take no more and declares: 'This far and no further.' That will be the case if the other one is seized by a passion that has a complete hold on him and causes him to forget every consideration of his companion. This point in our 'flyer's marriage' was reached due to my passion for aerial combat, which increased day by day. My interest in artillery ranging, photographic missions, and reconnaissance, dwindled to the point of complete apathy.

In the meantime the number of enemy fighter planes had significantly increased so one had now to keep a sharp look-out. Our two Fokker pilots, keen as they were, could not longer prevail against such superior numbers. One more reason for me to become a fighter pilot as soon as possible. I painted a picture for myself in romantic colours of man-to-man combat. It was a matter of courage and skill; a chivalrous duel. In my dreams I chased my opponents and did not relent, harrying them until they were forced to the ground. Then I landed next to them and generously extended my hand to them.

While we were flying on the front, carrying out some sort of mission, I forgot my good Rudno and thought only about the two fixed machine guns with which my new machine would be equipped and for which I sought a target. In a gravel pit near the airfield I had a target erected for shooting practice. In my free time I flew towards it in ever more daring dives with persistent fury. This alone had the result that I got together with Rudno less and less than before and so he often remained alone, sulking, and his mood got worse from day to day.

Whatever assignment Rudno had did not concern me. As soon as we were in the air my eyes bulged out of my head and I looked for a victim. What did the 'sandbag' behind me matter? By that I meant you, dear Rudno. Forgive me! How I must have terrified you when with a tremendous amount of speed and whistling wires I chased after some shadow of a lattice-tail aircraft. How much ammunition did I needlessly fire off at that time, because I always had to shoot and never gave you the opportunity to open fire. No one else would have put up with that. Anyone else would have had me relieved. But you took my youth into account and still took me, the little rogue, under your wing. It almost came to blows between us, but in the evenings we reconciled ourselves once more. That took a toll on our nerves and we wore each other down. Our quarrels, not fights against the enemy, made wrecks out of us. If only we could have known that a year later we would fly side-by-side, two fighter pilots, and I as your Staffel commander!

* * *

Once more we were flying towards the front, one of our last flights in the same aircraft. You had the task of photographing an area behind Verdun and, as always, you guided me towards the target. I can still see you today, you giant, as you lifted the heavy camera overboard in order to carry out your mission. Then three Nieuports which were flying about 300 metres below us caught my attention. Without asking you, without turning to look at you, without even thinking about you, I began to dive. I can still hear your shout. When I glanced around I saw you hanging far out of the aircraft. You frantically clung to the camera, your sacred relic, as would an infantryman his rifle. I had to level out the machine and fly calmly straight ahead in order to give you an opportunity to bring yourself and the camera back to safety. In this way I never got a chance to open fire.

The three Nieuports hung on our tail like three lovesick birdmen and twittered their bird-song in our ears to the tune of rattling machine guns. They shot us up to the extent that even today I still do not understand how we escaped with our lives. You were not standing at your gun, but rather sat slumped in your seat. If only I could have known that it was jammed! I was seized by the unreasonable fear that you could be wounded and I would perhaps bring you home dead. Then I would have been to blame for your death, dear Rudno.

I cursed my rashness, turned as never before, and in the process learned for the first time what turning really meant. The three lads conducted an aerial exercise that I would not have considered possible. How it came about that they suddenly broke off from us, as if by some secret command, neither of us knew. Even today I still have not forgotten the look you gave me when we had landed, Rudno.

It must have been horrible for you just to be left as a sitting duck with a jammed weapon. I thought you would have me locked up, but what did you say when I counted thirty-two hits on the machine? You said nothing but: 'That's enough. You have to become a fighter pilot.' But in the evening when we celebrated our lucky escape you attached a condition. You would only let me leave the squadron if you too could be trained as a fighter pilot.

The leave which we both had coming to us was to be used to initiate the necessary steps. Twenty-four hours later we were both sitting, as so often as before, in Moitrier's. After the departure from Metz we both came to a firm decision in the dining car. Only in Mainz did we separate. I had brought for my mother several pounds of butter, some ham, and a laundry basket full of eggs – all of which could still be purchased in some places, but rarely at home.

What more did I have to tell you at home, mother – of war, or Rudno my observer, my comrade, my brother? You often shook your head.

[Oberleutnant Hubertus von Rudno-Rudzinsky came from Dittmansdorff and was born 29 September 1893. He had served in the 8th Prussian Dragoon Regiment prior to moving into aviation. He would later become a fighter pilot and fly with Buckler again. We have not confirmed his death, one source saying it was 1971, but as Buckler infers that he died at sea(?) shortly after WW1, perhaps the date should read 1921, in which case 15 September of that year, at Rheinbrol would apply.]

Chapter Five

Jadgstaffel 17

Fighter pilot

Some days later I received a telegram – I knew who was behind it – with the enquiry as to whether I wanted to join the newly established Jagdstaffel 17. Certainly, I wired back, if Rudno could also become a fighter pilot, which is what we agreed. Our good Hauptmann Funck let us go with a heavy heart, as I may assume without being conceited. Rudno was transferred to the flying school and I myself to the Jagdstaffel.

On 11 November 1916, I reported to the commanding officer [Staffelführer] of the newly formed Jasta 17, Rittmeister von Brederlow, on the big Metz airfield at Frescaty. Here I saw for the first time Hermann Göring, who was then a Leutnant and is now Generalfeldmarschall and commander-in-chief of the Luftwaffe. There I also made the acquaintance of Loerzer, currently a general in the air service. The good Schmickaly was aleady dead.

[As referred to in the previous chapter, the German Air Service had developed its aerial fighter force after the Somme battles, by forming its first twelve Jagdstaffeln, which began assembling in August 1916. Although smaller in size to, say, a British squadron, of around eighteen pilots, with a CO and three flight commanders, and the same number of aeroplanes, Jastas were generally comprised of about a dozen pilots under the leadership of one commander and generally a deputy.

Following the success of the first dozen, more Jastas were formed in late 1916 and early 1917, Jasta 17 being one of them. A Prussian unit, this Jasta came into being on 23 October 1916 at Armee Flug-park Nr.5 as Frescaty, and became established on 11 November, Julius Buckler therefore becoming a founding member. His commander was Rittmeister [cavalry captain] Heinz Freiherr von Brederlow.

Von Brederlow had been a pilot with Kasta (Kampfstaffel or fighting section) 21 of Kampfgeschwader (bombing unit) Nr.4 in 1916, and along with several other more senior airmen had been chosen to form and lead these new Jastas. Air fighting, while now firmly established on the Western Front, did not necessarily mean that the more successful pilots flying those early Fokker monoplanes would automatically be put in charge of a new Jasta. Rank and position were still the order of the day, and although some new units did have a few of these successful fighters, most of the others merely had men who could command and lead.

The following is a list of pilots who were with Jasta 17 as it formed:

Leutnant d.R. Marcus	Adjutant
Vizefeldwebel Julius Buckler	From FA(A)209
Vizefeldwebel Eduard Ey	From Kek Metz
Leutnant Hermann Göring	From FA25
Vizefeldwebel Fritz Jacobsen	From FA1
Offizierstellvertreter Kern	From FA71
Oberleutnant Bruno Loerzer	From Kek Metz
Leutnant d.R. Günther Schuster	From FEA7
Vizefeldwebel Georg Strasser	From FA44
Vizefeldwebel Adolph Wellhausen	From FA25
Leutnant d.R. Jakob Wolff	From Kek Metz

As can be seen, the Jasta, including its CO, had six officers and six senior NCO pilots, all with a variety of experience. Loerzer and Göring had been a two-seater crew together, like Buckler and Rudno-Rudzinsky. Loerzer, a Berliner, had been an army cadet and infantry officer pre-war, then transferred to aviation. Once a two-seater pilot, he was joined by Göring from his old regiment and they flew together as a crew for some time. Loerzer then moved to single-seaters with Kek Jametz (Kampfeinsitzerkommando, based at Jametz airfield; a group of fighting aircraft, virtually a forerunner to the Jastas), while his observer took pilot training.

Göring, from Upper Bavaria, had also been a cadet before becoming an infantry officer and had seen some action in the early days of the war in the Vosges. Suffering from arthritis, he moved into aviation to fly with his friend Loerzer. After their two-seater days, Göring flew with Kek Stenay and Kek Metz.

By the time Buckler wrote his book in the late 1930s, Göring, as he relates, was head of the new German Luftwaffe and remained so throughout the coming world war that began in September 1939. He would commit suicide (aged fifty-three) after being captured in 1945 and put on trial for war crimes. His friend Loerzer was a Leutnantgeneral by the time

WW2 began and by that war's end he had risen to Generaloberst. He died in August 1960 aged 69.

Others in the list had all seen some flying with various Flieger Abteilungen, for it was generally the rule that pilots going onto single-seaters would have spent some time at the front on two-seaters. In this way most had gained some measure of experience in war flying, and were less likely to be 'war blind'. Throughout the war, very few fighter pilots came to a Jasta without having at least a taste of war flying, either as a pilot or an observer. This was in stark contrast to the British method of sending pilots from training to units that had a vacancy without, in the early years, taking into account a man's aptitude to single or two-seater machines. Thus many new pilots in fighter squadrons might not survive long enough to understand what was actually going on in the air, and be quickly picked off by the vastly more experienced (street wise!) German fighter pilots.

Jasta 17, based therefore initially at Metz-Frescaty, were on a section of the French front, supporting the German 5th Army, and would remain in this sector until the end of February, although from January to the end of February, its allegiance would be to Army Detachment 'A'.]

As for fighter planes, we at first had only old Fokker aircraft with rotary engines at our disposal. Three or four pilots had to share each machine, but at least one flew alone, had two machine guns – and was a fighter pilot.

Since none of us had ever flown rotary-engined machines [except those who had been with a Kek!], we had first carefully to try to taxi on the ground. However, during my first attempt to taxi, I suddenly found myself in the air through no fault of my own. I had not even 'blipped' [the engine]. That was one of the tricks of the rotary engine. My comrades did not fare any better. I slowly flew a large circuit and made the modest attempt to interrupt the engine and it succeeded. I landed in a glide, albeit somewhat roughly, and there followed a few more test flights.

* * *

Our life as fighter pilots, which had begun with so much hope, was now condemned to complete inactivity. The weather alternated between rain and fog and the daylight hours became shorter and shorter. At least this time I did not live, as I had a year before, in a cold corrugated tin barracks with rats and mice. I had a splendid room with central heating and running water. For the trip from the airfield to Metz we only needed a few minutes, and of course, money. We therefore arranged it so that twice a week we went out in style – that is, in Metz – and three times a week we stayed in

Montigny, a village in the vicinity. There we sat in the House of Three Maids. Thus we led wonderful and carefree lives.

> [This aerial inactivity did not suit everyone, for instance, Göring managed to get himself sent to Jasta 5 soon after Jasta 17 was formed, while Jacobsen moved to Jasta 9 in December. Loerzer left in January 1917, moving to Jasta 26. Their places were taken by Leutnant Wilhelm Gros and Oberleutnant Günther Viehweger in December, the latter posted from Jasta 2. Jasta 2 was now known as Jasta Boelcke after its famed first commander, who died following a collision with one of his pilots during an air fight with 24 Squadron RFC. Despite this supposed inactivity, the French had begun their first offensive action at Verdun on 24 October that lasted till mid-December, but obviously Jasta 17 were not heavily involved.]

Two of my comrades, Wellhausen and Rüdiger, were occupied at the same time with preparations for the school certificate required for one-year volunteers. Rittmeister von Brederlow suggested to me that I should participate in this and I agreed. We began a lot of cramming, and what I studied, I studied thoroughly. From December 1916 on I worked on with great enthusiasm day after day, as long as it was not flying weather. Günther Schuster, a dear comrade, instructed me in French. Schuster began flying with Skadta in 1923, an airline in Colombia with which the German Lufthansa is involved. Today I read in the newspaper to my great joy that he, together with Flugkapitän Henke, succeeded in a great flight to Brazil with the 'Kondor' from the Focke-Wulf factory.

One day I declared to von Brederlow that I had reconsidered the matter. Either I would become an officer in the war through my own abilities or I would do without it. Is it not said that every soldier carries the marshal's baton in his backpack? All attempts by the good Rittmeister and my comrades to convince me to continue working were in vain. Only a very few could understand what settled me in my decision. I did not want to have an emergency exam to thank if I should one day stand beside them equally as an officer, but rather my fitness as a soldier. I could fly and was a good shot. All the rest had to work itself out on its own.

From that point on I again concerned myself only with aerial combat. Every morning I checked the weather in a state of agitation. Finally it cleared up. He who is ruled by passion is no longer his own master, and if his passion is to torment others, then he will be the most tormented.

My first aerial victory

It was a winter day like any other when I took off in clear weather in a new machine, an Albatros DII, in order – driven by my demon – to scour the sky for the enemy, of whom I dreamt day and night. The sky was a bright empty grey expanse, a poor game preserve for a young, hot-blooded hunter. Damn, I thought, up here the sky is one big hunting ground, there are no borders and no hunting licenses. I pushed the engine wide open.

Below lay Verdun. My old comrades were quartered not far from there. I wondered whether any of them might meet me. Air combat and hunting fever were forgotten. I was only looking around to see whether I might catch sight of one of my comrades so that I could wave to him, and there, amidst the winter greyness, two machines appeared which I recognised. I flew towards them. The crew sat in the aircraft as a pair, just as Rudno and I had once done. I waved my hand at them as they flew past. I was alone again, feeling forsaken in the broad December sky.

Occupied with myself in this fashion, my aircraft drifted slowly, almost dreamily, onwards. What do the people down there know about the flyer? What does he know about them down there? Nothing, I was about to say, then two fist-sized cloudlets provided me with a different answer. Aha! The old flak was still there! They were well on their guard and they had irritated me for eleven months and I irritated them no less. If they thought they hindered us in the fulfilment of our photographic missions with their well-placed barrage fire, we let them go on believing that and once more flew towards the target just for show, although we had long since captured it on a photographic plate. One must have fun, even in war! So the good old enemy flak batter had me by the collar, or perhaps their shells were not actually meant for me. They were in fact much too low.

Then about 200 metres below me I saw one of the observation aircraft of my old Abteilung crabbing around, but at the same time I spotted directly over Fort Douaumont yet another aircraft – in fact, a lattice-tail. Without much deliberation I put my machine on its nose and raced past our observation aircraft into the depths below. That I did not ram the Farman remains a mystery to me. I sped past him too.

[All French and British pusher-types – that is aircraft with propellers behind a gondola which pushed the machine through the air – did not, of course, have a regular fuselage, so the tail section of fin, rudder and elevators, were attached to the gondola by way of struts and cross-members from the mid-wing area. This gave them the appearance of a lattice fence, which the Germans called *Gitterrumpf* (lattice-tail). As there were several different types of pusher machines, i.e: Vickers FB5, DH2, FE2b/d, FE8 amongst the British, and Bréguet 4 and 5, Caudron G.3 and G.4, Henri Farman F.20s et al, Maurice Farman MF.7 and 11, Voisin 1, 2 and so on, more often than not the overall term for them was *Gitterrumpf*. And with the French types, quite often the name Farman covered all pusher-types, confusing later historians when dealing with losses or combats with Voisins, Caudrons, etc. The German crews, in the same way, often called RFC and RNAS fighter types by the overall name of 'Sopwith' later in the war, even though there were several different types of Sopwith-built machines at the front, and ignoring machines such as SE5s, Martinsydes and DH5s.]

Missed! What was the meaning of this? I really was a fool. I tore the machine around on its wingtips, and now began the game of turning. The lattice-tail was slower than I, but the French aviator was by far the better pilot. His observer greeted me with a couple of decent bursts from his machine gun. What a laughable novice I was. Even today it makes me sick to think of how I conducted myself during my first aerial combat. When someone sees at a railway crossing that the barrier is already lowering, but still makes an attempt to dash through, this is called inexcusable recklessness. I had no presentiment of danger, I did not see the barrier, so I did not act with inexcusable recklessness, but rather out of complete ignorance of the matter. Who should have imparted the knowledge to me? In my time there were still no schools for fighter pilots, there was not even re-training for those going onto fighter planes. One was merely put in the crate and then it was 'off you go'. Everyone had to gain his own experience and perhaps that is the way it should have been.

Umpteen times I sped by the Farman and fired for all I was worth. Finally I noticed that the observer was no longer to be seen. Where was he? Was he hiding, wounded, or dead? Then I saw that the lattice-tail aircraft tilted and began to spin. I stuck doggedly behind him. A cloud of dust; the aircraft burst apart and was scattered in pieces. I came within a hair's breadth of running into the hill next to him. I was that low. There was a wild rattling and whistling of bullets as I was fired on from below. I had come down to within sixty metres of the earth, so now I had to open the throttle and get away, out of the whistling, hissing witch's cauldron. It was a matter of luck but I succeeded. Soaked to the skin from excitement, I sped above the ground, then I saw [the town of] Azannes lying beneath me.

It was my first aerial victory, yet I could not be glad about it. Now, after it was all over, I thought only of the two brave fellows who now lay on the hill, dead or with broken, mutilated limbs. I thought of their parents and brothers and sisters. Perhaps they were married and had children, or a fiancée. We were after all not machines fighting each other, but men. What we destroyed were machines – and men. Only a person who has never seen with his own eyes an enemy and fellow human being go to his death can thoughtlessly gloss over this fact. This has nothing to do with sentimentality. Sentimentality is an excessive squandering of emotion on something which is not worth it. Here, however, it was a matter of people's lives. This sympathy and compassion for the other, who as one's opponent is one's mortal enemy and as a living being is one's brother, is a problem of war that no one will ever solve. One cannot dismiss it with a claim of self-defence.

I admit that I was deeply sorrowful after my first victory, just as I was after my tenth, twentieth, and thirtieth. Yet to be quite honest, even though I am ashamed of it, the first thought concerning sorrow for my dead fellow aviators was mixed with a second very typical and selfish one. Will the aerial victory be recognised? Soon I so completely forgot about my defeated comrades that this thought alone held sway over me. How could I set about having this, my first victory, confirmed? Then I remembered once more my old comrades, who were located not far from here and I landed on the familiar airfield.

Although it was already afternoon, Hauptmann Funck, who greeted me warmly, had another plane take-off which snapped an aerial photograph of the wreckage of the lattice-tail aircraft. With the congratulations of my comrades, with 'Schnurps', the dog given to me as a present, and with eggs and butter on board, I took off again and flew back to the Staffel.

> [It seems this first victory was in fact a Caudron. The only lattice-tail aircraft in French casualty reports, is a machine from Escadrille C.74, which had a Caudron G.4 listed this day, with its pilot, Sergent Raymond Choisnet injured. The date was 17 December 1916. If it wasn't this machine, then maybe the crew survived.]

* * *

December 24, 1916. I arrived just in time for the distribution of presents. As a Christmas present I received my first silver goblet with the inscription [translated as]: *To the victor in aerial combat.* A year later it would have been made of iron, but its value would have been the same. A lot of champagne was drunk on this evening. Though I may have laughed outwardly, inwardly I remained sad and doubly so because it was the 'Holy Night', to which I had given no thought during the entire flight.

> [Buckler gives the impression here that his first victory was achieved on this eve of Christmas, whereas it was a week earlier. This is evidenced by the arrival of his cup of victory, which would only have been presented following the time it took for 'higher authority' to consider and confirm his victory. This victory cup, known as an *Ehrenbecher* (honour cup) was awarded to all airmen who achieved an aerial victory, accompanied by a certificate. There were no subsequent cups for further victories, although some pilots, such as Manfred von Richthofen, had a standing order with a jeweller to

produce small cups for each of his victories, although after the sixtieth such cup, silver became scarce in Germany so no others were made.

What Buckler does not mention, was that this first victory was also the first victory of Jasta 17, and timed at 16.20 hours, south of Bras, although the town of Azannes is further north than Bras, which is only four kilometres due north of Verdun, whereas Azannes is fourteen kilometres north-east of Verdun.

Confirmations were always difficult if the enemy machine went down on the Allied side of the trenches. Every Jasta endeavoured to have victories confirmed and would quickly contact the forward areas to see if anyone had seen a hostile machine go down. Gone down, perhaps, from the viewpoint of troops in the line, but not necessarily destroyed. For most of the war, confirmation for the German pilots was easier with most of the aerial activity occurring over the German side of the lines, where wreckage, bodies or prisoners were tangible evidence of a victory, unless of course, one victory was disputed between two pilots. There was, however, still a large proportion of victories credited that were seen to 'fall' on the Allied side of the lines, provided confirmation could be obtained from another pilot, or front line troops and observers, when asked if they had seen a hostile machine go down at such-and-such a time and at such-and-such a place.

However, front line troops were not just sitting around watching out for aircraft falling on the other side of the trenches, and one imagines few volunteered such information unless asked, generally by a telephone call from a Jasta adjutant. And few were trained observers of aircraft. If they saw an aircraft heading down and seemingly about to land or crash, they might say just that, without realising that the said aircraft's pilot headed away at tree-top height once he neared the ground, or perhaps landed without serious mishap. In these cases a victory was not one that could be said to be a permanent loss to the enemy. In the latter case, the aircraft may have been able to take off again later, or be dismantled and taken away by a squadron maintenance team, to fly again once repaired and reassembled. Yet the view taken by the confirming officer, was enough to produce a 'victory' claim.

To add to the overall confusion of dates, and Buckler does make errors in dates or the chronology in his story, while he made his first claim on 17 December, the Jasta's next victory came on Christmas Eve – the 24th. On this day Georg Strasser shot down a Caudron G.4 believed to be from Escadrille C.34, that fell in flames near Aspach, north-west of Fort Douaumont, in the late afternoon, and again inside French lines. Somehow, Buckler managed to confuse this event on 24 December with the receipt of his Ehrenbecher, received on the same day. This is why his next adventure appears to him in his memoirs to follow on Christmas Day!]

A failed attempt followed by a forced landing

All Christmas spirit and gentle sentiments aside, the very next morning – the first day of Christmas, with a temperature of 17 degrees below zero Celcius – I took off warmly wrapped up for a new pursuit flight. As a victim I had selected a balloon that had hung in the vicinity of Pont-à-Mousson for three weeks.

I had let the chief mechanic, who was an 'ace' in his field, in on my scheme. He had my ammunition [belts] re-filled, because for balloon attacks a special phosphorous-laden incendiary ammunition was necessary, for which one in addition needed a pass, which I had likewise procured.

With the same machine as on the day before, an Albatros DII, which I had christened 'Mops', I patiently climbed to 2,500 metres. At this altitude, at which the icy air made breathing a torture, I flew towards the balloon, hanging about twenty-five kilometres behind the enemy lines. While doing so it was difficult not to lose sight of it, because at this distance it looked no larger than a child's balloon. It temporarily disappeared in the grey mist, then I spotted it again, got closer to it, and finally rushed towards it in a dive, already with both thumbs pressing on the machine-gun triggers at ten kilometres range. *[sic. Buckler obviously did not attack the balloon at such a tremendous distance.]*

In spite of my continuous fire the balloon did not start burning. If I did not want to ram it – already it had taken on the size of a small single-family house – I had to pull the machine up and over it. I had done this, firing until the last second, without succeeding in setting it afire. Was it the fault of the ammunition, or the icy cold? The tack-tack of a machine gun left no time to think about it. With horror I noticed that my wings were once again perforated. In the same instant I saw three enemy flyers who were placing me in great danger with well-aimed fire. In order to throw off their aim I steered my Mops like a circus horse, back and forth, up and down.

Then there was a thud and the motor stopped. What else could I do but go into a glide? I was a sitting duck for my three opponents, but miraculously they suddenly eased off me and disappeared. For the second time I owed my life to a mysterious whim or kind providence of fate.

Mailly [Mailly-sur-Seilly] was the name of the snow-covered spot over which I found myself. I soared towards the church tower of the little village, while all the shimmering white fields seemed to invite me to land with equal kindness. The whole landscape was covered in deep snow. But how might things look underneath the blanket of snow? Since I really could not tell, in the end it was all the same where I put down. I was lucky. The snow, which was at least half a metre deep, quickly acted as a brake. My Mops had hardly come to a stop when machine-gun bullets whistled by my ears and light artillery began to range on her. With a leap I plunged into the deep snow and rushed to get away from the machine, always seeking cover in the nearest hole in the snow, as I had learned to do in the infantry. Now the morning sun shone down upon the fields, and bathed in sweat, I struggled to move forwards.

Looking around, I saw that my Mops had received a direct hit and lay as a wreck nearby. So there was nothing left for me to do here and I made my way towards Mailly. The snowfield across which I wearily plodded must have been under observation by the enemy, as again and again bursts of machine-gun fire sprayed into the soft mass of snow. I was soaked to the skin from the belt down when I arrived at a regimental headquarters, whose major received me in a friendly manner.

I had grave concerns because I had made a forced landing in a new machine which I had left behind, only for it to be shot to pieces by the enemy. What would Rittmeister von Brederlow say about that? But when the telephone connection to him was successfully established, he said nothing at all about it, revealing himself rather to be quite pleased that I had emerged unscathed from the forced landing, which had already been reported to him, and promised to have me picked up in the car at a particular crossroads. After that, I accepted with a hearty appetite the major's invitation to breakfast, which ended with an ample quantity of mulled wine.

Then I stalked along the edge of the village and ran double-time across a field two kilometres wide under the enemy's observation, towards the appointed crossroads, which was screened by a small wood. The French did me, a single man, the honour of accompanying me the whole way with fireworks in the form of machine-gun and shrapnel fire.

The car was already waiting for me and my comrades had thought of everything, food, cognac, cigarettes and chocolate. Since I had already eaten such a good breakfast, I immediately fell asleep during the trip home. I was greeted with a big hullabaloo by the unit and experienced how honestly pleased everyone was to see me again. My failed attempt against the balloon left me no peace. In my quarters I contrived theoretical balloon attacks, but each time stumbled over the 'yes, but what if's' and came to realise the uselessness of all air battles confined to a room.

> [As Buckler had found, it was no easy task to bring down an observation balloon. Even with phosphorous ammunition it did not always mean one could ignite these 'gas bags' and generally they were being rapidly hauled down by the winch men on the ground. Whenever they were up on observation

duties, fighters were on hand on their offensive patrols, giving some cover to them, and all balloon companies had a number of machine guns for defence, and nearby artillery might also join in. Some pilots, of course, seemed drawn towards balloons as a target and a number of aces on both sides ran up sizeable scores against these *Drachen*. Many fell to the defensive fire as would be expected, and it was a brave man who would go up against them. It can also be said that some aces never even contemplated attacking a balloon, acknowledging that the existence of a fighter pilot was dangerous enough without chancing one's life in this manner. As we shall see, Buckler continued his war against balloons from time to time, and had some successes.]

Looping serenade or mating dance in the sky

The monotony of winter days covered in snow or touched by the whirl of snowflakes was broken by the arrival of a Bombengeschwader [bomber group] that settled down with us for some time. I looked at the giant birds with astonishment and admired the pilots who were able to steer these mighty aircraft through the air. I admired just as much the courage of those men who penetrated deep into the enemy hinterland with these cumbersome machines in order to strike at the nerve of his armament industry. For quite understandable reasons they used the twilight or the night for these raids. Fly by night, how might that be? I could not imagine it.

At that time fighter pilots did not yet fly at night. In close formation, bristling with machine guns, bombers were hard for fighter pilots to attack. There were as yet no Jagdgeschwader, but woe to one of these mighty birds if he should stray, for then he would become all too easy prey for the agile hunting falcons which swooped down upon him by surprise from a great height. One day the Geschwader flew away, and we gazed after them sadly. Warm friendship had bound us with the bomber crews.

[Buckler does not make it clear that these night flyers did not fly in formation. It would be too dangerous to do so for collisions would easily occur. When on occasion they might fly on daylight missions, then attacks by opposing fighters would inevitably occur, but it would not be inevitable that they would suffer casualties, for their combined defensive fire could be effective.]

* * *

At the front everything was quiet in the air; the war was in hibernation. Protected by thick walls of mist which one could cut with a knife, we felt cosy and secure in our nest. We killed time mostly by drinking and playing cards like the troops. Besides that we engaged in sports, read or played music. A freshly arrived wine shipment was the occasion for us all to gather one day around eleven o'clock for a morning pint. In between hefty mugs, here a chess game was played, there a round of *Doppelkopf* or Skat.

In one corner sat the 'die-hards'. These were the ones who could not get enough of flying. They were Leutnant Gros, Vizefeldwebel Strasser, and myself. A paper model served us for the purpose of experimentation and had to put up with the wildest of aerobatics. In addition, we did some drinking and yet more talking.

Then through the fog a pale light fell upon the window pane. Was it clearing up? Were we going to have some flying weather? It was two o'clock in the afternoon and we placed bets about if there would be flying weather or not. The fog brightened, thinned out, dispersed, and left behind an almost forgotten blue sky. In spite of this, an order arrived by telephone from the Group that there would be no flying on this day, provided that no enemy flyers were reported.

However, Leutnant Gros had already obtained permission for a flight earlier from the acting Staffelführer and when we 'phoned the airfield he was already in the air. A short time later his machine roared away just above the roof of the officers' mess, and we charged outside to see what caused him to engage in this misconduct. Then we saw him pull up his machine and – *Donnerwetter!* – executed a genuine loop just the way we had tried to do earlier with the paper model. Our tumultuous admiration even attracted the chess, *Doppelkopf*, and Skat players. Gros described one loop after another, as he got the knack of it. The paper model had been his teacher.

Where was Strasser? Suddenly his machine too was racing towards us from the airfield. He yanked it upwards and slid down, but during the fourth attempt he made it all the way around. Two pilots in the unit who could perform loops! In our eyes this increased their flying prowess tremendously. In and of themselves, loops were nothing new. The Frenchman [Adolph] Pégoud had already performed them before the war in front of thousands of spectators, including in Germany, at Johannisthal, but who was supposed to teach us how to do them? Now these two were setting the precedent.

As the third, I pulled my Mops Number 2 out of the hangar. Chocks away and damn the crosswind! I had wanted to begin the loop at 300 metres, but then gave preference to climbing to 600 metres. Was I properly strapped in? Yes, indeed! So what could happen? I pulled the machine up, but then immediately returned it to a normal flying attitude. Then the necessary quantity of alcohol proved itself in this case to be a good ally. Again and again I stubbornly put the machine on its nose and on the eleventh attempt to thrust steeply into the sky I finally found the courage to pull the stick completely into my belly. Mops climbed vertically upwards and got into a position on its back. I hung with my head pointing towards the earth and stared despairingly downwards, with my legs pointing towards the sky. All attempts to bring the machine back into the proper position were unsuccessful. Out of sheer fear that the safety belts could rip, I had refrained from doing the one movement of the controls which could have brought me back into a proper flight attitude.

There was a jolt and the machine dived forwards and I thought the wings would break off. Then it flew on straight ahead as though all of this had been harmless child's play. This undesired inverted flight had lasted two or three seconds, which to me though had seemed like just as many hours.

With increased respect for the constructors of my Albatros, I repeated the whole manoeuvre without long deliberation. This time I raced at full revs towards the ground from the inverted position so that I feared the crate would completely fall apart with me in it. But the clever Albatros, which in the course of this desperate looping showed itself to be smarter than its master, did not fail in this case either and caught itself nicely at the right time. Now I practised until looping was no longer a problem for me, just as I had done during my time as a recruit with fighting and during my flight training with landing. In the end I did one loop after another.

In my stubborn pursuit of performing loops I had completely forgotten about my surroundings. As I now looked around I discovered to my amazement that a regular circus had opened up above the airfield, and the whole Staffel was in the air and trying to do loops. Only one of them actually had permission to fly and that was Gros. The rest of us were doing our loops illegitimately, so to speak.

We spent that evening in Metz fully conscious of having once more purchased courage from a dubious source. Without prior agreement, everyone had arranged with his girl that he would perform a couple of loops the next morning as though it were a 'serenade'.

Thus the next morning the inhabitants of Metz, whether civilian or soldier, got stiff necks from staring up in the air for an hour, because for an hour we danced around in the sky above the city with our aeroplanes like mating capercaillies. It was a wonder that in the midst of the wild confusion nobody collided with anybody else. However, on this occasion we managed to attract the attention not only of our 'nieces' as we called the girls below us, but also the authorities who supposedly said to themselves that such cocky youths could put their flying skills to better use in other places. So it came about that we were transferred, fourteen days later, to the Rheims area.

Chapter Six

A New Battle Cry

[There appears a gap either in Buckler's memoirs or memory, for while it seems to suggest a change of battle front in early 1917, it is obvious from the continuation of his narrative that he now jumps from the end of 1916 to the last day of April 1917. What is also odd is that when dealing with his next story, he mentions that he still has his single confirmed victory, whereas, by the end of April 1917, he has achieved six, while Jasta 17's overall score is now fourteen.

Buckler gained his second and third victories on 14 and 15 February, both noted as French Caudron machines, and both within French lines. One fell west of Facq Wood, the other near Pont-à-Mousson. French records indicate no obvious loss on the 14th so this may have been another that 'appeared' to fall. The second one too has no satisfactory French loss although one Voisin escadrille – VB107 – recorded men injured. On 21 March Buckler claimed a Nieuport 17 Scout shot down but on this occasion he did not receive confirmation. On 15 April he brought down a Spad VII and this, falling in the German lines, did receive confirmation. This was followed by a Nieuport Scout on 16 April, over Berry-au-Bac. It was a busy day for both the French and the Germans, as The Second Battle of the Aisne (the Nivelle Offensive) began, between Rheims and Soissons. There were a handful of Nieuport single-seaters downed this day, along with quite a number of two-seaters, but again it is difficult to pin any one of them down to Buckler.

Finally Buckler bagged his first balloon. This he attacked near the Bois de Genicourt at 09.20 in the morning, and it is confirmed. The balloon was from the 36° Cie Aérostiers (36th Balloon Company), and the observer, Sergent S C Saudet was killed.

Meantime, other Jasta 17 pilots had scored victories. Leutnant Schuster gained his first on 29 January – a Caudron.

Vizefeldwebel Wolff downed a Voisin for his first on 9 February, while Gros claimed his first on the 12th – a Nieuport. Leutnant Neumann, a recent arrival during March, downed another Nieuport on 25 March. Strasser got his second confirmed victory on 6 April, a Caudron, and then got his third on the 16th, another Caudron. A further Caudron fell to Wolff on the 28th. Then came Buckler's story concerning the events of 30 April.

The move of the Jasta is not made clear either, for it remained at Frescaty till 1 March 1917, and then moved to St Quentin-le-Petite on the German 7th Army front. It was nowhere near the town of St Quentin, but further to the south-east, close to the River Aisne, not far from the town of Rethal.]

The ruse

Our quarters were in a château. Growing in a magnificent conservatory were exotic plants such as one normally sees only in a botanical garden. Our predecessors were apparently big flower lovers, otherwise it would not have been possible that these beautiful, delicate plants would still be flourishing after almost two years of war, and bloomed as they would in the most peaceful of surroundings. I, who had never stayed in a château for more than a brief sightseeing tour, was oddly enough interested in only one thing – my bed. I also found it rather pleasant that one could bathe anytime one wanted to. Only two things are important to a flyer at the front: the airfield and his bed. Both were good, so I was satisfied.

During my first orientation flight seven observation balloons caught my attention which were hanging in the sky, calm and undisturbed, in a northerly direction, at about 1,000 metres height. The seven observers could carry out their work in utter tranquillity. It was immediately clear to me that this situation could not be allowed to continue any longer and I crafted my plans. For the time being we had other tasks to tend to and my comrades felt little enthusiasm for my balloon schemes, so I had no choice than to carry on independently.

I set out on a clear day. When I had made it half way to the balloons I noticed to my boundless surprise and disappointment that five of them were ablaze while the other two were being hastily pulled down. Someone else had got there first. Why had I not set out a day earlier? I cursed myself and resolved to be swifter in carrying out my decisions in future, otherwise I would probably roam around eternally with my single confirmed victory. The others were, as I afterwards heard, Leutnant Hahn of Jasta 19 together with his comrades.

[Jasta 19 had indeed assailed the French balloon lines on 30 April and claimed five in flames. Oberleutnant Erich Hahn had scored two, the others were credited to Leutnant Arthur Rahn, two, and Leutnant Walter Böning. Leutnant Rudolf Matthaei of Jasta 21 also claimed a balloon on this day, and French records show six balloon casualties, although most of the observers managed to parachute down without injury. All three German pilots would become aces, with six, seventeen and ten victories respectively, although Matthaei would not survive the war. Buckler continued his story of this day.]

Presumably nothing else was likely to be achieved on this day, but then suddenly all hell broke loose in the air. The enemy flak barked fiercely at me. Why our own then suddenly joined in on this outburst of fury was a mystery to me. Confound it, did the Herr Flak Officers have no eyes in their heads? Being shelled by one's own anti-aircraft batteries is no pleasure.

Turning around, I saw that behind me two observation balloons were burning. Quick revenge, but where was the one who got them? Damn! The shells from our own flak were getting closer and closer to me. Perhaps they were not shooting at me at all, but if so, where was the other aircraft?

He suddenly announced himself with the revealing tack-tack of his machine gun. A burst of bullets tore through my right wing. I whipped my machine around and now a fierce turning match began at 1,500 metres, during which we alternately fired and tried to avoid the fire of the other plane. While doing so we were drifting farther and farther behind the German lines until finally we were only 150 metres high and not far from my Staffel's airfield. Then the other pilot went into a glide. Had he been wounded? Had I shot-up his engine? Assured of victory, I followed him, not realising that I was dealing with an old hand who was luring me into a trap. As he was heading towards the ground above the wide-open field I was firmly convinced that he was about to land in. A cloud of smoke appeared briefly, coming from the forward part of his machine. Hopefully he will make it before he catches fire, I thought.

However, as I was about to go down next to him I noticed that he was not landing at all, but rather he continued to fly at full throttle and the cloud of smoke was coming from his muffler. I tore my machine around right in front of him, during which manoeuvre I presented him with the best possible target. That was what he had been waiting for; the whole thing was a ruse. He fired, but had no luck. I remained untouched and in turn shot him down from ten metres distance just as I was within shooting range. He was hit in the head, dying instantly, and the machine crashed on the field. The man bet everything on one card, either-or, and he had lost. This was my second aerial victory.

[Again we can see that Buckler is using his memory rather than a diary or even his flight logbook, for while the date of the balloon attack – 30 April – is a matter of record, Buckler did not make any claim on this day, and as mentioned earlier, his second victory was a Caudron two-seater on 14 February 1917, and not a single-seat scout. While there is a possibility that the German confirmation system may be misleading us, it seems odd that it took so long, therefore, to have the intermediate victories confirmed too. That is to say, chronologically the Caudron was his second victory, but does it mean that 'higher authority' confirmed this single-seater as his second 'officially' confirmed success? And were his other victories – namely those on 15 February, 15 April, 16 April, and 26 April – confirmed later still? To be clear, the German fighter pilots listed their victories in confirmation order, not necessarily in date order. Therefore, some victories were confirmed later than the date on which they occurred. Buckler seems so certain about this single-seater. It fell in German lines, the pilot dead from a bullet in the head, yet it is not clear who the Frenchman was or what his unit was. He does not, unfortunately, tell us what type it was, Nieuport or Spad or…?]

Three flyers, three jams

I had really wanted to shoot down one of the seven balloons – all seven if possible. The fact that I had arrived too late vexed me. These big air bags which hung around so pretentiously in the air annoyed me. There was no better way of letting someone peek at one's cards than by allowing them to do so from these elevated observation posts. That is also why the fire of the enemy batteries was so well directed. Other balloons had already appeared to replace the five that had been torched, and they were still hanging in the sky as dusk fell.

I forgot about the approaching night and the difficulties of flying back in the darkness and rushed at one of the balloons, firing only when I had reached a distance of 100 metres. Because it did not immediately catch fire I turned sharply and fired again. In the meantime, the observer had bailed out with his parachute and I saw him disappearing below me as a tiny dot.

I did not concern myself with the small clouds of anti-aircraft fire that appeared in ever greater numbers around me in the semi-darkness. Even enemy flyers made no difference to me now. I did not think about them at all, as I had but one thought: it must burn. When the flames finally shot out of the balloon I very nearly burned up as well, so close had I approached it.

On the way home I thought: someone had definitely seen the burning balloon, but had they also seen who shot it down? It was to be assumed that at this late hour no other aircraft were so close to the front. The late hour which was so welcome to me as an aid to my third victory proved to be less favourable when it came to orientation and landing. I wandered around for some time, then signal rockets showed me the way to the airfield. So someone had heard me coming. In the coloured light of the rockets the landing was successful.

The Hauptmann was in the best of moods. We had every reason to celebrate this evening. My friend Strasser had shot down his first opponent in the afternoon and I had bagged a balloon just before the closing of the gate, as it were. On this night we both looked forward to a rosy future and agreed to set up a joint account, splitting the victories between us fifty-fifty. The next victory would be credited to Strasser so that he could catch up somewhat.

Just twenty-four hours later the agreement would have gone into effect had you not insisted that it be cancelled, dear Strasser. This came to pass in the following fashion. We took off after dawn with four machines. We still had not learned how to fly against the enemy in close formation. After ten minutes we had been scattered to the winds, and I flew west, the rising sun behind me. Since nothing was going on at the front I soon turned back again. Then two machines came towards me that were flying at almost the same altitude. I cautiously turned away to one side until I recognised Strasser and made up my mind to join the two of them. This decision saved Strasser's life.

I thought I was dreaming when I got a closer look at the machine flying behind and somewhat lower than Strasser, for it had a red, white and blue cockade on its fuselage. It was a Nieuport!

> [Buckler is incorrect here for French aeroplanes only carried cockades, or roundels as the British called them, on the wings, not the fuselage. He probably meant the wings, but with the passage of time had no doubt forgotten that it was the British that carried cockades on wings and fuselage sides.]

The Frenchman must have been stalking him unnoticed and was now waiting for the favourable moment to strike, so there was no time to lose. I charged at the lower flying Nieuport and opened fire, but without success. A jam forced me to break off from him. It was at this critical moment that Strasser pounced on him from above. [Presumably Strasser had now become aware of the danger and pulled up and round.] The Frenchman went into a dive with Strasser and myself behind him. I was enraged to discover that despite all my frantic efforts the jam could not be cleared in the air. In the meantime the Frenchman had managed, in an incredibly skilful manoeuvre, to get above Strasser and now almost sat on his neck. Apparently Strasser also had a jam, as he made a run for it and the Frenchman followed him, oddly enough without firing. Could he also have a jam?

I wanted to find out and disregarding the fact that I could not shoot, went after him. The Frenchman turned to look at me and when he saw that

Top left: A youthful Julius Buckler, the *Pour le Mérite* at his throat and the Iron Cross 1st Class on his breast pocket.

Top right: Buckler began his operational flying as a two-seater pilot. Here an Aviatik B comes into land.

Middle: A two-seater Aviatik C1.

Bottom: One of Jasta 17's original pilots was Jakob Wolff, seen here in a Fokker Eindecker with Kampfstaffel Metz, the unit that supplied the nucleus of pilots for the new Jasta.

Top: A mix of Albatros DII and DIII fighters lined up at Metz-Frescaty in early 1917.

Middle: An upturned Albatros DII, similar to the machine crashed by Buckler on Christmas Day 1916; his DII was shelled by artillery.

Bottom: Rittmeister Heinz Fr von Brederlow, Jasta 17's first Staffelführer, climbing out of his Albatros DIII.

Top: Buckler's Albatros DIII D.2033/16. White rudder, black and white fuselage bands and the name Mops on the fuselage.

Middle left: Another view of Mops with Vfw Rieger standing by it. Rieger had been wounded on 16 April 1917.

Middle right: Another of the original pilots who became firm friends with Buckler was Georg Strasser. He achieved seven victories and remained with Jasta 17 until May 1918.

Bottom: Alfred Träger, also a close friend, seen here in a DIII.

Top: Messrs Buckler, Heinz Sachsenberg, Gros and Strasser at St Quentin-le-Petit, spring 1917. Sachsenberg served with Jasta 17 from December 1916 to June 1917.

Middle: Buckler's fourth victory, a Nieuport Scout on 12 May 1917, surrounded by the usual mix of soldiers and field police.

Bottom: Buckler standing by Papeil's crashed Nieuport, 15 April 1917.

left: The man with the bandaged eye is Sergent Achille
›eil of Escadrille Spa3. He is standing with Georg Strasser,
helm Gros, Alfred Träger and Julius Buckler, who brought
ı down.

right: Alfred Träger in his earlier days as a two-seater pilot.

Bottom: Jasta 17 in May 1917. Rear left to right: Ltn Wolff, Ltn Gros, ----?---, Rittm von Brederlow, Ltn Sachsenberg, Ltn Schröder; sitting: Vfw Buckler, Ltn Zschunke, Oblt Viehweger and Ltn Träger.

Top: Hauptmann Eberhard von Seel took over Jasta 17 on 10 May and was killed just over a month later. The Albatros appears to have black stripes along the fuselage, black spinner, wheel covers and rudder.

Bottom: Von Seel standing in fron[t] another mainly black Albatros wit[h] white circles around the fuselage.

) left: Leutnant Ernst Wendler came in from Jasta 2 to take mmand of Jasta 17 after von Seel was shot down. Note black d white horizontal stripes along the fuselage and two rear-view rrors.

) right: Leutnant Wilhelm Gros in his Albatros named Fips. os was killed on 22 August 1917.

ddle: OffStv Adolf Schreder by his Albatros DV. Note white lplane with coloured rudder, a coloured lightning bolt along fuselage, and a coloured spinner.

tom: Vfw Gustav Schniedewind scored four victories with Jasta then moved to Jasta 1F in January 1918, bringing his score to en. Most of the medals he is wearing were awarded whilst with ta 1F in Palestine.

Top left: Buckler and Strasser. Buckler is wearing his stocking head-gear.

Top right: A more formal portrait of Julius Buckler.

Bottom: Buckler with another Mops, this time the name is in white.

Top: Jasta 17 pilots at Ghistelles, summer 1917. Centre, in boots, is Ernst Wendler, while to his left is Günther Schuster. The others, from bottom to top, are: Gustav Schniedewind, Alfred Träger, Wilhelm Becker (KIA 26 August), Erich Zschunke, Ltn Ehlers (wounded 16 August), Walter Brachwitz (DoW 23 December), Buckler, Otto Fitzner, Jacob Wolff (wounded 27 July), Adolf Werner, Georg Strasser.

Middle: Ernst Udet of Jasta 37. Their strange meeting in the air, while seemingly true, cannot be verified by the date or location Buckler supplied.

Bottom: Jasta 17's hangars at Wasquehal, near Lille.

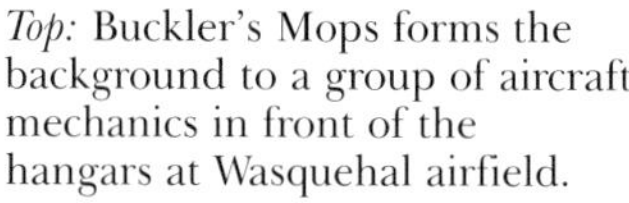

Top: Buckler's Mops forms the background to a group of aircraft mechanics in front of the hangars at Wasquehal airfield.

Middle left: Leutnant Alfred Bauer, killed in action 16 September 1917.

Middle right: Buckler and a DV at Wasquehal – possibly his other Albatros Lilly?

Bottom: Strasser, Träger, Becker and Werner.

p left: Buckler downed seven
illoons. This picture shows a
illoon with one of its occupants
aving taken to his parachute.

p right: Two observers in a
illoon basket, equipped with
eld glasses and a large-scale
ap. They could radio
iformation down to the ground.

iddle left: Jasta 17 had two
onkeys Heini and Rieke for a
hile, similar to these two with
nother unit sharing a bottle.

iddle right: The Jasta car (left to
ght): Wilhelm Becker, Träger,
dolf Schreder, Strasser, ---?---,
Adolf Werner; Richard Grüter and Alfred Bauer sit on the running
board.

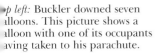

Bottom: Buckler's seventeenth victory, a Camel (B6314) of 70
Squadron, forced down on 11 October 1917.

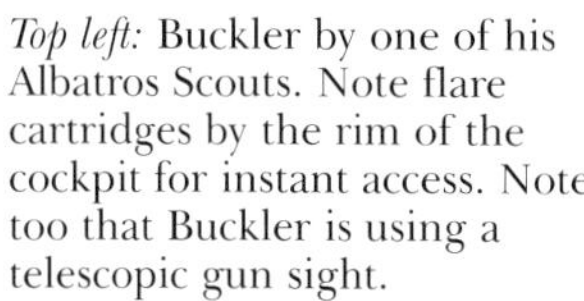

Top left: Buckler by one of his Albatros Scouts. Note flare cartridges by the rim of the cockpit for instant access. Note too that Buckler is using a telescopic gun sight.

Top centre: Two of Buckler's victims: Lt C M DeRochie, shot down on 14 July 1917...

Top right: ... and Captain C W C Wasey MC, 28 October 1917.

Bottom left: Buckler chopping wood after the party following his commissioning.

Bottom right: Jasta 17 pilots late 1917. Bottom to top. Left row: Rudol von Esebeck (CO), Wilhelm Becker, Alfred Träger, Richard Grüter, Gustav Schniedewind. Right row: Kurt von Rudno-Rudzinsky, Walter Brachwitz, Konrad Brendel, Adolf Schreder and 'Ltn' Buckler.

Top: Rudno-Rudzinsky in an Albatros named Gisi (short for Giselle) with lightning flash.

Middle: Vfw Koch of Jasta 17.

Bottom left: Shaven-headed Buckler with Rudno-Rudzinsky.

Bottom right: Strasser with his Albatros DV which he named Ly.

Top left: Leutnant Buckler wearing his 'Blue Max'. Apart from his Iron Cross 1st Class and his pilot badge, he is wearing the small Warriors' Honour Decoration in Iron. The ribbons depict the Iron Cross 2nd Class, the Hessian General Honour Decoration for Bravery, and the Prussian Golden Military Merit Cross.

Top right: A reproduction row of Buckler's medals where ribbons only would be worn. Iron Cross 2nd Class, the Golden Military Merit Cross, the Hessian General Honour Decoration 'for bravery', the Württemberg Silver Military Merit Medal, and the Hamburg Hanseatic Cross. The actual decorations that he would wear are the Blue Max, Iron Cross 1st Class and the Hessian Warrior's Honour Decoration in Iron.

Middle: Jasta 17 pilots, spring 1918. Standing l to r: Becker and Träger. Seated: Ltn Spindler, Alfred Fleischer, Georg Strasser, Julius Buckler, Adolf Werner, Konrad Brendel, Vfw Schumann (adj) and von Esebeck.

Bottom: Buckler wearing his Blue Max, visits comrades in Kest 8.

Top left: Alfred Fleischer arrived on Jasta 17 on 12 April 1918. The aircraft now carry the Patée Cross national marking.

Top right: Karl Bohny arrived on 18 January 1918 and scared Buckler with his flying when bringing him back to the Jasta in May 1918. Bohny achieved eight victories.

Middle left: Another pilot to join in April was Oberleutnant Hermann Pritsch, seen here in front of his Fokker DVII. The white nose of the DVII uses the air intakes to form a face, with eyebrows and teeth centre below.

Middle right: Another shot of Pritsch and his DVII. It carries a yellow swastika – used then as a good luck charm – and chevron, with the name Boroke! in black. Pritsch took temporary command of Jasta 17 following von Esebeck's death.

Bottom: Buckler claimed two French Salmson two-seaters, like the one shown here.

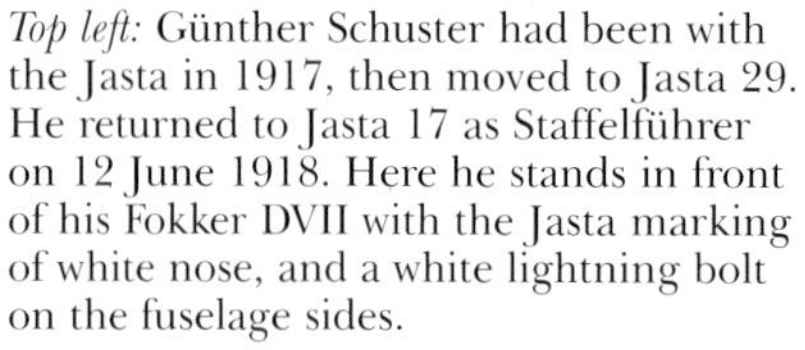

Top left: Günther Schuster had been with the Jasta in 1917, then moved to Jasta 29. He returned to Jasta 17 as Staffelführer on 12 June 1918. Here he stands in front of his Fokker DVII with the Jasta marking of white nose, and a white lightning bolt on the fuselage sides.

Top right: Alfred Fleischer in his Fokker DVII(Alb). It is believed the pennant marking is yellow, which is also the colour of striping to top and bottom of the fuselage. Nose i black and the radiator shell, white.

Bottom left: Buckler and one of his 'circus' trailers.

Bottom right: Julius Buckler wearing the rank of Hauptman in the 1930s.

I was setting a determined course for him he became nervous, side-slipped, regained control of the machine just above the ground, and prepared for a landing, during which he flipped over. Strasser also landed and a minute later my machine was standing next to the other two. This all took place about six kilometres behind the front.

[Before we deal with the Frenchman, there are several things to clarify about Buckler's narrative. Firstly there is no record of Buckler flaming a balloon on 30 April following the earlier efforts by Jasta 19 and 21. As for this also being the day on which Strasser gained his second victory, his second claim came in fact on 6 April, and indeed, by the 30th he had three victories to his name.

Generally, by this time, the Germans were fairly good at flying in a formation, which was the whole reason for the Jasta to be formed and used. The main tactic was designed for the leader, and not necessarily the Staffelführer, but mostly the most experienced pilot and or the pilot whose firing ability was better than most. Once the formation engaged hostile aircraft, this leader would attack first, covered by the rest of the pack. In this way, the man with the proven ability to bring down opposing aircraft could concentrate fully on his target, knowing his back was covered. Once the attack had been made, and hopefully the target hit, then a free-for-all might well ensue, giving the rest of the pilots a chance to engage. So to give the impression that Jasta 17 would lose each other once airborne is incomprehensible.

Far from being the day after the 'balloon victory and Strasser's second kill' this action, if a matter of fact, occurred on 15 April 1917, and the Frenchman, whom we will shortly hear more about, was flying a Spad, not a Nieuport. Buckler was obviously getting confused with a photograph he had in his possession when writing his book, showing an overturned Nieuport Scout, with a number '9' on the fuselage, a victory that he achieved in May, and about which we shall read later. In the meantime, Buckler recalls now the meeting of this French pilot who had force-landed. Although Buckler recalls his name as being 'Papaine' it was in fact Papeil, Sergent Achille Papeil of Escadrille N 3.

Spa 3 was in fact one of the elite French fighter squadrons within the French Groupe de Combat No.12, led by Commandant Félix Brocard. It was comprised of four escadrilles, Spa 3, Spa 26, Spa 73 and Spa 103. French squadron numbers were prefixed by a letter or letters denoting its equipment, thus the 'Spa' in this case denoted Spads.

> Among the aces in this escadrille were Georges Guynemer, Albert Deullin, Alfred Heurtaux, and René Dorme.]

The prisoner Papaine

The prisoner was a nice young fellow, a sergeant, and a real Frenchman. His name was Papaine (*sic*) and I was truly thankful that my bullets had missed their mark. It was my greatest victory and there is no other that I think of with such pure joy.

Why had Papaine landed? A grazing wound on his left cheek alone could not be the cause of it, but now it was revealed that he had in fact been the victim of a jammed machine gun and that during the fight we had both been bluffing in the same way. However, I had had the better nerves. Besides that, I had put two bullets through his fuel tank and that was the compelling reason for his landing.

While we were taking Papaine to our Staffel in a car which headquarters had put at our disposal, Strasser declared to me that our agreement from the previous evening did not apply in this case. First of all, I had saved his life and secondly, it was not a matter of shooting someone down, as I had forced Papaine to land without opening fire. I could say what I wanted, but he stuck to his point of view, so we abolished the agreement.

> [In fact the Germans had no system where victories were shared between pilots, unlike the British, French, and later the Americans. A victory could only be credited to a single pilot and in the event there was a dispute over which man should have the credit, and a toss of a coin did not satisfy either party, the claim would go to arbitration by a 'higher authority' whose verdict would be final.]

Papaine behaved in every respect like a good soldier and patriot should. One could not get a word out of him regarding military matters. Since he saw that we completely understood this and regarded him as a comrade, he soon became sociable and told amusing stories of which I admittedly understood only a little, and we spent a merry evening with him in our mess. Late in the evening we delivered Papaine to the rear. His machine, which apart from the [fuel] tank and some holes in the wings had remained fairly intact, served us for a long time as a touring machine [squadron hack!].

I met Papaine again in November 1918, at a tram stop on the way from Mainz to Wiesbaden. This is the only time when I have seen one of my opponents again after the war. He was still in the uniform of a French sergent aviator, which was reason enough for me to take a closer look at him. I recognised him immediately by the scar on his cheek, which was caused by the grazing shot he had received during our aerial combat.

To the astonishment of the other passengers there followed a warm, friendly greeting. Papaine had learned excellent German in the meantime and we had so much to talk about that the trip to Wiesbaden passed quickly. We had dinner together at Lösch's. Germany's fate had been decided by then. We two front line soldiers bore no hatred towards one another in our hearts. We expressed the hope – and it was sincere on both our parts – that our countries would be bound by friendship and would never again go to war with one another. I have not given up this hope to the present day, though there are repeated attempts to sow mistrust between the two great European nations, which together have so many valuable cultural assets and should be called upon to secure a just European peace forever.

The birth of 'Malaula'

In the high-spirited mood of our victory celebrations the word 'Malaula' was born. Was it that after Papaine had left some [of my] comrades imitated him, who spoke French with a Gallic temperament and with a broad singing accent? Was it some sort of garbled word? Had he referred to his machine, of which he spoke with great love and passion, as *ma Lola*, which had sounded like Malaula? I do not remember.[1]

The word pleased us and we liked it so much that from that night on we used it first in reference to Papaine, then all Frenchmen, and finally the entire enemy front. [To us] Malaula meant, go after the enemy! Malaula simply meant, Charge! This word, the longer it flourished amongst us and the more often we used it in difficult and ticklish situations – perhaps just ground through one's teeth – had an almost magical effect on us.

It became a signal, a battle cry! The battle cry of our Staffel!

> [Officially this was Buckler's fourth victory. Achille Louis Papeil came from Raffenville, born on 27 July 1890, so was getting on for four years older than Buckler. He entered military service in October 1911 in the Reserves (3e Régiment de Zouaves). A mechanic in civilian life he was mobilised on 2 August 1914, in an artillery unit – 15e Régiment d'Artillerie – and transferred to aviation during October 1915. Military Pilot Brevet No.3437, 29 April 1916. He had been assigned to Spa 3 in early 1917 and appears to have been credited with two victories plus another forced to land. Papeil had been flying a Spad VII, number S.117 and had come down near Prouvais, having taken off on a patrol at 05.20 that morning. In

[1] It has been suggested that it was not Papeil who said something like "ma Lola" but another French pilot Buckler shot down, Albin Joussaud (see later). The only problem with this is that Papeil was alive to say it, Joussaud died when he was shot down.

September 1917 he managed to escape from his prisoner of war camp and by December he was with GDE and then in the new year was an instructor at St Cyr. Papeil had been designated a Maréchal-des-Logis (cavalry or artillery sergeant) on 8 April.]

Detached and shot down

In the following weeks I shot down two more aeroplanes and a balloon. Since the course of these aerial combats did not involve any particular complications, but rather took place in a normal fashion, so to speak, there is nothing further to say about them. Every victory was celebrated and though I may have seemed outwardly happy, I felt sadness within. I thought of the men who had to lay down their lives and of their relatives whom I did not know. How would they bear the news of their fate? I thought of my mother. If the same fate were to overtake me, she would be grief-stricken, but brave.

Sometimes I felt a certain glee when I failed to score. If I had shot down everyone against whom I fought the number of my aerial victories, but also the burden of my private sorrow, would be much greater.

As soft-hearted as what I write about my sorrow and compassion may sound, as soon as I was in the air and the battle was joined, I thought only of one thing: victory. My comrades called me 'Bull'. 'Steer' would have been closer to the truth. When I was riled up, I forgot everything. The red, white, and blue cockades had the same effect on me as the red cape [of the bull-fighter]. So I led a sort of double life. In spite of all my inner gentleness I was quite the furious fellow. In the meantime I became a Vizefeldwebel.

Then something happened which did not suit me at all and which I almost perceived as an insult and yet in light of future possibilities of promotion worked only to my advantage. I was detached to a fighter pilot school for four weeks. With seven victories I held first place in Jasta 17, so why of all people was I being sent to a school for fighter pilots? To me this measure seemed both extremely illogical and unnecessary. But orders were orders.

[It is a pity Buckler shoots ahead and makes no mention of his two victory claims in May, although only one was confirmed. On 6 May he had a scrap with a Spad VII near Pont-à-Vert and was credited with a *zlgzw* 'victory'. This stood for *zur Landung gezwungen* – forced to land. It is not always clear what this is. Obviously one can understand it is an Allied aeroplane that has been forced to land inside its own lines, and, presumably not shelled to destruction by German artillery. However, considering the number of pilots claiming victories that only 'appeared' to go down inside Allied lines, and as we now know did not in fact land or crash, how is it that some victories were credited, while others were not? After all, a machine that was shown as *zlgzw* may well have had a dying pilot on board, or may indeed have been so badly damaged or inaccessible for recovery, that it was a loss, yet a pilot who caused this to happen was not given credit for a victory. Thus Buckler forced a Spad VII to land, but it was not added to his victory score.

It is possible, however, that the Spad was a machine from N 69, flown by Lieutenant Gaëtan de la Brunetière, who had been wounded during the encounter and had to make a rapid landing inside his lines. To give him his full title, Gaëtan Pierre Marie Dimier de la Brunetière came from Senlis, born 10 August 1893. He enlisted into the military in November 1913 and after graduating from the Special School at Saint-Cyr, served with the 4e Régiment de Hussards (Hussars). He moved to aviation in November 1915, gaining his Military Pilot Brevet No.2689, on 10 February 1916 as a sous-lieutenant, and was promoted to full lieutenant in August. His first assignment was to N 68 on 28 June 1916 but two days later he was wounded in combat, although he did claim a Fokker shot down. He won the *Croix de Guerre* with three palmes in WW1, and had become a *Chevalier de la Légion d'Honneur* for his actions on 30 June 1916. His citation recorded: *Sous-lieutenant pilot, Escadrille N 68. A young officer who on his first sortie gave proof of audacity, composure and courage above praise. Surprised by a Fokker and hit twice, he resolutely gave combat and downed his adversary in his lines; attacked by a second aircraft he was wounded again, he succeeded, although his motor had stopped, to put to flight the enemy aircraft then returned his plane in free flight to our lines.* (German casualty possibly Gefreiter Otto Schneider). Brunetière was in hospital until January 1917 and after a period at GDE (Groupe de Divisions d'Entraînment) was posted to N 69 on 9 February 1917. Having survived the encounter with Buckler, he continued flying but was reported missing on 25 September 1917 during a fight with a German two-seater.

On 12 May Buckler gained his seventh official victory, a Nieuport XXIV No.3674, at 18.40 hours at La Malmaison. This was a machine from Escadrille N 75 (X Armée) flown by Adjudant-Chef (Chief Warrant Officer) Albin Joussaud. Joussaud came from Tornac, born 24 January 1888 and he had been a trader pre-war. Entering military service in October 1909, he served with the 2e Régiment du Génie (Engineers) and when mobilized in August 1914 joined the 7e Régiment. With the engineers he was promoted to adjudant in April 1916 and had won the *Croix de Guerre* with 1 *étoile d'argent*, and 1 *étoile de vermeil*, plus one *palme*. Transferred to aviation in 1916, gaining Military Brevet No.5313 on 3 February 1917. Posted to N 75 on 26 April and was reported missing on 12 May having taken off on a patrol at 17.00 hours.

By the time Buckler left on 17 June, Jasta 17 had achieved a total of nineteen victories in air combat. Individual scores were:

Vfw Julius Buckler 7
Vfw George Strasser 4
Ltn Jakob Wolff 3
Ltn Günther Schuster 2
Ltn Wilhelm Gros 1
Ltn Neumann 1
Ltn Albrecht Crüsmann 1

The Jasta had suffered two casualties. On 9 February Vfw Adolf Wellhausen had been wounded and died as a result on the 11th. Vfw Rieger, who had joined in March, was severely injured on 16 April following a crash-landing after combat. What Buckler does not record prior to his leaving is that his old observer Rudno had become a pilot and was assigned to Jasta 17 on 8 July. Albrecht Crüsmann had joined in May while a future ace, Vizefeldwebel Gustav Schniedewind came to the Jasta on 17 June.]

The Jagdfliegerschule lay far to the north, about 280 kilometres from us. That was a longer cross-country flight than I had ever made before. I drew the flight path on my map but as simple as it appeared on paper, I knew how difficult it was to navigate over unfamiliar territory. How much would I have liked to have had Rudno, my old observer, with me.

I thought of my first cross-country flight from Metz to Briey with Leutnant Parisius as observer. Normally it would have taken one and a half hours but after three hours I noticed that something was not right and finally Parisius confessed with an emphatic shrug of the shoulders that he had no idea where we were. There was no time for lengthy deliberations. We had [almost] run out of fuel and the motor was beginning to quit on us. We would have to make an emergency landing. At an altitude of 3,200 metres it looked as though there were very nice places to land everywhere. Yet when the machine was at 800 metres I saw that there was nothing but hills below us and that we were right over a hollow. How thankful I was to you Höfig, that you had taught me to 'corkscrew' so well!

Using every trick imaginable, I finessed my way over several obstacles and only in this way did I still succeed at the last moment in pulling the machine up over a two-metre-wide ditch filled with water. I set down just on the other side, but now saw to my horror a wall, which seemed a good distance away, racing towards me awfully fast. Since from experience I could not assume that it would prove to be smarter than I and give way, after I turned off the engine I jumped out of the machine, grabbed the end of the left wing and tore it around, so that the right one swung around just a millimetre from the wall and everything remained intact.

German soldiers and Luxembourg farmers ran over and congratulated us on everything turning out so well. Since heavy fog had set in, we stayed put for three days in Luxembourg at a regimental headquarters. They were three wonderful days and our hosts spoiled us in every way. When finally on the third morning the longed for sun mightily parted the thick ground fog, we took off in the thin golden mist and flew in the brilliant sunshine under a blue sky to Metz. That evening Parisius had to pay dearly in the mess for getting us lost. Now I was supposed to make this much longer flight with no observer at all.

A comrade from the fighter pilot school had asked me in a letter to bring along some medicine for him that was not available there. I had our medical orderly get some and equipped with this bottle of medicine, a lot of coffee, and a lot of more or less good advice from my Staffel mates, I climbed into my machine and set off on my trip. I had marked all the prominent points on my map and during the first forty minutes everything was going wonderfully. Then I ran up against a thick bank of clouds that forced me to fly lower and lower until finally I was only fifty metres high and racing at great speed above God's green earth. Things were going past so quickly that I had no more time to check the landmarks I had marked. Purely by instinct my right foot kept pushing the rudder bar and steered the aircraft away from the west. My only remaining guide were the shell holes below me. At last the thick snow clouds came to an end and the way they dissolved in a whirling motion under the sway of the piercing sun was a magnificent sight to behold. Blue sky appeared. I had been flying for two hours and had kept a constant look out for the airfield of the fighter pilot school.

Then I saw a couple of dots coming towards me. Were they aeroplanes from the school? Before I came to my senses there was a rattling of machine-gun fire and the carburettor in my machine caught fire. I felt a blow against my head and when I awoke I was sitting in a pile of wreckage literally on bare ground. I took my cigarette case out of my left pocket and the lighter from my right and began to smoke. At the same time I moved my legs and discovered to my reassurance that they were not broken. Then I saw drops of blood on my coat and when I felt my face I had bloody fingertips. I heard a female voice address me in German and then I fainted.

* * *

I awoke in a military hospital. I felt something wet on the left half of my face and saw two women and a German flying officer standing next to me. So I had not fallen into captivity, which was my main concern. The woman who spoke German – she and the other women were French – had been in Wiesbaden for several years and thus quite close to my hometown of Mainz. She told me that she and her friend had been busy in the garden of her farm when she saw three French pilots dive on me and I suddenly went down in a steep dive. Then there was a terrible crash and pieces flew around in the air, but the enemy machines were driven away by my comrades. Together she and her friend brought me to the farm and made a makeshift dressing until my comrades came and took me away.

Due to my bandaged head I was taken to the head-wound section of the hospital. What horrible things I experienced in the next few days I spent there I cannot describe. All of the soldiers who lay there had wounds to the head or face. Some screamed and acted like madmen or were driven crazy with pain. I was wheeled into the operating room. My upper lip was closed with fourteen stitches, the gaping laceration above my left eye with twenty-four. Six men had to hold me.

An hour after my operation the German-speaking French lady visited me and brought me all sorts of titbits. She did not look at all like a French woman, for she had blonde hair and was without make-up. Only now did I notice how pretty she was. She asked me to give her my flying cap, which she had found in the pile of wreckage and brought along.

'How much blood you must have lost, you poor man,' she said.

I only understood what she meant when she showed me the cap which had been coloured reddish-brown through and through as though from coagulated blood. Yet I did not have my cap on during the entire flight. It had lain well-packed beneath my seat together with the bottle of medicine. So the medicine must have been reddish-brown. However, I left the beautiful girl alone in the belief that the cap, which she requested as a relic, had thus been steeped in my noble blood.

I was also visited by my comrade for whom the medicine had been intended. He was quite sad about its loss and I felt so sorry for him that I promised I would see to its replacement.

After I had lain for seven days in the hospital I was shipped out en-route to the Staffel with the left side of my head covered in bandages. It was a good thing I made an appearance there because wild rumours about my crash had caused my comrades a great deal of anxiety. Even though they knew I was not dead, they nonetheless had to assume that I was so badly wounded that I would not return to them and resume my duties as a fighter pilot. For this reason, their joy was all the greater and the three days of leave and convalescence which I spent in the circle of my comrades contributed much to the fact that I returned to the

Jagdfliegerschule with fresh courage and a new bottle of medicine in my little suitcase. Of course, this time I went by car.

> [It is strange that this story, told in so much detail, and seemingly enhanced by the business of the medicine, does not appear to fit into the chronological sequence of actual events. There is no evidence of a posting to the school, although this need not be significant, nor is there any report of Buckler being shot down and wounded in the assumed period of which he is speaking. As far as is known, his first aerial wounding did not occur until 17 July, so once again, while the basic story may well be true, it cannot be verified by records.]

Soon [at the school] I had to confess to myself that my assumption that this whole detachment was highly unnecessary and superfluous for an old hand like me with seven victories, was very premature and unjustified. It was only here that I discovered the higher techniques, so to speak, of aerial fighting. Every single type of aircraft available at that time was flown here and indeed without dual control. It was a matter of getting in and getting a handle on it. This form of self-instruction was still the best way to learn. Because of Höfig, my first instructor, that is what I was used to.

Besides excellent training in aerial combat, I also came away with a lot of theoretical knowledge from the fighter pilot school. My initial period of flight training had been of such limited duration that theoretical matters received scant treatment. Here I enjoyed receiving the same instruction as the officers and later, when my dream of becoming an officer was realised, I was often grateful that I became acquainted with concepts here which concerned not only aviation, but also subjects typical of a liberal education. The camaraderie was exemplary, so it was not easy for me to say farewell to the Jagdfliegerschule, however happy I was to return to my Staffel.

Chapter Seven

In Flanders Skies

An unmanned balloon and an armoured opponent

Hauptmann Freiherr von Esebeck had taken over the leadership of the Staffel. From the first day of my return onwards, his relationship to me was one of such sincere warmth and such unconditional trust that the position I had gained under von Brederlow not only remained the same, but rather became more independent and recognised. As before, as soon as the Staffel was in the air I took command. Not once was there any disagreement. This significantly increased my self-confidence.

[Perhaps because they were only with the Jasta for a short time, Buckler does not tell us that following von Brederlow's posting on 10 May 1917, to Idflieg (Inspektion der Fliegertuppen – Inspectorate of Aviation), two others had led the Jasta while he had been absent. Hauptmann Eberhard von Seel had become Staffelführer, posted in from Jasta 2 (Boelcke) as von Brederlow left. Von Seel came from Wallmerrod, born in January 1885 and had served with the Prussian 176th Infantry Regiment till transferring to aviation. His stay with Jasta 2 was brief, so obviously his age, he was thirty-one, and rank took precedence over experience. He lasted just a month with Jasta 17, before falling in flames on 12 June in combat with a Spad near Montigny. He probably fell to Adjudant-Chef René Fonck of Escadrille Spa 103, who claimed an Albatros near Cauroy-Cormicy at 09.00 hours for his 6th victory. Fonck was destined to become France's Ace of Aces with seventy-five confirmed victories by the war's end.

Von Seel's replacement was Leutnant Ernst Wendler a week later, another former Jasta Boelcke pilot. Wendler came from Ulm, where he was born in April 1890. He had become a pilot in March 1916 and was sent to Kampfstaffel 14 of KG3. He was wounded on 1 July 1916 – the first day of the Somme offensive – and his observer killed, in a fight with Major L W B Rees MC, CO of 32 Squadron flying a DH2 pusher scout.

Rees engaged several German aircraft on this occasion, shooting down one and forcing another machine to land (Wendler), and although wounded himself, drove off a third, possibly with a wounded observer aboard. For this action, Lionel Rees was awarded the Victoria Cross. Wendler had been awarded the Württemberg Gold Military Merit Medal on 29 June 1916. Despite what Buckler recalls, Wendler remained with Jasta 17 till October, even surviving a shoot down on 16 September 1917, so von Esebeck did not arrive to command Jasta 17 till 8 October. It is somewhat surprising that Buckler should omit mentioning at least Wendler, having been, therefore, under his command for some three months.

Rudolf Frhr von Esebeck came from Karlsruhe, born in March 1888. He had served in the Garde-Regiment zu Fuss 2 (2nd Foot Guards) and had been awarded the Iron Cross 1st Class. He had been a pilot with Jasta 8 for most of the first half of 1917, then commander of Kest 7 (a home defence unit) until posted to command Jasta 17 on 4 October 1917.

Buckler relates that in the air he took command. This is what we referred to earlier, that the most experienced air-fighter usually led in the air, and not necessarily the senior pilot or even the Staffelführer. With his seven confirmed victories and despite his brief absence, Buckler was still the top scorer in Jasta 17.]

During my absence three of my comrades had fallen in aerial combat, which hit me hard. Only those involved in the war can appreciate what comradeship meant at that time. We opened up to one another and trusted each other implicitly. We were always ready to comply with one another's wishes and even whims, not knowing whether there would be time to do so the next day. If someone had had a falling-out in the evening, mostly over something foolish, it was forgotten when one returned from a fighter patrol the following day. The shared closeness to death brought about a quick reconciliation. [The only casualties at this time were Leutnant Wolfgang Günther, a former pilot with FA(A)205 whose stay was brief, arriving on 16 March and being severely injured on 21 May in a crash whilst taking off, plus von Seel's death on 12 June.]

Only during my schooldays did I know of a similar unconditional friendship. I am sometimes reminded of a little incident which took place when I was thirteen years old and, amongst other things, was still an acolyte [assistant or attendant to a priest; an altar boy]. At a rehearsal for confirmation, about forty of us boys had to enter the church with wooden candles to practice the procession. In the darkness behind the altar I stepped on the heel of the person in front of me. Disregarding the sanctity of the place in which we stood, he turned around and hit me on the head with his wooden candle. I lay in wait for him on the way home and repaid him in full for that blow to the head. Suddenly I was surrounded by his twin-brother and some others who belonged to the same clique, all coming to the aid of the candle-wielder. I found myself in a very pressing situation. Then a friend of mine came along whom I had stuck by faithfully for six years, until four weeks previously when we had had a terrible argument. At this very moment all quarrels were forgotten. He bailed me out and we probably would have given the gang a thorough thrashing had not the priest intervened, at which point we all ran away.

* * *

In the first ten days after my return to the Staffel I was considerably hampered by my bandaged eye. In spite of that I continued flying with enthusiasm, not with the Staffel, but on my own. I was not credited with any successes at this time until a quite dubious special circumstance that could have cost me my entire career. Our observation post reported that an enemy balloon was drifting over our lines at 1,800 metres. I suspected some sort of devilishness was behind this, jumped into my Mops, which was already running at full revs, and raced towards the balloon. Although some of my other comrades had joined in the chase, I was the first one on the scene. I owed the speed of my machine to my first mechanic, Unteroffizier Roth, who was a first-class engine specialist and an extremely skilled rigger. Whatever machine I happened to get, after Roth had taken it into his charge it soon became the fastest machine in the Staffel.

I circled the balloon suspiciously and determined that the basket was empty. I feared, however, that it might be loaded with explosives. In the meantime the balloon had climbed to 2,800 metres and, caught by another stream of air, changed direction and drifted westwards, whence it had come. I did not allow the French this triumph, not wanting them to be given the chance to recover it. So I fired a couple of bursts at it from some distance and it began to burn, but the flame went out again almost immediately. Then it slowly swung lower and lower until it finally landed, still not completely deflated, on the southern edge of our airfield.

[As I had seen] the basket was completely empty and the situation became clear. The balloon had torn free and its observer had either taken all his instruments with him when he bailed out or had previously thrown them overboard. My only regret was it was not a genuine victory. However, a short while later I was to regret having shot the balloon down at all.

After I returned to my quarters I was told that the Kofl had called; Kofl meant kommandeur der Flieger [officer in charge of all flying units assigned to an Army] and I was to report to him immediately. Instead of the praise I thought I had earned, I received a very thorough dressing down, as I had disobeyed an order that prohibited the downing of unmanned balloons. I knew nothing about this order, as it had been issued during my detachment to the Jagdfliegerschule. So why had I not read the orders in the file folder? It served me right.

At least it was limited to a dressing down, for a formal reprimand would have made any further promotion more difficult, if not questionable. I could have told myself that a burning balloon posed a great danger if one did not know where it would go down. In any event, I was determined to prove to the Kofl as quickly as possible that I could do more than just blow up un-manned balloons floating around harmlessly.

I was to succeed in doing so the very same day. I received permission for a special flight and patrolled along the front. Everything was quiet, including the enemy flak. Then a few exploding cloudlets appeared in my immediate vicinity which could only have come from one of our own flak batteries. Was someone trying to warn me and bring something to my attention? Was there an enemy somewhere nearby?

Then I saw the 'Invisible One' coming towards me obliquely from the side. We had given this honorary title to an enemy two-seater which we had already attacked several times in fours and fives and thus fired upon with eight to ten machine guns. He had stubbornly resisted every attempt to get the better of him and in my opinion he must have been armoured.

However, I attributed our failures to the fact that during our combined attacks we were much too pre-occupied with ourselves, taking care not to ram into each other, and getting in each other's way robbed us of success. In accordance with the proverb 'the strong man is most powerful when alone', perhaps I would have a better chance of handling him without my comrades.

We now got involved in the usual dogfight. During our twisting and turning I concluded that my opponent's aircraft was in fact armoured. Besides that, I soon realised that I was dealing with two really strong-willed lads. They put me in such a dire predicament that I lost my instinct for self-preservation. Without firing a shot, I approached my armoured opponent within ramming distance and only then did my machine guns crack. The pilot and observer collapsed and the aeroplane went into a spin and crashed.

In many aerial combats I had approached the enemy very closely, but never so deliberately and with such calmness and cold-bloodedness as with this one – my eighth victory. The Kofl was so pleased with my accomplishment that he arrived as our guest in the evening and while dining I had to take a seat between him and the Staffelführer.

[This again makes no sense when dealing with a chronological event, for Buckler's eighth official victory was a Sopwith Triplane. In the *Nachtrichtenblatt* – the equivalent of the British and French *communiqués* – a pilot's victories were now being shown in date order and followed by its order of confirmation. As was mentioned earlier, victory confirmations were not necessarily in strict date order, so that a fifth victory could be credited at a later date than a sixth, simply because of the time it took to receive confirmation, i.e. a victory, say on 1 May, may be credited as No.6, due to the fact that a victory on 2 May took less time to confirm and became No.5. However, Buckler's accredited eighth victory was a single-seat Triplane and not a two-seater – armoured or not. His eighth victory was dated 11 July, which is roughly in the right place if we are following Buckler's story chronologically, so if he is talking of some other machine – a two-seater – it has to be on another date entirely.]

Changes on a quiet front

Spring had come, but while nature awakened, our sector of the front fell more and more quietly asleep. May of 1917 was for us the most calm and peaceful May of the war.

Two monkeys, Heini and Rieke, and a giant eagle with clipped wings provided our entertainment, Hagenbeck having sent them as a gift from Hamburg. We kept them in a shed we constructed in our beautiful conservatory. In just a few days some of us could go into the cage without hesitation to play with the monkeys, while others were rejected by them with loud shrieks and bared teeth. The old eagle became a good companion to us young eagles. He would observe the childish antics of the monkeys with majestic serenity. If things were getting a bit too rowdy for him he would beat his wings, instilling some respect in Heini and Rieke and causing them to behave properly for a while. Later we allowed the monkeys to run around freely and they jumped from tree to tree in the garden, came begging to us in the mess, or romped around with the dogs.

One day when we returned from a patrol we found a fine mess. The monkeys had climbed into our rooms through an open window and had torn, smashed, and thrown into confusion everything that was not nailed down. They had [even] gobbled up the soap from the wash-stands. Heini sat in a cloud of bed feathers and was trying, without much success, to get rid of a clump of feathers which he had greedily stuffed into his cheeks.

Infuriated, we attempted to apprehend the offenders. At first they thought we wanted to play with them, then they realised it was serious and became nervous and enraged. Rieke took flight and we had to hunt after her for a long time until we were able to lure her down from the tower of the village church with a wartime ruse. We tied Heini to a long rope while we lay hidden in ambush. It took many hours before Rieke could no longer resist Heini's mute supplication and came down. From then on the monkeys were again locked up in the cage. If it had been up to me, the animals would have been sent back to Hamburg, then we and they would have been spared hours of sadness.

Later, we took the monkeys along to new quarters in another area. There, during a renewed escape attempt, Rieke was wantonly shot by an infantryman. Heini took this so much to heart that he would no longer eat and died soon thereafter. Having to watch this otherwise lively monkey die was more than torturous for us. We left the eagle behind in the château conservatory for our successors, as we feared we would not be able to secure any comparable accommodation for the regal bird.

* * *

A special mission brought some variety to our life of flying. Each day we had to accompany a certain aircraft thirty to fifty kilometres behind the enemy lines. This was not accomplished without aerial combat. Because we were not permitted to leave the plane however, it did not lead to any victories. This 'claret show', as we dubbed it, because during this period we drank red wine in the morning instead of coffee – not to give us courage, but to cheer us up – lasted four weeks. [Jasta 17 scored no victories between 16 June and 9 July.]

More entertainment was provided by the military hospital which was set up in our village, with whose doctors and nurses we soon stood on a good neighbourly footing. A charity show was to take place one Sunday for the benefit of poor wounded soldiers and we flyers were asked to contribute in some way. We did so by entering a 'Vizefeldwebel Buckler aerial exhibition'.

On the day before the event I had terrific pains in my left eye and therefore went to my room early. Since I could not fall asleep, I felt around my eye until I detected something hard and pointed. After a lot of futile efforts it could finally be pulled out and revealed itself to be a glass splinter of eight millimetres length. I went down to the mess in my pyjamas to explain the cause of my pain to my comrades. The successful operation was properly celebrated and the sun was already rising when I returned to my room. A few hours later it was time for my flying exhibition.

At 500 metres I began to loop my aircraft and with thirty-two consecutive loops definitely established a world record for that time. Following this, Strasser and I presented an intense mock dogfight. I had no idea at the time that ten years later I would make a living with such stunts.

As nice as this period was for us, it did not entirely suit our taste. We wanted to be where the action was. One of us heard that something was brewing up north and then we received orders to move to Flanders. We packed up quickly and did not even have time to say farewell to our friends at the military hospital, but as we flew away above the hospital we waved to those below.

We had flown about 200 kilometres in formation when we came across the famous Flanders fog. For the sake of safety we had to separate and in spite of that landed in short intervals behind one another on the assigned airfield, which disappointed us with its small size. After three days we were permitted to leave it again and were deployed yet further to the north.

[Jasta 17's new airfield was Ghistelles just a few kilometres south of the port of Ostende. The Jasta had been moved to this 4th Army front in response to a request for reinforcements in view of the British Ypres offensive actions, including the Battle of Messines, which began on 7 June and ended on the 14th. The date of the move was 24 June so if Buckler had earlier been talking of his eighth victory which occurred on 11 July, it could not have been a RNAS Triplane in any event.

Being based at Ghistelles would mean Buckler and Jasta 17 being up against the British Royal Flying Corps for the first time, as well as units of the Belgian air force. Much of the British air operations in this general area were also undertaken by the Royal Naval Air Service, as well as the RFC. Although the RNAS had been supporting the RFC further south, with a succession of fighter squadrons, the RNAS had something of its own private war along the Channel/North Sea coast. RNAS aircraft in both France and Belgium, as well as from England, had to cover enemy operations over the sea, against U-boats and shipping, as well as aircraft belonging to the German Naval Air Service and the German Marine Korps aircraft. These used both seaplanes and land planes.

Ghistelles airfield had, in 1915, been the home of a German bombing squadron, under the code-name BAO – Brieftauben-Abteilung, Ostende, or Carrier Pigeon Section. One of its observers was none other than Baron Manfred von Richthofen, before he became a pilot.

No doubt Buckler and his comrades knew only too well that fighting against the British would be a tougher proposition than they had been used to whilst being up against the French. German Jasta pilots generally accepted this, and it was not unknown for units that had been heavily engaged on the more northern sectors, to go down to the French front for a breather. Jasta 17 had achieved a total of eighteen victories thus far on the French front, balloons and aircraft, but would quickly adapt to fighting the British.

Georg Strasser opened the Jasta's account on this front on 8 July by shooting down a Sopwith Camel that went down on the Allied side, south of Nieuport, timed at 21.00 hours. Not only was this the first victory for the Jasta on the British/Belgian front, but it was the first Sopwith Camel brought down by a German pilot. The Camel was from 4 Naval Squadron, a patrol having flown out that evening and been engaged by four Albatros Scouts over Pervyse at 19.50 (the German time at this period was one hour ahead of Allied time). It had crashed near Ramscapelle, which is south of Nieuport. The British pilot was Flight Sub-lieutenant E W Busby, the Camel's serial number being N6361. Busby did not survive and Strasser had achieved his fourth confirmed victory.]

Two events prevent a duel in the air

The Flanders town to which we moved was called Ghistelles. One could hardly imagine a nicer airfield than the one we found here, with spacious tents and even a hangar, while the seaside resort of Ostende lay right next door. Nevertheless, I have only seen the town from above. Already the increased roar of the artillery fire indicated to us that there would be plenty for us to do in this sector.

The first orientation flight of the Staffel was an experience for me, as I saw the sea for the first time. While the others flew behind the Staffelführer out towards the open sea without hesitation, I first had to fight against a very unpleasant feeling inside which wanted to prevent me, the landlubber, from flying over the water. On the return flight we encountered warships and flew towards them with joyful greetings. From now on whenever we went into our glide we found ourselves above the sea, which crashed and foamed below us. [We were all aware that] With our land planes, if the motor were to stop running prematurely an emergency landing upon the stormy waters would probably turn out quite badly for us.

Since our mess was not yet completely set up, we took an excursion in the evening through Ghistelles. Strasser and I ended up in an *estaminet*, a small, comfortable inn. We both fell in love with Eugène, the owner's daughter, at first sight. She spoke good German and I imagined that she was in love with me and therefore out of sheer happiness bought everyone drinks time and again until, overcome by a lot of alcohol, I fell asleep still sitting at the table. When I awoke and glanced around with sleepy eyes, I caught Strasser and Eugène by surprise in a tender embrace. Filled with mindless fury, I paid the bill, then Strasser and I walked beside one another through the dark streets in silence. It was clear to us that this affair could only be settled by a duel and it was equally clear that this duel had to take place in the air.

Today I laugh at this childishness, but at the time we were both deadly serious about the duel. We established the conditions: a single exchange of fire with ten rounds of machine-gun ammunition. Upon our arrival at the airfield we had Hennicke, our faithful old armourer, change the machine-gun belts. Perhaps he had not slept well, but in any event he performed the task of changing them over so slowly that in the meantime,

Leutnant Gros, our flight leader, appeared at the field. He was happy to come across us here so early and suggested we all take off on a patrol together. Accordingly our diabolical plan had to be postponed. Strasser and I did not look at one another and spoke not a word.

We flew towards the front just beneath a solid layer of cloud. Apparently the enemy anti-aircraft batteries were still asleep. Our own were all the more lively and agitated, but it could not immediately be determined what they were actually shooting at, if we were not to assume we were the intended target. I searched along the chain of small exploding clouds that stretched out for about a kilometre. I thought I was dreaming; an airship was steering its way through the morning light. Just as suddenly, it disappeared again. It must have gone back into the protective layer of cloud and could not be found again. Furious about losing the giant but elusive prey, we continued to roam around for a while. If Gros and Strasser had not also seen the airship, I would have perhaps considered the whole thing to be a hallucination. [Later] we received confirmation [of its presence] from some anti-aircraft units, whose quarters had been bombed by the airship.

[Back on the ground] even at breakfast neither Strasser nor I spoke a word to each other. Then two events occurred, either of which would have been enough to make me forget any sort of quarrel, especially such a ridiculous affair of jealously.

Hauptmann von Esebeck walked into the officers' mess and informed us that in a few days the Staffel would receive a new pilot. His name was Rudno-Rudzinsky. I could hardly believe it, my dear Rudno, thus was our fondest wish to be fulfilled! Side by side we would fly against the enemy, each in his own aeroplane, just as we had dreamt of doing during the days of our topsy-turvy flyer's marriage.

> [Considering von Esebeck only joined Jasta 17 on 4 October, while Rudno-Rudzinsky arrived on the 5th, there is again a question of Buckler's memory. However….]

As far as I was concerned, the episode with Eugène was forgotten, for I could have hugged Strasser with joy. However, the matter of the unsettled duel was still stuck in his head and in order for him to forget it as completely as I had, a second event was necessary, which was indeed of quite different character, and for all of us of a much more painful nature.

Just after breakfast a report came in that an enemy bomber formation had been sighted over Bruges. Malaula! Malaula! We dived into our cars and raced over to the airfield. As with all pursuit flights, after taking off the leadership of the Staffel was turned over to me. Under my leadership we flew towards the enemy formation, to discover that it consisted of ten bombers and six fighters. The bombers were flying at 4,000 metres while the fighters were at 4,800 metres. With a cry of Malaula we dropped down on them.

Our thirteen machines dived on the bombers. Remarkably, the higher-flying fighter planes did not react. I took on the lead machine of the bomber formation and greeted it with a burst from both machine guns, resulting in it going into a spin. I saw the observer quite clearly squatting down on his seat; he must have been wounded. I was so certain of my prey that I followed without firing. At 100 metres the enemy pilot succeeded in regaining control of his machine and hastily turned for home. Then, when I wanted to open fire, I suffered a jam. In addition, during the dive behind the spinning machine I lost my goggles and my eyes were completely sticky from spraying oil. So I escorted him brave and true, up to the enemy lines. He may have believed in a miracle or a whim of fate, as I did in similar circumstances. I then turned away and landed back at our airfield.

We had agreed that as soon as the purpose of the flight was fulfilled and the [enemy] formation had been dispersed, everyone would immediately return to the airfield. During this attack my comrades shot down three opponents, Strasser obtaining his fourth aerial victory.

Half an hour later we were in the air once more. We had received orders to fly a 'barrage patrol' which meant seeing to it that no enemy flyers flew over our lines, behind which some preparations were underway for a ground assault. During this patrol, Leutnant Gros led the first flight [Kette], I the second.

Whilst flying back and fourth we ran across six English Sopwiths in the immediate vicinity of our airfield and at once a most wonderful aerial battle broke out. We were equal in numbers and the one I took on began to smoke after a few seconds but – thank God – without catching fire, landed with a total smash-up on our airfield. The other five got away.

Leutnant Gros did not return from this offensive patrol and we were all badly shaken by the news. Strasser forgot about his fourth victory and I my ninth. We approached one another and silently shook hands. With that our old friendship was sealed once more. The fuss over the woman at the *estaminet* was forgotten. We no longer visited Eugène and became much better friends than before.

Gros was safe. The English pilot in the meantime had been pulled from the wreckage of his aircraft with a nasty wound to his right thigh from a ricochet and he was taken by car to the military hospital in Ghistelles. On the next day we visited him, bringing champagne, wine, and cigarettes from the officers' mess. From then on, one of us attended him daily. I visited him for the last time after fourteen days. On this day the poor fellow's right leg was amputated. I would not have been able to see him again, so much did I suffer with him. He was a charming, strapping fellow and three days later he was transported away. [Sadly] I have forgotten his name.

[At last we can record a date for an action. On 17 July, Buckler brought down a Sopwith Pup (B1713) of 54 Squadron, whose pilot did indeed lose a leg. However, we have now travelled back in time from October to July, and despite what he says, this was a morning victory and not an afternoon one. Also, Jasta 17 did not bring down three enemy bombers that morning, just one Bristol F2B two-seat fighter, claimed by Vizefeldwebel Adolf Werner, for his first victory. The BF2b, from 48 Squadron (A7166), force-landed on the beach at Middlekerke, its pilot mortally wounded and the observer captured. There is no record of Gros having been brought down, so perhaps it was little more than a forced-landing away from base and he quickly turned up. Either that or Buckler has merged two events together in his mind.

Fortunately we have the British pilot's report of the action, taken from the form he was asked to fill out upon his repatriation from prisoner camp in January 1918. He was Second Lieutenant Clifford Twyford Felton, from Ivy Hall, Solihull, near Birmingham. He recorded:

'I was with three other scout machines on an Offensive Patrol at daybreak on 17 July 1917, when enemy machines were sighted. We attacked and during the fight, when I was behind an enemy machine, I was hit by a piece of high explosive shell which badly shattered my leg. The shock was great and this made it impossible to continue. I turned off towards our lines although unable to see and being very dazed. Just then I was attacked unobserved and apparently at close range by an enemy machine, and bullets hit my petrol tank and set the machine on fire. I side-slipped down at a steep angle trusting it would bring me to our lines and to try and extinguish the flames. However, a few seconds before I reached the ground the flames appeared to have died down with part of the machine only smouldering. I switched on [the engine] again with the idea of making sure of reaching our lines, but nothing happened owing to the loss of petrol. Just at that moment I thought I saw a dark shadow and I pulled back on the control expecting it to be the ground. Much to my surprise the machine pulled up and slowly turned over on to its back. I unfastened my belt and dropped into what turned out to be water. I then guessed where I was and in about a quarter of an hour's time one of the enemy waded in and I was conveyed to a barge along the canal, which runs close by the floods at Nieuport and taken to a field hospital when I became unconscious for a time. On regaining consciousness I was informed that my leg would have to be amputated. This they did and I remained for three weeks in the field hospital until I was transferred to Munster Hospital, where I remained for about a month before going to a camp at Karlsruhe. Subsequently I was moved to Trier and finally exchanged on 22 January, to England.'

Felton had fallen into the area that the Belgians flooded earlier in the war, an area that ran from Dixmude to Nieuport, by the Iser Canal. This was some distance from Ghistelles airfield, where Buckler says the Sopwith came down, but otherwise, Felton's story runs pretty much as Buckler stated. 54 Squadron does not appear to have made any claims, so Gros, if indeed he did not return to the airfield after this particular action, was not hit by any of the Pups. It was Buckler's eleventh official victory.]

A fateful victory

Then one day Rudno arrived [officially he was posted in on 5 October, so from a story about 17 July, we have shot forward to October]. Our friendship had in no way changed. The self-assured giant, always inclined towards all sorts of mischief, also quickly won the hearts of my comrades. He fit so well into our circle that already after a few days no one could imagine that he had not always been with us. If however on the following pages I do not say much about him, the only reason is that events got the better of us and we now performed our duty separately and I want to tell the story of my own flying life and my air battles here, not the story of our friendship. The reader will discover in another passage how well this friendship also proved itself during our time together as fighter pilots.

Rudno also got along splendidly with Strasser. A very young Leutnant by the name of Alfred Träger became the third member of the alliance. He came as a replacement for Gros (*sic*). At war's outbreak Träger was the youngest cadet, while his brother was a U-boat commander.

[Alfred Träger had come to Jasta 17 from Kampfgeschwader Nr.4 – posted in on 30 January 1917.]

Träger had a special preference for sheep dogs, but unfortunately no talent in properly handling these beautiful and clever animals, lacking the patience for training. When he went on leave he entrusted his dog, called Greif, to me. Later I had two more sheep dogs that answered to the same name, but I will never forget Greif No.1. He was really a remarkable animal and my efforts to train him were quite fruitful. He devoted himself to it with joy and enthusiasm. His outstanding achievement was to climb up a simple ladder onto the roof of our hangar and back down again. His intelligence or, if you wish, his instinct, was so great that he detected the approach of enemy airmen by the sound of their engines before any listening post did. He would prick up his ears, turn around on the spot, and disappear into the dugout.

Greif's astonishingly sharp hearing once helped me win a bet. We were sitting in the mess when he suddenly became restless and bolted. On the strength of that I made the assertion that an enemy bombing raid was impending and that Greif had already reached the safety of the dugout. One of my comrades laughed at me and maintained the opposite. We bet a bottle of champagne, and the bombs bursting a short time later, plus the fact that Greif was already lying in the dugout when we hastily fled there, won me my bet hands down.

> [There is an anecdote regarding another wager between Buckler and his fellow pilots, in which the stakes once more concerned bottles of champagne. It appeared in *Luftkämpfe im Westen* (*Aerial Battles in the West*), by 'Wilfried Eck,' the apparent pen-name of an Unteroffizier Vahldieck serving in Jasta 50.
>
> On the morning of October 4, 1918 the commanding officer, Leutnant Hans von Freden, led an offensive patrol on the French front. They encountered a Spad two-seater, which was forced to land behind German lines near St Morell, its crew being captured.
>
> Leutnant von Freden decided to have the enemy aircraft flown back to the Staffel's airfield. A Gefreiter Röhr volunteered to drive to the scene of the downed aircraft in the company of two mechanics, who would prepare the Spad for take-off and paint black crosses on the undersides of the lower wings. Gefreiter Röhr would then pilot the French two-seater, being escorted back to the Jasta 50 airfield by twelve fighters from this unit.
>
> The rendezvous at 5:00 took place as planned and everything proceeded smoothly until the German fighters and their charge encountered a dozen aircraft from Jasta 17 led by Buckler. Leutnant von Freden and his pilots were forced to protect the Frenchman, by keeping the Jasta 17 fighters at bay. What afterwards transpired is related by the author:
>
> 'In the evening the pilots of Jagdstaffel 50 are sitting with a glass of beer in the general mess at Attigny, when Leutnant Buckler also appears. He shouts to Leutnant von Freden: "Well, gentlemen, you know I've never seen such a slack performance. You have the Frenchman right in front of your guns and don't blow him out of the sky? You should've let us do the job. You could learn a thing or two."
>
> 'But Jagdstaffel 50 has in Leutnant Herbst not only a

> competent special duties officer [*Offizier zur besonderen Verwendung*], but also a keen defender. "My dear Buckler, you have absolutely no say in the matter. The Spad in question, of which it pleases you to speak, was attacked by the Staffel at the front, herded along, and forced to land at our airfield. Has your Staffel ever managed to do that?"
>
> "Herbst, I'm aware that you are capable of telling a whopper, but you really can't fool an old warrior."
>
> "He who wants to bet, cheats, Buckler; therefore I suggest we bet five bottles of champagne that the Spad is standing on our airfield. Agreed?"
>
> 'Because Buckler had just visited the Staffel in the morning and had not seen a captured aircraft, he accepts the wager, only, of course, to lose it. Only when the champagne has been drunk does he learn the truth and, laughing, he adds another bottle.']

Greif's loyalty and his devotion to me had a tragic end. Once I had taken off, he would lay by the trestle and wait until I was starting to land. He recognised my machine from amongst all the others and the mechanics said that every time he saw it coming he jumped up and yelped joyfully. I landed last for his sake, then the mechanics would let him loose and he was allowed to run towards me, jump onto my lap, and taxi with me to the hangar.

After my eleventh victory he did not do so and this came about in the following fashion. On this day I was flying alone and encountered two Sopwiths at the front. They thought that with their combined force they would make short work of me, but they were fooling themselves. It did not take long for me to gain a height advantage and therewith the upper hand. After a few rounds one of them was ablaze. To this day I hope the Englishman was already dead when his aircraft shot earthwards, burning like a torch. The other appeared to turn away, but did not think at all of flying home and instead started to climb. I observed him closely and likewise climbed. At 4,500 metres we had approached to within 150 metres of each other. I wanted to wait a bit more, but at this distance – my opponent was definitely using a telescopic sight as he fired – my machine was hit by a salvo and I felt a horrible blow to the left side of my chest.

My opponent sped away above me while I dived down at full throttle. I raced at about 2,000 revs down to 100 metres, levelled the machine, and began to glide. I was rendered temporarily unconscious during this dive, but like a miracle I came to at the right time. The lining of my coat was turned outwards and blood oozed red out of the hole. I could hardly lift my left arm. This was no time for an emergency landing amidst the shell holes!

Without the customary circuit of honour around the airfield which usually signified a victory, I landed with my last ounce of strength. Later the mechanics said that during my landing Greif did not bark, but rather howled as though he knew what had happened to me. After the machine came to a halt before the hangar he greeted me, but not boisterously as usual, and did something that he otherwise never did. He jumped onto the fuselage of the aircraft, licked my forehead, and jumped back onto the ground howling. This so moved me that tears came to my eyes.

'Stretcher!' I yelled to Roth. The medical orderlies were already rushing over with the stretcher, lifted me out, and carried me to the truck. The moment the stretcher was to be stowed in the interior of the ambulance, Greif had a rabid seizure, not wanting to be separated from me. I was brought to the military hospital in Bruges, while Greif was put into his grave.

> [Buckler was no stranger to wounding during the war, but at this period – presumably around July – he was wounded on the 17th, possibly in the scrap with the Pups of 54 Squadron, although he makes no mention of it during his description of the fight with Second Lieutenant Felton. The only similarity is that he saw his opponent dive headlong, leaving a trail of smoke and flame. Nevertheless, one has to wonder if he confused the story of being wounded by three Allied fighters on his way to the Jastaschule, (see Chapter 6) with the scrap with those three Pups.]

Chapter Eight

Fateful Encounters

The thirteenth

After five weeks I returned to the Staffel at Ghistelles. The third summer of the war clearly revealed a deterioration of our position. The airmen on the opposing side were appearing in greater numbers and with better and better machines. For Germany the war had already lasted too long. Germany was like a single fortress under siege from surrounding enemies, while to the enemy the whole world stood open.

[This summer 1917 period was indeed a time when new and better Allied aircraft were reaching the Western Front. The British were equipped with Sopwith Camel and SE5a scouts, as well as the Bristol F2b two-seater fighter, while the French had improved Nieuports but more importantly, the Spad XIII was replacing the old Spad VII. Meanwhile the German fighter force was struggling on with the Albatros DIII and DV/DVa, with little on the horizon apart from the Fokker Dr.I Triplane which would reach the front in September, together with the Pfalz DIII, which was really no better than the Albatros types. It would be late spring 1918 before the ultimate fighter, the Fokker DVII, would come into service.

The Allied airmen may have appeared to be in greater numbers, but squadrons on the British and French fronts tended to fly in small formations, mostly in just flight sizes of five or six. They only turned out in squadron strength of twelve to sixteen for big shows supporting offensives. The German Jasta was still smaller in size but often now began flying in at least two Jasta strengths as grouping of these Staffeln came into being. The most famous, of course, was Baron Manfred von Richthofen's Jagdgeschwader Nr.I (JGI), which was formed in June 1917, comprising four Jastas. The Germans also formed Jagdgruppen during the spring and summer of 1917, and while these could be also up to four Jastas in strength, they only operated for limited periods and usually for a specific purpose of support. Mostly, of course, these formations were, if anything, for administrative purposes, although the aircraft could combine to make a larger fighter force. It is amazing that Buckler perhaps gives the impression they might be starting to be overwhelmed in the air, because the Allied side too, if all their reports are to be believed, seemed always to be outnumbered by German fighters, suffering losses accordingly.]

One day in midsummer I flew out over the sea, but with no particular goal in mind. I just wanted to wander around a bit. At 4,800 metres and about 70 kilometres off the coast I heard machine-gun fire behind me. Glancing around I saw that four Sopwiths were following me. This surprise attack by these four aircraft came so suddenly that initially I just throttled back and went into a dive. Taking on four enemy aircraft all alone and way out to sea did not seem to me to be a good idea.

However, to them I probably seemed an easy and certain victory. They pursued me for such a long time that they probably assumed that the rough seas would complete their work of destruction upon me, but not one of their many bullets inflicted any serious damage on my machine. Flying close above the misty water, I quickly eluded my pursuers.

Then shrapnel exploded about me – I was being fired upon from the sea. Climbing rapidly again, I saw below me a swarm of enemy ships. I counted no fewer than thirty-nine monitors which supposedly were planning a raid on our coast. Malaula! I had to submit a report as soon as possible, but where was I? Water, water as far as the eye could see. I did not have a compass and the sun had hidden itself behind some clouds. So off I went, trusting to luck.

After a while I noticed that I had flown in a circle as the ships appeared again in the distance. The contents of my fuel tank would only last for a short time. Then I could pick the spot in the sea where I wanted to drown. I was not a sailor and if I had to die I would rather do so up above in aerial combat. Malaula! However, I managed to land safely.

My report about the monitors, which was confirmed by the navy a few minutes after my landing, brought the Staffel to its feet. Since I had the direction in my head, we succeeded in sighting the enemy ships after a short flight, but they were already proceeding at full steam far out to sea towards the English coast. With our landplanes we could not fly too far out to sea, so we turned around and flew along the front.

My thirteenth was due. I was free of superstition for neither the number thirteen nor a Friday could deter me in my purpose. On three Fridays, and twice on the thirteenth, I would leave a military hospital and return to the front. Although I did not go to church, I still felt myself to be in union with God and lived trusting in the fate that was determined for me. Being inwardly prepared for one's fate was, so I thought, all that a person could do. If he had conscientiously fulfilled his duty, then he would be able to die in peace.

At about 4,000 metres I saw one of our observation aircraft being attacked by two enemy machines. Joystick into the belly, and with a cry of Malaula, I dived to the aid of my hard-pressed comrades! The other members of the Staffel had been no less attentive. We all met up with one another again here and would probably have prepared a swift end for the two attackers, who had to abandon their ill-treated prey at the last moment, had not a terrible, never-before-seen spectacle held us spellbound.

The observation aircraft, a Rumpler CV, lay on its back and slowly spun down. It was horrible to see how the heads of the two crewmen hung downwards. Without being able to help and hoping for a miracle, we remained close above the unfortunate crew in order to at least prevent any Tommy who happened to come along from chalking up these poor doomed men as a cheap aerial victory.

At a little less than ten metres something miraculous happened. The machine lay first on its side and then returned to its normal flight position. We saw the two men wave to us and then hastily fly home. For a long time afterwards we spoke of this horrible inverted flight.

On the following morning I took off very early. At 4,000 metres I encountered an enemy flyer. We were by far and wide all alone in the sky – he and I. Without any further ado, we immediately started a fight. I would really like to know who my opponent was, for if I thought I could fly, then this stranger demonstrated a perfection in flying ability which astonished me. The whole feverish bout of turning seemed to be an enjoyable bit of sport for him. He was engaging in a merry joust with me while I struggled desperately for a chance to open fire. The battle ended indecisively at 300 metres, both of us having to give up due to a lack of fuel. You taught me a lot, strange foe, but it was a damned tough lesson for me. Tired and battle-weary, I flew home.

* * *

A storm was in the air. Thick black clouds gathered threateningly and a first bolt of lightning flashed on the horizon, while distant thunder became audible. The mess was empty. I removed my jacket and stood in shirt and trousers at the window as the streaks of lightning multiplied. In a fiery zig-zag they tore through the bank of cloud as the thunder roared more loudly.

There in front of us lay Ypres, a name like Verdun and Douaumont! A name which burns in our memory as though written in blood. What was everything we flyers did compared to that which had to be endured by those who lay opposite each other day and night in trenches and burrows?

What great accomplishment had I, Offizierstellvertreter Buckler, achieved? What were my few victories compared to the thirty or forty of the great fighter pilots like Boelcke, Richthofen, Schäfer, Voss or

Löwenhardt? [At the time Buckler was talking of, Löwenhardt had scored but one victory, although he would go on to bring down fifty-four opponents.] Fine, I led the Staffel in the air and was asked whether one should do this or that. The good von Esebeck granted me a lot of freedom and in the meantime I had also received the Iron Cross 1st Class. But when I thought of Boelcke I felt small, extremely small. I could not forget his serious countenance. There was but a single goal to be seen in this face, that of victory. Boelcke had fallen on 28 October 1916, but he lived on in each of us. For us he was the model, the great admonisher. Boelcke had met his end undefeated, having been in collision with his friend's machine.

I had been together with Böhme, his unfortunate friend and successor in the leadership of the Boelcke Staffel [in fact he did not command Jasta B until August 1917], in Leipzig-Lindenthal. Like myself, he was a flight instructor there, only he was much older. Wüsthoff was also one of the younger instructors there. [Leutnant Kurt Wüsthoff, twenty-seven victories, PoW 17 June 1918.] Both names had been cited in the army reports. It was not the vain longing to became famous and well-known which filled me in this stormy hour as I stood at the window of the officers' mess. No, it was the burning desire to accomplish as much as these other men, to match their achievements.

Anti-aircraft fire startled me out of my thoughts. The report came in from the airfield: Enemy flyer over Bruges! Because everyone was asleep and no order followed, I drove alone to the airfield, climbed into Mops with just shirt, trousers, scarf, and goggles on, and flew towards the old Flanders town. There was still lightning and the raindrops stung my face like needles. At 200 metres I plunged into the clouds. I saw a hole, pushed through, and then entered the clouds again, climbing even higher. Finally at 3,200 metres I had blue sky and brilliant sunshine above me.

A solid white sea of cloud cut me off from the earth below. Here above one could almost forget that there was an earth at all and that on this earth there was so much misery and sorrow. It was so beautiful flying up here in the sunshine over the peacefully slumbering clouds that I entirely forgot about the war below them. In this solitude I met an enemy airman. He came from the direction of Bruges and was apparently about to fly home. So he was the one reported, the enemy I was looking for. He was flying 200 metres higher than I, and as I followed him and while doing so, pushed my Mops to 2,000 revs. Then I pulled up and shot at him from below.

He immediately turned around, which was just what I wanted. I pretended to make a run for it and he dived after me. Then I made a sudden turn and he raced past me and, sitting on his neck, I fired a few well-aimed rounds from 15 to 20 metres range.

His machine emitted smoke and then burst into flames. Now came the most horrifying thing I have ever experienced in my flying career. I saw the pilot stand up – the brave man did not want to burn – preferring a leap to his death from 3,000 metres rather than endure a death by fire. I cannot describe my emotions as I watched this person plunging into the depths before my eyes. I cursed the war. If all this had not been for the Fatherland I would have been close to hurtling myself after him. First my fellow aviator and then the burning machine plunged into the sea of cloud, with me following. When I again appeared from out of the clouds I just managed to see the burning motor with the spark-scattering remains of the airframe whirling around it strike the earth.

The spot below me – it was our airfield – was black with people. Then I realised that they were infantrymen who, probably just as paralysed with horror as my Staffel mates, first saw a person and then a flaming aircraft plummet from the clouds. None of them could know who the vanquished was.

Therefore the relief when they saw me coming from behind, turned into such a frenzy of joy that they lifted me out, having remained sitting in my machine after landing, deeply disturbed and pale with horror, and carried me on their shoulders in triumph to the hangar. They were just glad that I was alive, not that the other was dead. They did not think of him at this moment, but I thought that this triumphant reception, such as might justifiably be prepared for successful sportsmen by their enthusiastic supporters, was very inappropriate here. In any event, it did not suit my mood at all and I was glad when I was able to get away from the reception. Rudno and Strasser almost squeezed me to death.

I jumped into the car and drove to the crash site. The English flyer lay there as though he were sleeping. Someone had fished his corpse out of the Yser. Everything was crushed internally. His trunk and thigh were torn up by bullets that had passed right through him. What tremendous energy this person must have possessed to still find the strength to jump out of the aeroplane with these frightful wounds! I could endure everything again if I had to, but I would not want to experience my thirteenth victory a second time.

> [Buckler gives us few clues as to who this British pilot might have been, but the likely candidate was Second Lieutenant Curtis Matthew DeRochie, a Canadian from Cornwall, Ontario, lost on a bombing sortie on 14 July 1917. He was a member of 27 Squadron which flew Martinsyde G100 'Elephants'. They looked more like a fighter but their main role was that of a bomber, the machine being capable of carrying a bomb load of 336 pounds (153 kg). Its speed of around 95 mph was a little less than the new Camel and SE5 fighters, but about the same as the Sopwith Pup. It carried two Lewis guns, one fixed to fire forward, the second on a mounting just behind the pilot's left shoulder, which he could

operate on a flexible mounting, although this was more a 'scatter gun' than an accurate weapon.

On this day, 27 Squadron had suffered. The Martinsydes were sent to bomb Zarren and Quiéry-la-Motte, but ran into aircraft of Jasta 30 and Jasta 6, losing two machines on a dawn mission. Buckler's victim was on a later sortie, leaving base at 15.00 hours in Martinsyde A6266. His claim was timed at 17.50 (16.50 British time) at Leffinghe, about three miles inland from the coast, south of Ostende, where DeRochie was buried. There was only one squadron equipped with Martinsyde machines in France so it is not particularly surprising that Buckler reported downing a BE2, which one supposes does not look totally unlike a G100 in the air.]

It was Udet!

My twelfth victory was mentioned in a confidential report, and in the same report was the name of Udet, who shot down his thirteenth. So it came about that we each had a desire to make the acquaintance of the other. That came to light when we did in fact meet each other a short time thereafter, and it was memorable enough.

It was near Armentières. One morning – I still remember the exact time, it was about 10.40 – I saw an enemy aircraft going down in flames in my immediate vicinity and indeed it was at the very same moment that my sixteenth victory fell apart before my eyes, and the left wing broke away. He plummeted, following his burning comrade into the depths below.

I flew home, accompanied by the other, unknown victor, who did not belong to my Staffel. We landed almost at the same time, climbed out of our machines, and introduced ourselves. 'Buckler' – 'Udet'. As though we had known one another for a long time and were old friends, Udet said, 'You're coming with me now to my Staffel for breakfast.' I was more than glad to accept this half-grumbled invitation. As a budding 'ace' I had two machines at my disposal, so I had the other one quickly made ready for take-off and we roared away together.

The breakfast was brief and we were both alone [obviously a late breakfast for as Buckler relates above, the combat took place at 10.40!]. For me it was both very amusing and very instructive. Why and how remains known only to Udet and myself, but I have put his teachings to the test and made profitable use of them. I owe many of my later successes to you, dear Udet, and this brief breakfast.

We then flew off together. Udet wanted to head to the front and I to my Staffel but he was hardly six kilometres away from me when I saw an enemy machine dive on him from out of the blue. A frenetic series of turns began, then I saw one of the two climb out. I could not determine who, but thank God, he had a parachute. An hour later I knew who it was. It was Udet!

[Here again we have a strange mix of fact and either fiction or confused memory. Buckler gained his twelfth victory on 9 August (a Camel at 07.45 in the morning), while Udet gained his thirteenth (one of two Camels at 18.00/18.05 hours) on 28 September. Udet was with Jasta 37, although he did not command it, at least, not until November 1917.

In Armand van Ishoven's book on Udet, *The Fall of an Eagle* (Wm Kimber, 1977), he tells of the above story of the two aces meeting, but gives the date of the combat and subsequent meeting as 1 October, a date on which neither pilots scored victories. The day Buckler scored his sixteenth (and seventeenth) on 11 October, Udet did not score. Although Buckler refers to parachutes several times during his recollections of events in 1917, German pilots did not use these devices until 1918. Udet did on one occasion save his life by jumping out of a fighter with a parachute, the date was 29 June 1918.

Van Ishoven refers to the action where both pilots were 'introduced', recording that Udet was flying alone when he saw two LVG C-types below being attacked by a pair of Camels. Udet shot one down near Deulemont, south of Ypres at 10.35 and then, as he flew home he observed another combat below which ended with the British machine breaking up in mid-air. Udet followed the victor home (to Wasquehal by this date), although he says it was to Ghistelles, from where Jasta 17 had left on 28 August! Udet landed to congratulate the pilot, who turned out to be Buckler, and then both men flew to Wynghene for breakfast, Jasta 37 having moved to this airfield on 10 October.

In fact Udet's victory was on 18 October, so Buckler has merged two events. He himself did not claim a victory on this date, although Udet did attack two 'Camels' that were going after an LVG. One of the British pilots saw the German machine and dived for the lines but the other continued on and fell to Udet's fire. It was not a Camel but an SE5a of 56 Squadron.

After both had left the airfield, Buckler to fly home, Udet to take a look at the front, the latter found an RE8 but in attacking this he was hit in the knee by a bullet from the two-seater's observer. As Udet tried to locate a place to land, petrol streaming from a holed fuel tank, some Camels came into view but he managed to keep ahead of them and finally force-landed, crashing into a water-filled trench. So Udet did not use a parachute, and this has become a very convoluted story, which one imagines has some basis in fact, but several things have been confused. Perhaps van Ishoven read Buckler's book, tried to confirm the story, but was caught out by the locations and timing.]

Boelcke's friend Böhme visits us

The superior strength of the opposing forces became greater and greater. Even on our airfield they no longer left us in peace. Every night they came and dropped bombs. This had to come to an end, yet how was one to get at the nocturnal enemy in the blinding rays of one's own searchlights and amidst the shells of one's own anti-aircraft fire? 'Don't think about it too long,' I told myself, 'get Mops out and take off.'

It was a pitch-black night. Of what use was it to me that I was familiar with the irregularities of the airfield? I could not have avoided them in the darkness anyway. The 'legs' of an aircraft are as fragile as those of a deer, but in spite of that I got off the ground.

As I hunted around in the night amidst the searchlight beams, threatened all around by flak fire, there were some frightening moments. It was damned eerie when a shadow then raced past me! I was so startled that I forgot to open fire and the danger of colliding in the darkness caused me to forget any other thoughts. I landed feeling furious, but took off a second time, although again it was in vain. I had to realise that it was no simple matter coming to grips with the enemy at night. However, I had at least got my first night landings behind me, and this in a fighter plane in the year 1917.

* * *

At this time – it was 31 October 1917 three days after the anniversary of Boelcke's death – Böhme paid us a visit. He was now leading the Boelcke Staffel [Jasta 2] and wanted to clear up some questions. We had not seen each other since 1915. He was as composed as ever, good old Böhme. Yet the tragic stony calmness in his face un-nerved me. One had the impression that he never thought, or wanted to think, of anything other than his dead friend.

On this very day I shot down my twenty-third victory, an observation balloon. At that time Böhme had twenty victories under his belt, and his modesty was just as great as Boelcke's. After he had taken care of the official business with von Esebeck, he sat down with us in the officers' mess, and I was supposed to tell him about my latest air combat.

'There's not much to tell,' I began, 'it was the downing of a balloon, just like many others. The situations repeat themselves; they're almost always the same. I think a fighter pilot needs three things: guts, calmness, and some luck. Guts to approach the enemy, calmness while firing, and luck not to get shot down while doing so.' This was nothing new to Böhme, and he listened quietly and just nodded in agreement. I said it more for the young comrades sitting around us.

Almost a month later, after his twenty-fourth victory, Böhme was surrounded by an English formation behind enemy lines above Zillebeke Lake, in the vicinity of Ypres, and was fatally wounded by a bullet. Amongst the mail waiting [in a box] on his desk for the Staffelführer in vain this day, lay the *Pour le Mérite*.

> [Buckler did shoot down a balloon this date – 31 October – one from the 42nd Section, 4th Company, 1st Balloon Wing, at 16.20 pm near Laventie, which became his twenty-fourth victory. Buckler's twenty-third victory was achieved earlier that morning, at 11.30, near La Bassée. It was an Armstrong-Whitworth FK8, a two-seater bomber-reconnaissance machine from 10 Squadron, which came down in 'no-man's-land' and was initially credited only as *zlzsw*.
>
> Böhme fell in combat with a two-seat Armstrong-Whitworth FK8 of the same 10 Squadron RFC, on 29 November, near Zonnebeke, just east of Ypres.]

The twenty-seventh, twenty-eighth and twenty-ninth

On 18 November 1917 thick fog lay over the entire Flanders front. Three days previously I had shot down my twenty-sixth opponent [an RE8]. During the daytime enemy flyers had descended from a layer of grey cloud to attack us at our airfield. I had jumped into my Mops, the motor of which happened to be already running, and caught one of them who carelessly appeared once more out of the clouds. Without opening fire, I literally forced him into the ground and his machine smashed to pieces, but the pilot remained uninjured and was immediately brought to headquarters. As a result of this raid, Ehlers, a brave fighter pilot, lost his right leg due to a thigh wound. He did not receive it in air combat, but rather in his barracks where he was sleeping.

> [More confusion I'm afraid. Leutnant Ehlers, who arrived at Jasta 17 on 8 July (and was wounded in combat on 16 August), was indeed injured in a bomb raid on the airfield at Erkeghem, but on 15 November, not the 18th. Jasta 17 had moved to Erkeghem, near Bruges, Belgium, on 6 November, and would move again on the 20th. Buckler had scored on the 15th, an RE8 on an artillery observation mission near Ypres, with both crewmen fatally wounded – falling in Allied lines.]

As usual, I was the first at breakfast in the morning. In the prevailing fog an operational flight was unthinkable. I tried to read, but it did not work. I took out a letter from my mother, in which she had asked me to write more often and to be more careful. She was proud that her son was so brave, but she was prepared every day to receive the 'inevitable news'.

'Inevitable news' – I could not get those words out of my head.

I had now been a fighter pilot for a year and had twenty-six victories. During his visit Böhme had asked me why I was not yet commissioned. Yes [I thought] why not? I did not have the one-year volunteer certificate and had not wanted to take the exam. I quite deliberately avoided it as I wanted the attainment of the rank of officer to be based on my own flying ability, not a certificate or an exam. Should that really not be possible? In the meantime I had received the Military Merit Cross. In order to get over these broodings, I went to the airfield.

All the tents were closed; only mine stood open. My machine's motor had just been overhauled and was being test-run. It was running so smoothly that I was itching to open it wide. In a few minutes I was in the air and flying an extended circuit around the airfield, although I could not fly higher than 100 metres, but at this height the visibility was still relatively good.

Why not take a little trip to the front [I thought]? When I was about five kilometres from the front I saw an enemy balloon floating over Zillebeke Lake, near Ypres. The number '27' popped into my head. The balloon was hanging at a distance of about ten kilometres from me, so with a speed of about 160 kilometres per hour, I needed just a few minutes to reach it. I tested my guns then I plunged into the mist.

Those few minutes of blind flying seemed so awfully long to me at that time that I left the 'pea soup' again four times in order to be able to breathe freely for a moment. When those minutes passed the balloon was still hanging far behind the enemy lines – I had underestimated the distance. If I were now to dip back into the mist I might fly over it or not find it again, so I sped directly towards it at a height of about fifty metres. They were hauling it down as I opened fire and it burned. In the same instant, three enemy aircraft came to greet me. In addition, the guns on the ground were firing everything they had at me, but then the 'soup' was my salvation, as it cut me off from view.

Now, as I chased through the grey mist I no longer had any idea where I was. When I ventured outside of it I saw below me shell holes, shot-up terrain, and ruined villages. Without a compass and without the aid of the sun, I had no point of reference indicating in which direction I should fly. So trusting in my [lucky] star, I flew on haphazardly in some sort of direction and after a few minutes spotted an airfield below. I throttled back and began to glide.

What's this? Enemy aircraft in the air beside me! Enemy planes below me on the airfield! I gave the engine full throttle and yanked the joystick into my belly, again disappearing into the 'soup'. When I came back out of the muck after a few minutes I saw before me – no my eyes were not deceiving me – an enemy observation balloon! I quickly surveyed the situation. Below me lay Dickebusch, so my home was over there. This gasbag had served for a long time directing fire into our trenches so at full speed I pounced upon it, although it was already going down in a hurry. After a few rounds it was ablaze, its observer hanging peacefully from a parachute and swinging to and fro to earth. That was an unexpected and un-hoped for victory – my twenty-eighth.

I did not wait for a parting 'blessing' from below, but rather swiftly took to my heels or, more accurately, to the mists from whence I came. For five awfully long minutes I raced along blindly until I broke through the grey cloud and discovered an airfield directly below me. I recognised it [immediately] – it was the airfield of the Flashar Staffel.

> [Oberleutnant Richard Flashar commanded Jasta 5, based at Boistrancourt, east of Cambrai, on the 2nd Army front. This was some way south of the general Ypres area so it is uncertain if Buckler in fact landed here during this period.]

I landed and could not refuse an invitation to breakfast or a cigarette, especially because with the best of intentions I could not have immediately flown any further. The mechanics had determined in the meantime, that I had in fact landed with my last drop of fuel. With this announcement a cold shiver ran down my spine. It could have damned easily been the case that after my twenty-eighth victory I would have been forced to land on enemy territory due to nothing more than a lack of fuel.

To my joyful surprise, while we sat at breakfast, two reports came in from an artillery observation post with the message that the fighter plane Mops had shot down an observation balloon in flames both at 10.30 and 11.20. With the confirmation of my twenty-seventh and twenty-eighth victories in my pocket, I gratefully bid farewell to the Flashar Staffel and took off for home.

> [These two balloon claims were timed at 09.10 and 09.25 hours. The first location was Jeperen, near Ypres, the second at Dickebusch. The first one has been identified as being from the 36th Section, 17th Company, 2nd Balloon Wing; the second balloon has not as yet been identified.]

On the way home – I had about twenty minutes flying ahead of me – the most recent events went through my head once more. During this it occurred to me that some weeks ago, on the occasion of the Staffel's forty-second, we had agreed that whoever achieved the fiftieth victory of Jasta 17 would receive a silver cigarette case. I counted it up and determined that my last two victories represented the Staffel's forty-eighth and forty-ninth. I wanted to keep this discovery as my secret, but my comrades could probably do the maths better than I. Therefore I considered how I might be able to dupe these better mathematicians. Only chance could help here.

When I landed everyone was assembled on the field feeling nervous. Where had I been for so long? Some had already feared the worst but now everyone revealed themselves to be very glad that I was back again and the good Freiherr von Esebeck suggested we head as quickly as possible to the officers' mess for breakfast. Otherwise the weather might clear up and we would then have no time for it. We departed in three trucks.

Behle and Lackner, the lords of the mess, were no less happy than the cook that my place would not remain empty during breakfast, as everyone had believed. I acted tired and taciturn, although I found it difficult to remain silent about the two victories. Fortunately, right after soup, a report came to my aid stating that there was lively aerial activity to be observed at the front. Von Esebeck asked, 'Buckler, what do you think, should we eat first or should we take off immediately?' I quickly responded, 'Take off!' With that, I was able to overcome the temptation to reveal my secret at the last moment.

* * *

Perhaps the report had been transmitted late, as when we arrived at the front there was practically nothing going on. I gave the signal to split up, which meant everyone could do what he wanted to. With one exception, I had shot down all of my opponents entirely alone. Therefore I was also glad now that I could remain alone. About ten kilometres behind enemy lines I espied an RE, a French [*sic*] observation aircraft, which I selected for my twenty-ninth.

The cloud layer hung at about 600 metres and was fairly solid. Using it as cover, I flew towards the enemy and during the duel that ensued I forced him down to thirty metres, then victory was mine. He caught fire and crashed. I had no time to flee back into the clouds so I allowed the hell-fire that broke out from the earth to pass over me and flew at full throttle towards my own lines. Gunfire crackled from all sides but as long as the engine and myself remained intact, it was all the same to me.

Then I suddenly saw an aircraft appear close behind me which I thought was an enemy and cursing I braced myself for a new battle, but when I took a closer look I recognised Rudno, my old observer. He waved to me and it was revealed after landing that the faithful soul had stuck with me during the entire flight in order to not leave me by myself.

If after the landing I gave the good man hell for it, it was merely out of concern for him, as he had quite needlessly exposed himself to the danger of being shot down from the ground. Actually, I had to be grateful to him, as quite apart from his good intentions to help me, in this way he had also become a witness to my twenty-ninth victory. So this would not have first required the confirmation of a balloon observer which arrived a short time later.

When I announced to von Esebeck, 'Offizierstellvertreter Buckler reports the downing of two observation balloons and an RE, with this last one making the Staffel's fiftieth,' there was a great hullabaloo. Von Esebeck hugged me and there was no end to the congratulations from my comrades. But then the Staffel commander ordered: 'Buckler, go to bed immediately.' It was 2.20 in the afternoon.

[The RE8 (A339) came from 9 Squadron, RFC and crash-landed near Bixschoote, on the Allied side. The two crew scrambled clear without serious injury and the machine was then shelled by German artillery fire. According to records, Buckler did in fact claim the Jasta's fiftieth victory, an RE8, but it was one he forced down into Allied lines on 15 November. However, with three in one day, and the circumstances behind the story of 18 November, it is a far better tale to record in one's book.

Buckler mentioning his award of the Military Merit medal earlier in this chapter needs explaining. Rather than paraphrase the words of the late Neal O'Connor, whose work on German aviation decorations awarded in the Great War is second to none, we shall quote from his Volume VII of *Aviation Awards of Imperial Germany in World War I and the Men who Earned Them*. Neal O'Connor was a well respected aviation historian, a decorated US army veteran of WW2, a friend to many, and a generous sharer of information and photographs. He wrote:

> …no roll of recipients of the Warrior's Decoration in Iron seems to have survived, but one related document in Buckler's case has. From it, we learn that on 11 October 1917, a proposal was made to Darmstadt that he be awarded the decoration. On 5 November, in a letter of transmittal to a headquarters command in Buckler's area, the badge itself and the certificate of possession were forwarded for presentation. Also returned was proof of Buckler's Hessian citizenship, one of the requirements for earning the award. Exactly one week later, on 12 November, Buckler's Golden Military Merit Cross was approved in Berlin. He was only the fourth aviation recipient in the war so far to be given what was also commonly referred to as the 'Order for Merit for the Little Man' ('Little' here meaning not an officer but a man in the ranks). Concerning it, Buckler merely wrote, "In the meantime, I had also received the Military Merit Cross." (Here Buckler is being quite correct, 'Military Merit Cross' was the full legal name of the decoration but the word 'Golden' or 'in Gold' came to be attached

> to it in almost every instance to distinguish it from the Military Honour Decoration 1st Class which was an identical badge but in silver, also awarded in World War 1). Buckler's use of the word 'also' here is interesting. It would seem to refer to his just-awarded Warrior's Honour Decoration in Iron which he otherwise ignores in his writings but which he proudly wore thereafter as several photographs show.'

Neal O'Connor had earlier written: 'The Warrior's Honour Decoration would never be awarded in large numbers since no proposal for the award would be accepted through official channels unless there was proof supplied that all four conditions had been met. These were:

1. A recipient had to have held Hessian citizenship since at least 1 August 1914.
2. A recipient had to have served more than two years in units active in an area under enemy fire with the exception of temporary stationing in rest or reserve positions. During the two-year period, beginning with the day of deployment, any time in hospital or at home lasting more than two months did not count.
3. A recipient had to be wounded at least once.
4. A recipient had to have displayed bravery and good conduct.

The badge itself was a black lacquered wreath of laurels on which the silver crowned initials EL were superimposed. At the foot of the L there was a small silver plaque with the numeral '25'. The back of the badge was plain.

The 25 represented the date of the inauguration of the medal (13 March 1917) on the twenty-fifth anniversary of the death of Grand Duke Ludwig IV and the succession to the throne of his only surviving son. The badge itself was worn on the left side of the torso, at the base of any breast pocket, and just below and to the right of a similarly positioned Iron Cross 1st Class. Just below these, in the case of aviators, would be pinned the flyers badge.]

Chapter Nine

Desperate Glory

Promoted to officer

[At the end of the last chapter we left Buckler, tired out, being sent to his bed. He now continues:]

I was in fact quite honestly exhausted. The aerial combat and the downing of the balloons had put less of a strain on me than the unpleasant and difficult circumstances accompanying them, frequently flying blind and being heavily fired upon by the ground defences.

In spite of the deep calm which presided over the entire household I could not sleep. I was excited and pre-occupied with the fact that my plan to dupe the superior mathematicians had succeeded in such a surprisingly swift manner – on a single day and with three victories – and that my score was now approaching thirty. I was also unable to leave the room as Rudno had locked it from the outside, so in order to finally redirect my thoughts elsewhere, I played the gramophone.

Late in the afternoon things got lively down in the officers' mess and the table was being set for a banquet. The clinking of glasses and clattering of silverware reached my ears upstairs. I began to change my clothes and was just shaving when there was a knock at the door.

'Offizierstellvertreter Buckler to the telephone. There's a call from general headquarters. It's the commanding general of the air service, His Excellency von Hoeppner!'

'Then unlock the door. Quickly!'

'I can't – there's no key.'

I shook the door in vain. This was a fine situation. A commanding general was on the telephone and a warrant officer was in his pyjamas unable to get out of his room! Finally Rudno, who had taken my key for safekeeping, stormed up the stairs. He unlocked the door and like two little rascals we raced downstairs taking several steps at a time. I pounced on the telephone. A few seconds later I heard the voice of the general. His Excellency congratulated me 'in the name of His Majesty the Kaiser' on my three latest victories and at the same time on my promotion to active flying officer in Flieger Bataillon Nr I.

I simply answered: 'I humbly thank you, Your Excellency'. With that, the telephone conversation was concluded. Rudno was nearby bursting with curiosity:

'Did he…? Are you…?

'What?' I replied.

'Well, did he finally promote you?'

'To what?' I said innocently.

'For heaven's sake, to Leutnant! We had already selected you after your twenty-fourth victory.' He had let the cat out of the bag.

'Great! But his Excellency merely congratulated me on my three aerial victories.' I wanted to save at least one surprise for the evening's festivities.

Rudno took a deep breath and then began to utter a stream of nonsensical blasphemous curses. One might say that this was a mean trick to play or even an outright injustice. Perhaps it should not have been allowed to continue. Rudno's righteous indignation and well-intentioned fury nearly dissuaded me from my pre-conceived plan. However, that would have spoiled the evening's surprise. Pulling myself together, I bound past him up the stairs and now locked myself in my room.

The noise below me increased. I heard the mess officer shouting and the orderlies running. From the window I saw the Staffelführer driving up. He had raced over to Brussels to shop for 'a few nice things' for the banquet. He had already declared at midday that one could not manage such an affair with just noodles and spice.

An orderly whom I had summoned, and ordered to maintain a strict silence, procured a couple of officer's shoulder tabs for me and affixed them to the tunic I wore when on leave. When the dinner gong sounded, I noticed that the dried shaving cream was still sticking to my cheeks so I quickly finished shaving. Thus I was automatically the last one to enter the dining hall.

Von Esebeck had been waiting for me and everyone was already standing behind their chairs at the table. I strode towards him quickly and reported for the second time on this day:

'Offizierstellvertreter Buckler promoted to active flying officer in Flieger Bataillon Nr I.'

The effect of this report far exceeded that of the first. For a moment there was an almost solemn silence, but then there arose a tremendous and prolonged cry of joy. Von Esebeck's face beamed with pride and satisfaction. I believe that if he had been given the opportunity of choosing the *Pour le Mérite* for himself or promotion for me, he would not have hesitated in picking the latter. Like every true leader of a community, he saw in every decoration and promotion that was bestowed upon an individual, at the same time an acknowledgement of the whole which enhanced their reputation. Rudno fell upon my neck and chided me thoroughly for leading him by the nose. My other comrades shook my hand with hearty words of congratulation.

We had hardly sat down when von Esebeck began to talk. He spoke in his warm and heartfelt manner of the threefold occasion for the day's festivities: the fiftieth aerial victory of the Staffel, my three victories, and my promotion to officer. This brought legitimate outside recognition as well for something that we had long considered valid within our own circle. He added that the bonds of comradeship could not be made stronger by this, as they had already always been closely tied to mutual respect and trust. They all rejoiced with me concerning such a rare and high distinction. I was moved by this and could only stammer a few words of thanks. Then the celebration took its course.

During the meal a wireless message arrived which conveyed the following words from the army report: 'Leutnant Julius Buckler, who due to his bravery in the face of the enemy was promoted to active flying officer by His Majesty, shot down two observation balloons and an enemy aeroplane, therewith achieving his twenty-seventh, twenty-eighth and twenty-ninth victories.'

It often seemed odd to me that on this evening and in the days that followed my old comrades addressed me as 'Herr Leutnant'. Strasser, Schröder, Schniedewind, and Brendel held the rank of Feldwebel or Unteroffizier, and Strasser and I addressed each other as *du*. When he stood up and addressed me as Herr Leutnant I found it so ridiculous that I requested of von Esebeck that we be allowed to continued saying *du* amongst our group of friends and he consented to this. There was probably not a single wish he would have denied me on this evening.

I got to see Alfred Träger mount a bicycle and ride through four rooms, during which he ran into every edge and corner and scratched himself badly. Poor Alfred, what a sight you were! Then it knocked me down. This was all too much for me. And so it came about that while my comrades were celebrating in my honour I was already lying in my bed by 11 o'clock.

[At this time, while Buckler had brought his score to twenty-nine, the other pilots in the Staffel who had achieved victories, had totals of:

Vzfw Georg Strasser – 5
Ltn Jakob Wolff – 4 – wounded July 1917
Ltn Walter Brachwitz – 2
Ltn Otto Fitzner – 2
Ltn Günther Schuster – 2 – posted to Jasta 29 September 1917
Vzfw Gustav Schniedewind – 2
Vzfw Adolf Werner – 2
Ltn Albrecht Crüsmann – 1 – killed in action 28 July 1917
Ltn Neumann – 1 – posted to Jasta 31 in May 1917

As mentioned earlier, this reflected the situation in most of the German Jastas where the pilot whose 'eye was in' and who had achieved several victories, not only became the leader in the air but by having the rest of the pilots behind him during attacks, was protected to a large degree, therefore being able to concentrate on shooting down an opponent in the initial attack before all the aircraft became mixed up in any resultant dog-fight. If the attack had been on a lone machine, there was a good chance the victory could be achieved by him alone, and then the pilots would again reform behind the leader before hunting for further targets.

Another development that Buckler does not impart in his book, is that by mid-to-late 1917, the German fighter units were often grouped together. This did not necessarily mean they fought as a whole group, as explained earlier, but by this time, Jasta 17 had become part of Jagdgruppe Nord which comprised four Jastas and a Kest. These were Jastas 2, 17, 20 and 28, plus Kest 8. (A Kest was a Kampfeinsitzer Staffel – Home Defence unit – that operated mainly against long-range enemy bombers attacking either the rear areas of an army group or even targets in western Germany.) Leader of JGr Nord was Hauptmann Otto Hartmann, leader of Jasta 28s – the small 's' standing for a Saxon unit, as did 'b' for Bavarian or 'w' for Württemberg. This formation operated between 28 August and 6 November, at which time the Jagdgruppe disbanded.

Jasta 17 then became part of Jagdgruppe Houthulst, under Hauptmann Rudolf von Esebeck, Jasta 17's 'boss', comprising Jastas 12 and 17, between 6 and 20 November, while both units were based at Ergekem, Oostkamp, south of Bruges. Houthulst was a small village half way between Dixmude and Ypres, the local forest bearing this name being a well-known feature and therefore a good identification spot when a pilot needed an instant check on his position. (It was probably to Bruges where von Esebeck drove to pick up some extras for Buckler's party rather than faraway Brussels.)

On 20 November, two days after Buckler gained his three victories, Jasta 17 became part of Jagdgruppe 2, in company with Jastas 8 and 35b. This included a move of airfield, from Ergekem to Neuvilly, near Le Cateau, on the 2nd Army front. Neuvilly was about eighteen kilometres east of Cambrai and five miles north of Le Cateau, so a new front for Jasta 17 and Buckler.]

Invited to dine with von Richthofen

On the following morning, it was a Sunday, I was not the first one in the mess as I usually was. Most of my comrades had not gone to bed at all and were still sitting there while continuing to celebrate. Breakfast was excellent and just as on the day before, there was thick fog outside. It was also cold and damp.

Perhaps it would suddenly clear up again as it had yesterday, so I made my way to the airfield. If there had not been guns roaring in the distance I would have felt like a Flemish peasant on the way to church. Somewhere an imposing bell was tolling, but I did not come across any other people.

At the airfield I saw both of my machines, Mops and Lilly, standing before the tent. They were draped in green foliage and above the entrance of the tent hung a banner [on which was written]: *Leutnant Buckler is forbidden to take off today*. The good von Esebeck had even anticipated my steadfast desire to fly.

The fog prevented me from any breach of discipline, and in the evening it was just as thick as it had been in the morning. God, this was boring. In order to at least do something, I took an axe and chopped wood into small pieces for two hours. Afterwards I realised that I had not actually done any manual work for many years, as all my bones and muscles were aching.

The fog did not relent. Day after day passed without us getting a chance to fly. Then something happened which filled me with a special sense of pride. I was twice invited by von Richthofen to dinner and took my place between the two brothers. Both of them had worn the *Pour le Mérite* for some time already.

Manfred von Richthofen had been named commander of the first German Jagdgeschwader back in June. With that, the Geschwader had received a commander, as General von Hoeppner later wrote about his: '…steadfast determination to fly relentlessly against the enemy was soon transferred to every member of the Geschwader. Richthofen's refined modesty, his openly chivalrous nature, and his military ability secured for him within the army an unshakable trust which in spite of his youth [he was twenty-five, two years older than Buckler] was coupled with reverence.'

Everyone who was fortunate enough to be a guest amidst his company could sense this boundless respect for their young commander. Manfred von Richthofen's unaffected, serene, and charming nature had to win anyone over. In Lothar's pale face one could still see traces of the period he endured in a military hospital, from which he had just returned to the front. A bullet had smashed his hip. Actually, Lothar had achieved his greatest successes only in the few weeks in which he had been free of wounds. Richthofen's adjutant was Oberleutnant Bodenschatz, the present-day generalmajor and chief adjutant of Generalfeldmarschall Göring.

[It was not unusual for von Richthofen to invite other

successful pilots to his table, for quite often he was seeing if there was any possibility he could recruit them into one of his four Staffeln. Sometimes the guest indicated he would rather stay with his existing unit, for despite the honour of being asked, the guest probably felt he would rather be a big fish in his own 'pond' than a smaller one in von Richthofen's 'lake'. Buckler does not tell us if he was invited to join him, so we can only speculate.

Manfred von Richthofen's brother Lothar, like the Baron, was a former cavalry man, but while he did not have the finesse of his brother in the air, was nevertheless a successful air fighter. Even so he had his share of wounds, several of which occurred on the 13th of a month. Two years younger than Manfred, once he became a fighter pilot Manfred had him posted to Jasta 11, which the Baron commanded, in March 1917. Later, when Manfred was given command of JGI, Lothar took command of Jasta 11. Wounded on 13 May, he had scored twenty-four victories in those two months, his twenty-fifth victory coming on 9 November, just after returning from hospital, as Buckler says. Manfred had won the *Pour le Mérite* in January 1917, Lothar's came in May. Lothar would end the war with forty victories, exactly half the number his elder brother achieved.]

Shot down in a shell hole

On 27 November [records indicate 20 November] we received the order to move immediately to the vicinity of Cambrai. Due to the low-lying mist we took off at three-minute intervals. Two hours later we had all landed smoothly at the new airfield assigned to us.

Towards evening, with improving visibility, we also undertook an exploratory flight. We used the two foggy days following to have the machines examined and the engines overhauled. The purpose was to be fully prepared to engage in the counter-offensive that was to take place on 30 November. We had difficult tasks ahead of us.

[Jasta 17 and Jasta 8 had moved to Cambrai to support the battle of Cambrai, in which the British made their first major use of tanks. JGr2 was commanded by Hauptmann Constantin von Bentheim, the Staffelführer of Jasta 8, that also shared the airfield at Neuvilly.]

In spite of the bad weather I wandered along the front alone on the 29th. In the vicinity of Bapaume I spotted a balloon about twelve kilometres behind the enemy lines. The cloud ceiling hung down to about 200 metres, so there could not be more favourable weather for an attack on a balloon.

However, it seemed to me that the approaching flight was taking forever and as so often happens, it took some effort to overcome my inner agitation. Halfway to the balloon I unexpectedly came across an RE two-seater [RE8]. I dived upon it and the matter was quickly decided. It went down after a single turn although I do not know if it hit the ground or not. I did not bother to follow it, as I had something else to do. The balloon was still hanging in the sky.

> [Buckler does not claim, or at least, is not credited with a victory over an RE8 this date, and there is no attributable loss on the British side.]

I wondered whether the balloon observer still had no idea what was in store for him. It was now high time for him to bail out! However, this time I was the one who was surprised, as I had never before seen an observer remain sitting calmly in his basket greeting me with machine-gun fire. I was so shocked at first that I thought an enemy aircraft had made a sneak attack on me from behind. I turned aside, but saw nothing. I only heard something smack into Mops and immediately turned again towards the balloon.

Now I noticed that the observer was the brave machine gunner. I now hammered away furiously at the gas-bag and also aimed my machine guns at the man in the basket. Fortunately I did not hit him and the brave man was able to use his parachute at just the right moment before the balloon caught fire.

During my return flight I looked for the two-seater I had dealt with so quickly, but I could not find it anywhere. Perhaps it had escaped after all, so I just reported my thirtieth victory.

> [The balloon was from Section 31, 18th Company, 3rd Balloon Wing, and burned at 12.05 pm British time near Bapaume. Its two-man crew, Lieutenants Weeks and Gordon, survived. It was Buckler's sixth balloon victory.]

On the evening of the same day we were ordered to Le Cateau where a long discussion took place concerning the deployment of our Staffel for the next day, the day of the [counter] attack. Punctually at 23.00 hours we were all lying in bed, for the next morning we were to meet other units at 08.30 at a pre-arranged spot. I got practically no sleep during the night and then I was startled awake by troubled dreams in which I was constantly wounded. In the morning when Meisenbach came to my room – as a Leutnant I now had a batman – I said full of foreboding: 'Today I'm going to get it!' Neither breakfast nor a cigarette tasted good to me.

The units met punctually at the agreed location. Two fighter planes each took on the protection of a lower-flying aircraft whose duty it was to range the artillery. Since we had appeared in an uneven number, I assumed the duty of protecting my lower-flying comrades alone.

The outward and return flights went smoothly the first two times. During the third approach [to the front] I thought to myself that if the English were smart they would cut us off this time. Below me I saw two Sopwiths, but before attacking them I took the precaution of looking to the right and left. I did so too late.

From the left an enemy pilot was charging my flank and was less than ten metres from me. His machine guns hammering away wildly at me could not miss their mark. I experienced a blow to my back and felt both of my arms get hit. Before they dropped limp and useless I was able to push the control column into the corner and kept it there with my right foot. My machine turned vertically around its own axis with the ground approaching at a furious speed. Mustering all my strength, I succeeded in turning off the ignition at the last moment, then the machine crashed in the middle of a field of craters.

I do not know if I was conscious upon impact, but in any event, when I was able to survey my situation I was hanging upside down staring into a shell hole. Despite tremendous pain I loosened my belt and let myself fall.

* * *

My machine lay on its back with broken wings on the sloped side of a shell hole, partially sticking out of it, while fuel was dripping on my head from above. All attempts to even slightly alter my position, which caused me horrible pain, were futile. I lay in my hole cringing like an animal that someone had wounded in its burrow. If someone did not find me soon I would have to perish here.

How was someone supposed to find me, since I was lying between the lines? I heard bullets whistling over my shell hole and in addition shells were impacting all around me. I remembered hearing that two shells never landed in the same hole, which comforted me and could have been my salvation.

What was that? I heard the roar of an engine which grew louder and louder. There was a sliding and grinding sound while the ground trembled. Then my gaze, which was directed towards the sky, fell upon a black monster rolling past the edge of the crater. A tank! It was rolling in the direction of the enemy – our troops were advancing.

Earth and stone began sliding and threatening to bury me alive. I lay there and prayed. I continued to lie at the bottom of that crater for many hours while the attack passed over me. Then silence set in. Medical orderlies found me and pulled me out of my hole with infinite care and kindness. The attack had succeeded and strategically important territory had been wrested from the enemy.

The brave fellows carried me on a ground-sheet to a temporary military hospital [casualty clearing station]. They did not leave me until it was my turn to have my wounds dressed. Besides Germans, there were also a lot of Englishmen. Lightly wounded English officers sat and stood around and smoked, while I longed for a cigarette.

A priest arrived at my bed at the same time as the doctor. He got me a cigarette and allowed me to smoke by holding it between my lips and letting me take one puff after another, the same way one might feed a baby. In the meantime I received an injection against gangrene, then I requested my Staffel be notified by telephone.

Three hours later von Esebeck, Rudno, and our faithful Unteroffizier Koch were at my bedside in order to pick me up with the largest car of the Staffel. Rudno had also brought along champagne and cigarettes. The stretcher was laid across the car and as carefully as possible it set off on its way to Le Cateau. While en-route, von Esebeck and Rudno told me that Brachwitz, one of our comrades, had already brought home the report that he had seen my aircraft lying shot down between the lines and they had little hope of seeing me alive again. Now their joy was all the greater and by the time we arrived at Le Cateau, the champagne and cigarettes had all been polished off.

> [Buckler had come down by Vaucelles, south of Cambrai, near the St Quentin Canal, at 12.05 hours German time – 11.05 British time.]

Pour le Mérite

A short time later I was lying on the operating table. What they did with me there I do not know. What I was later told about it I would rather keep to myself, but for a long time the rumour circulated that both of poor Buckler's arms had been amputated!

On 3 December – I will never forget this day as long as I live – after the doctor visited me, the nurse again came and tidied up everything around me, carefully smoothing out my bed and placing down a glass of milk for me. I smiled at her gratefully. Oh, I was so glad to be alive and lying in a soft bed! I was just horribly tired and weak.

After that a Hauptmann appeared who in a soft, gentle voice prepared me for a high-ranking visit. Then the door opened and a general with a snow-white moustache entered. It was General von der Marwitz.

> [General der Kavallerie Georg von der Marwitz, Commander-in-Chief (Oberbefehlshaber) of the German 2nd Army, had a son in Jasta 30. Hans-Georg von der Marwitz would end the war with fifteen victories only to be killed in a flying accident in 1925.]

The old gentleman sat on the edge of my bed. He observed me for a little while thoughtfully, almost affectionately. Then he began to tell me about his life. He was, and always had been, a soldier. In March 1915 he received the *Pour le Mérite* [*mit Eichenlaub* – Oak Leaves]. 'Not for myself, but for my troops,' he said with a good-natured smile. 'But how wonderful it must be for youth to receive such an order entirely for their own accomplishments.'

With these words he pulled a small black case out of his pocket, opened it, and took out the blue cross that hung upon a broad black and white ribbon. Then he bent over me and while tears of emotion fell on my face, he laid the *Pour le Mérite* around me so that the blue cross now hung out of the collar of my nightshirt. For a long time he held my hand, until I fell asleep from exhaustion. As a precaution, since one feared the consequences of any sort of excitement, a morphine tablet had been put in my milk. When I woke up again three hours later I felt around for the cross at my neck in order to convince myself that the whole thing had not been a dream.

Many years later the son of the general, the young von der Marwitz, was buried after meeting a fighter pilot's end. It was the most horrifying way to go – burned to death. After seven years I saw the general again, on his estate at Klein-Romin, near Stolp, where I was his guest.

My left arm is saved

While I was lying in the hospital with both arms in casts, my comrades visited me daily. Each time they brought along something different and showed a kindness and caring which I will never forget. Rudno cared for me like a father.

Then Christmas approached. Since I wanted to celebrate this holiday with my mother, von Esebeck arranged to get me transferred to a hospital in Mainz. On the night of my transfer my Staffel mate Brachwitz was brought in with a thigh wound and in my room in terrible pain he departed from us forever. [Walter Brachwitz died on 23 December following wounds received on 1 December, possibly in a fight with DH5s of 68 Squadron, Australian Flying Corps.]

On the 23rd I was taken to the private hospice of Doctor Castell in Mainz. Unfortunately nothing came of my wish finally to be reunited with my mother on Christmas Eve again after four years. My condition worsened during the trip and on the Holy Night no one was allowed to see me. One of my old friends in Mainz by the name of Baesier took over the night watch. He eased my pain with morphine tablets to the extent allowed by the doctor's prescription. He was compensated in turn with the good wine that I received in great quantities from known and unknown contributors.

The most beautiful flowers were standing in the room. Look at all the people who were suddenly thinking about me! In the days following when I was again allowed to receive visitors, people dropped in to see me who would not even have said 'hello' to me back when I was still a roofer's apprentice. However, I was not an exhibit to be gaped at, so except for my mother, my sisters, and some good friends, I no longer allowed anyone to see me.

After I had lain on my back almost motionless for eight weeks, my right arm was freed from its cast. It was completely stiff but with great strength of will I got it to the point, within a few days, where I could bend my wrist in all directions and could move my fingers individually.

My doctor's greatest concern was my left arm, the artery of which had been shot through. Two days before the decisive operation I was given almost nothing to eat. I was dying of hunger, or at least that is what I imagined. In reality the fasting did me a great deal of good, as it is the best thing for one's health. At 07.30 in the morning I was laid upon a stretcher and carried to the operating room. Four hours later, Doctor Colignon had completed his masterpiece. The suturing of the artery had succeeded and my arm was saved.

When I awoke from the anaesthesia around 2.30 that afternoon, my single concern was that I get something to eat. I felt like I was starving, but no one wanted to assume responsibility for it, so I had to wait until the doctor came. He had known me since I was six years old and addressed me with *du* and called me Julius. After he was convinced that everything was perfectly fine, I finally got something to eat and drink. I have never since devoured a meal with such voracious appetite.

* * *

Fourteen days later I was allowed to stand up for the first time in twelve weeks. Pale and weak, I staggered around in the hallway and then crawled back into my bed, only waking up again after sleeping for fourteen hours. This long sleep did me an extraordinary amount of good. I felt as though I were reborn.

That same morning I received a telegram from Hauptmann von Esebeck informing me that he was going to land at Gonsenheim airfield around 1 o'clock and then pay me a visit. This airfield was the former parade ground of my Mainz infantry regiment and had been, so to speak, my home for two years. Von Esebeck was coming from the Pfalz factory at Speyer. Without much further thought, I had myself driven to the airfield by car.

About the same time as my visitor took off from Speyer, I pushed the throttle and flew towards him. We met over Worms and flew together to Mainz. Only when I was preparing to land did I notice that I had over-exerted myself. My left arm was still in splints and I had been very much weakened by the long period of lying in bed and the loss of blood from the operation. However, summoning all my energy, I landed the machine intact at the airfield.

The reunion celebration ended only the next morning, as the good von

Esebeck had to give me a report down to the most minute detail about everything that had transpired in the Staffel during my absence. Every new victory was celebrated once more belatedly. In the meantime, nothing had happened to my comrades so we were therefore in the best of spirits.

> [While this is true in part, the Jasta had lost a pilot while Buckler had been in Le Cateau, in addition to the death of Brachwitz. On 18 December, Leutnant Stanislaus Zentzytzky who had joined the unit in July, was severely injured flying a two-seater machine which crashed at Bohain. His passenger, a Leutnant Gruschwitz (not an airman), also died. On 7 December, Jasta 17 had moved its base to Retheuil Ferme, near Bohain (midway between Cambrai and St Quentin) and shortly after Christmas became part of Jagdgruppe Nr.1, in company with Jastas 8, 24s and 48, again commanded by von Bentheim, under 18 Army control. However, Jasta 17 claimed no victories between 12 December and 5 March 1918. The last three in 1917 had been an RE8 by Schniedewind on the 1st, and two balloons, both by Strasser, on 10th and 12th December.]

That night I went to a bar for the first time in my life. Up to this point I had known this sort of mundane place of entertainment only from hearsay. Everything seemed nice and wonderful to me, and for the first time I was wearing my *Pour le Mérite* at the collar of my new officer's uniform. From everything that von Esebeck told me I gained a sense of how sincerely my comrades were devoted to me and how closely my life was bound to theirs.

* * *

On a bright morning, carrying a giant bouquet of lilies, I took a tram to my hospice. The only other people sitting in the tram were workers on their way to their wartime production jobs. On this particular morning I definitely did not look like an old soldier. Even the orders and decorations did not help in this regard. I must confess that I honestly felt ashamed in front of these people whose faces betrayed how difficult and rough each day of work was for them. It was impossible for me to stand up and tell them that I had spent twelve weeks in the hospital in horrible pain and with the prospect of losing my left arm, and that today, or rather yesterday, I was once more amongst people for the first time and really had cause to celebrate with my Staffelführer and comrades. So I got off the tram somewhat sheepishly, but at the hospice I was greeted like a long-lost son.

I could only take it for three more days in Mainz, then I had to get back to my comrades at the front. The day before my departure I visited my old regiment. As I approached the gate to the barrack square a voice bellowed: '*Rrrraus!*' I suspected the approach of the regimental commander and rushed to get through the gate. The guard lined up in ranks and the order rang out: 'Form up! Eyes straight! Shoulder arms! Attention – present arms!' I saluted and hastened my step but I had hardly passed the guard when the order rang out: 'Order arms – fall out!' I looked around in bewilderment and discovered that I was the only officer in the vicinity.

Only now did it occur to me that the guard must step out for the *Pour le Mérite*. I was deeply moved by these proceedings. They had taken place for the first time in my life at the very gate before which I myself had often stood guard in the years 1912 to 1914. I sent two cases of beer from the officers' mess to the guardroom and therewith rendered my thanks.

Chapter Ten

The Début of Circus Buckler

The night-bombing of Retheuil

Once again without actually saying farewell to my mother, with whom I had spent many happy hours – how proud she was of my *Pour le Mérite* – I departed for Metz the next day. Here I received an invitation from Oberleutnant Göring, who a short time later took over the leaderless Richthofen Geschwader and was destined to create our new Luftwaffe.

> [Richthofen's JGI was not, in March 1918, leaderless. The Baron was destined to fall on 21 April 1918 and his successor, Willi Reinhard, survived till he was killed in a flying accident on 3 July. Göring took over JGI five days later.]

In the meantime my Staffel mate Bohny, 'little Bohny' we called him, had come to Metz to pick me up in a touring machine. I sweat more from fear during the flight from Metz to Retheuil than at any other time during the whole war. Bohny immediately soared away with me in a cavalier take-off. That he did not graze the tree tops while doing so was not to his credit. Because I had always only flown solo since 1915, I only had a feeling for aerobatics that I myself performed. What Bohny called 'flying' was to me simply incomprehensible.

We gradually rose to 2,800 metres and below me I could see Verdun, Fort Vaux, and Douaumont. Memory wakened within me everything associated with these names. Suddenly I heard a rattling sound like that of a machine gun and I ducked down on my observer's seat. I did not even have a flare pistol with me. Then the clattering stopped. As I cautiously straightened up again it immediately appeared once more. This guy seems to be aiming just at me, I thought, and quickly disappeared again. When the same game repeated itself for a third time, I found out that a strap on my leather helmet had come loose, which as a result of the strong slipstream was slapping against it.

That was not the last of the frightening events. Over Retheuil, Bohny went down in such a God-awful corkscrew that my hair stood on end beneath my helmet. I decided to pilot myself from Retheuil onwards. I did not think about showing off to him because it is during the flights in which one wants to show what one can do, that things usually go wrong.

Bohny made a smooth landing, but due to engine trouble we could not fly any further and had to stay overnight at the Armee Flug Park [AFP 18]. The commander, Hauptmann Palmer, was just as good a comrade as he was a host. Just as we were sitting down to dinner, the report arrived: Air Raid! I was quite astonished when everyone jumped up and cleared out. I had never witnessed this before.

During the twelve weeks in which I had been away from the front a lot of things had changed. Now formations of twenty to thirty [enemy] machines attacked the rear areas by night. So, while everyone disappeared into the air-raid shelter, Bohny and I rushed outside. It was a silvery clear moonlit night but before we had a proper chance to look around the enemy aeroplanes were already there. Now it was too late to run – bombs were bursting.

We had thrown ourselves down and had to remain lying like that for half an hour waiting to see whether the bombs would hit us or not. To me being torn to bits here on the ground would have been a terrible way to die. I would much rather meet my end up above in aerial combat. The enemy bombers flew so low that they almost grazed the rooftops. By doing so they were not able to intimidate our brave men who provided defence at machine-gun posts on top of the roofs. Their machine guns rattled away at the sky without interruption and two enemy planes tumbled down upon Retheuil. A house caught fire. After thirty minutes the nightmare was over.

This was repeated three more times that night. Bohny and I bravely rode out these other raids with the rest of the men in the shelter. As a result of this night, we climbed into our machine the next morning, tired and worn out. We did not even have time to shave. After three quarters of an hour we landed – that is to say, I landed – on our old airfield.

The only machines still standing on the airfield were Bohny's and mine. All the others had taken off, as we found out, in order to move to a new airfield located closer to the front. We had breakfast and then took off together. Both of our machines had machine guns, but no ammunition. We flew directly towards the new field at about 2,000 metres, until we saw it below us.

What was going on over there? One little cloud after another appeared in the sky. Our flak was shooting like crazy. *Donnerwetter!* There were enemy machines above and below us. One bomb after another was hitting our new airfield. We had wandered into the middle of an enemy formation that was paying the new base a visit after it had just been moved into. Bohny was more sensible than I. He immediately turned away and got out of the witches' cauldron. I wanted to land and load up with ammunition, but while levelling out received such a blow from below – this was no ground gust – that I thought my Mops would burst asunder. I quickly opened the throttle and flew onwards. A few minutes later when the sky was clear and the raid was over, I landed after circling the field a couple of times as a precaution in order to view the locations of the bomb craters. Otherwise there would most definitely have been a crack up.

The joy of seeing one another again after such a long separation was great, but we had not even finished our initial greetings when there was a new air raid alarm. Everyone cleared out, just like at Retheuil and only I remained out of habit. Behle, the mess orderly, tugged at my arm: 'Herr Leutnant, let's go down in the dugout!' However, it was too late. There were explosions all around us, a hellish spectacle. When finally everything was quiet once more we were both still lying flat on the ground. This raid cost us twelve men dead and thirty-two wounded.

My comrades told me, as I had already seen and heard in Retheuil, that the 'good old times' at the front were pretty much over. The French and English were flying in larger and larger formations. Whoever did not immediately disappear into the dugout was no longer a hero, but a fool. I had to relearn a lot of things pretty quickly, but I soon adjusted.

[It is not clear when Buckler returned to the Jasta. One source records the date as 4 March 1918, but the unit was still at Retheuil Ferme till 26 March, so he would have no reason to land there and then fly to the 'new' airfield. On 26 March the Jasta moved to Douilly, but only remained there for two days, then moved to Balâtre, east of Roye, on the 18th Army front. This location is south-west of St Quentin and south-east of Amiens, so is well in the area re-taken by the Germans in the successful 'Operation Michael' which began on 21 March, so we must assume Buckler returned much later in March than is sometimes noted or once again the event has no relation to a known date or period. The Jasta was part of Jagdgruppe 11, commanded by von Esebeck, along with Jastas 22s and 63.

Jasta 17 might well welcome Buckler back, for they had only achieved six victories since his departure at the end of November and had suffered some losses. As we noted earlier, on 1 December Leutnant Walter Brachwitz had been shot down and died of his wounds just before Christmas. On 17 March Offizierstellvertreter Adolf Schreder was shot down and killed, and of course Zentzytzky's death had been reported to Buckler whilst in hospital.

Leutnant Karl Bohny had joined the Jasta in mid-January 1918 but was already an experienced pilot. He had been with Jasta 5 and then Kest 7 where he scored two victories. He was about to gain his third victory and would go on to bring his total to eight by the war's end.]

Circus Buckler

One day when I was picking up a new machine from the Armee Flug Park at Retheuil I saw three old circus trailers standing in a yard for which no one apparently had any use. The idea popped into my head that such mobile trailers were more suitable quarters than stationary buildings, considering the present conditions at the front where one could count on a disturbing bomb raid every night. In the evening one could have them moved to some spot in open country and spend the night in them peacefully. This would substantially increase the effectiveness of the crews, as men who have slept poorly [are usually less effective compared to] those who have slept well. Besides that, since childhood I had a soft spot for those gypsy caravans and imagined this sort of living as being very romantic.

Once I got back I sent my raiding party, Unteroffizier Koch and four sturdy fellows, into action. A couple of hours later we were the owners of these 'private homes'. Next day they were painted in accordance with military regulations and twenty-four hours later they had been comfortably furnished.

From now on as dusk fell each evening the trailers were moved about six kilometres from the airfield to the most secure possible location and were well camouflaged. We could now sleep peacefully in spite of the nightly bombing raids. From then on our Staffel was known in the vernacular as 'Circus Buckler'.

Wounded for the fifth time

On 8 March 1918, four days after my return to the front, I made my first flight again with the Staffel. I was leading it in the vicinity of Montdidier and we crossed a ghastly field, the stench of which rose all the way up to our level. It was covered with thousands of dead men and horses. It looked as though a horrible earthquake had wreaked havoc here. What must have taken place in this area?

This was a relatively quiet front and it was half an hour into our barrage patrol before an enemy observation machine ventured forth. We were about 500 metres above it and I led the Staffel during the approach, but then turned aside prematurely. This was something we had previously arranged in order to give others a chance to score. While my comrades were attacking I allowed my machine to climb in order that I might be able to protect them from above, if necessary. To my horror I saw one machine after another attack, fire, and race past the enemy machine without success. The last man to do so did not fare any better. The enemy crew, now above all of them, flew onwards.

Burning with rage, I dived down from above, approaching to within twenty metres of it and opened fire. The pilot of the enemy machine tore his machine around in a frantic turn and began to glide. I flew close behind him. Nothing was to be seen of the observer. Feeling I had the situation well in hand, I was actually thinking only about where in heaven he might want to land. Down below was nothing but gaping shell holes, so out of concern for my opponent I searched around for a spot where he could make an emergency landing. If he had now dived down 100 metres I would probably have sped over him and he would have been well able to get away from me. However, he continued to glide peacefully onwards, now about 600 metres up. In my mind's eye I could already see him somersaulting down below and just hoped that nothing serious would happen to him.

However, at this precise moment something happened to me that I had in no way predicted. A murderous machine-gun fire began and as I looked round I discovered, pale with horror, that seven aircraft were following me. How odd! None of the seven machines were attacking. Then I saw it was my comrades. In spite of that, the machine-gun fire did not cease. I looked forward and noticed that the observer in the two-seater was now suddenly standing at his gun and kindly aiming at me. That spelled an end to my equanimity. With a racing engine I charged at him and finished him off. The enemy machine with its heroic crew dived vertically from fifty metres into an infantry position [in the front line].

[Despite one of Buckler's rare moments of actually recording a date, also giving us the date he returned to the front, which, as referred to above, is in doubt, this victory is not one that is recorded in either the Jasta records or the *Nachtrichtenblatt*. His first victory upon his return to Jasta 17 was not recorded until 16 April, and noted as his thirty-first. If his story is real then not only must front line observers have seen it but so too must his seven comrades. Also, in early March the Jasta was flying on the British front, but in mentioning Montdidier, which was south-west of Péronne, and on the French front, he was many kilometres from where he should be patrolling – and the British front was rarely 'quiet'. An incident similar to this may well have happened, but not on 8 March 1918.]

* * *

I was invited to dine this evening with Menckhoff. While there I also made the acquaintance of Pütter. Both had the *Pour le Mérite*. A short time later poor Pütter was shot down in flames.

[If Buckler is still talking about March 1918, then his memory in the late 1930s is again at fault and he is merely remembering that both men had received the Blue Max during the war. Karl Menckhoff received his Blue Max on 23 April 1918, and Fritz Pütter was given his on 31 May. Menckhoff had scored twenty victories with Jasta 3 by early February 1918, at which time he was given command of Jasta 72, where he brought his score to thirty-nine before he was brought down and captured on 25 July. At this time he was thirty-four years old.

Pütter was younger – twenty-three – and had taken command of Jasta 68 in March 1918 with a score of ten whilst flying with Jasta 9. He would go on to down twenty-five Allied planes and balloons by 16 July, the day his incendiary ammunition exploded, badly burning him. He managed to get down, but died of his severe injuries on 10 August.]

* * *

It was soon so quiet in our sector that we found almost nothing more to do. In the meantime I had shot down another opponent, my thirty-second, but we now roamed around for fourteen days without catching sight of any prey.

[Buckler is definitely talking about April 1918 now, although one would not have thought their front was that quiet, as Balâtre was just south of the main British sectors and on the edge of the French. The March offensive had petered out like all previous offensives, running out of steam because the Germans ran out of support and supplies. Nobody ever seemed to think success would happen and when it did, no one was ready to support the front line assault areas. Buckler's thirty-first and thirty-second victories were over French aircraft, both Bréguet XIV bombers. The first he had downed in the afternoon of 16 April near Vaux (presumably Rubescourt-Vaux, south of Montdidier), the other on the 21st over Mareuil, north-west of Montdider, and well into French territory, half an hour past noon.

Whether either of them was the action described above is unclear. It appears, according to French records, that the first Bréguet may in fact have been a Salmson 2A2 of Sal.225 (but perhaps both types and the unit designation had yet to be changed; German pilots in any event often confused French bomber types) who lost a machine on the III° Armée Front this day. The crew were Caporal André Honoré Henri Ricard and Sous-lieutenant Paul Pruvot. Ricard came from Aix-en-Provence, born in June 1897. Mobilised into the 157th Infantry Regiment in January 1916, he transferred to aviation a year later and won his pilot brevet (No.6707) on 30 May 1917. He joined Br.225 on 27 September.

Pruvot was born in February 1894 and came from Trouville. Mobilised as the war started, he served with the 15th Artillery Regiment and later the 270th Field Artillery, winning

> the *Croix de Guerre* with silver star. He was moved to aviation as an observer on 4 October 1917. There are no obvious candidates for the crew of the Bréguet on the 21st, and it probably came down inside French lines without injury to either crewman.]

There was an observation balloon hanging somewhat far behind enemy lines and at a considerable height. The more often I saw it hanging there, the more firmly my mind was made up to do away with it and put a stop to the observer's activities. So, on 6 May [it was in fact 3 May] I flew off at five o'clock in the morning and crossed the trenches at 2,000 metres. I acted as though I did not have my eye on the balloon and kept my course somewhat to the east of it. In spite of that they did not appear to trust me over there and I noticed that the balloon was getting smaller and smaller, so they had started to haul it down. Malaula! There was no time to lose, so I swooped down upon it at full throttle.

At about 200 metres I had it in front of me at full-size. The observer had already jumped out and I was welcomed with flak and machine-gun fire, but that did not disturb me. I aimed very calmly and fired twenty rounds at the balloon, then I had to tear the machine upwards, otherwise I would have rammed it. I had hardly passed over it when I went into a left turn, and cast a furtive glance at the envelope to see whether there were any small burning holes. It was still not on fire! I was just about to fly towards it again when I finally saw the little orange tongue of flame shoot out. I could fly home with my mind at ease.

However, those on the ground in no way seemed to go along with this, apparently wanting me to stay forever. The flak was thick and every shot signified an invitation to stick around. I had to fly in a zig-zag in order to dodge them and staggered around in the sky like a drunkard. Climbing meant slowing down and slow aeroplanes make good targets, so I tried to get out of the danger zone as fast as possible while remaining at the same height. I was only 150 metres up and was still about 12 kilometres behind enemy lines.

Then my left ankle was struck by a terrible blow. The pain was great but fear of getting hit a second time was greater. Greatest of all was my dread at the thought of falling into captivity. I could only steer with my right foot, as the left one was as good as dead.

A little invention which I had attached to my rudder-bar a year earlier, out of purely theoretical considerations, proved its usefulness on this occasion and saved my life. In any case, it saved me from captivity. We had once discussed what a pilot should do if one of his legs got shot-up. One of us had said that there was no remedy for it, one cannot steer with one leg. There would be nothing left to do but to glide, even at the risk of landing in hostile territory. This thought pestered me until one day I did find a remedy, indeed a very simple one. I had Unteroffizier Roth attach a leather stirrup for each foot on the rudder-bar. If one shoved one foot into the stirrup, one could operate the rudder by pushing and pulling, even if the other foot was out of action. This simple safety device was quickly imitated and stirrups were attached to the rudder-bars of all the machines in the Staffel. I felt it to be an especially kind act of fate that, of all people, I the inventor was allowed to put this invention to a practical test.

With my right leg I steered Mops not only over the front lines, but all the way to the airfield. It was a good thing that the maddening pain did not cause me to lose consciousness. I looked for the exit wound on my left foot, but did not find one, so the bullet had lodged in me. That was a nuisance, because such a wound generally took longer to heal than when a bullet passed through cleanly. Having hardly escaped from the hospital, I now had to prepare myself once more for a boring and inactive period of lying around. Then the war might be over!

I therefore swore and cursed every which way after the landing as the good mechanics lay me on the stretcher once more and carried me away, having once again been put out of action. The truck quickly arrived on the scene, and someone brought my little suitcase. Von Esebeck, Rudno, Strasser, and my other comrades once again said farewell to me.

> [Apart from the action occurring on 3 May and not the 6th, Rudno would have had difficulty in saying farewell to his friend as he had left the Jasta back in early January. He had been given command of the newly-formed Jasta 60, based at Ercheu, part of Jagdgruppe 4, on the 7th Army front. (Ercheu was only about five kilometres to the east of Jasta 17's airfield, so it might have been possible that he was visiting his old unit.) One has to wonder what Buckler thought of this move and promotion. Despite Rudno being such a good friend and very much his senior in all things, he had not yet scored a single victory, whereas Buckler had a score of thirty at that stage. While Buckler led Jasta 17 in the air, due to his experience and expertise as an air fighter, Rudno had been made leader of Jasta 60 on seniority, rather than his air fighting prowess.
>
> Buckler's balloon was from the French 67° Cié Aerostiers and burned at Tricot on the III° Armée front, to the south of Montdidier. Its two observers, Lieutenant Weiss and an aspirant (officer candidate) he had with him, both bailed out safely.]

I had been lying in a bed at a nearby field hospital for less than ten minutes when a bombing raid took place, although a large red cross was clearly painted on the roof. Killing badly wounded, defenceless soldiers was a mean thing to do. Fortunately we were loaded onto a hospital train as quickly as possible, given our wounds, and transported to the closest base.

I was temporarily accommodated in a Bavarian hospital. A nurse there who was especially concerned about me always filled the syringe with water for fear that I might become a morphine addict. Afterwards I went to Lindau on Lake Constance, where I found a beautiful, well-maintained hospital with charming nurses. However, that did not help me get over the fact that I was lying there idly, while reading in the army reports of how other pilots were achieving higher and higher scores. Now the Americans had arrived at the front and with the mass deployment of enemy planes every single German airman was needed.

'You already have the *Pour le Mérite*, what more do you want?' people sometimes said to me. As though my whole reason for fighting was to get the *Pour le Mérite*, and as though everything did not depend upon victory – the final victory!

The wound to my foot was more painful than all four of my earlier wounds put together. First thing each morning I got a morphine shot and then slept until eleven o'clock. As soon as I awoke, the pain returned, so then came more morphine shots. So it went on day after day.

In my sleep I was tortured by horrible dreams, which were almost always about air combat. In my dreams I saw my Staffelführer, the good Freiherr von Esebeck, surrounded by three enemy flyers. I rushed to his aid like a wild man, but the distance between us stayed the same. I saw von Esebeck fighting desperately and even saw the grimace on his face and yet I could not help him. Suddenly his machine was ablaze. Why did he not bail out? Despairing over the fact that this dear person was burning in his machine before my eyes, I woke up. My shirt was thoroughly drenched with sweat. I related my horrible dream to the nurses who were standing around me full of concern.

On the next day I received a telegram: 'Esebeck shot down in flames at 10.50 over Montdidier.' Even the time indicated coincided almost to the minute with the time of my dream. One never heard an ill word spoken about von Esebeck. He stood up for every man in his Staffel whenever it mattered. What luck to have had him as a superior! Even today after twenty-two years I think of him with the same love and respect.

> [Von Esebeck was lost on 27 May 1918, probably while attacking Bréguet bombers of Escadrille Br217 near Rambercourt, one of two fighters and a two-seater claimed by one of its crews – Lieutenant Charlet and Caporal Gérard, north of Noyon.]

A second piece of news that shook me up was the report that Leutnant Schröder had fallen. The death of this young comrade especially tortured me because I imagined that the reproaches I had administered to him shortly before my wounding had driven him to recklessly risking his life. As I later found out, during the combat in which he fell he had acted entirely against the tactics I preached. Every flyer, whenever he sees no chance for success, must make a run for it. This is not cowardice, this is his responsibility to the Fatherland.

My tactics, clear and simple, were: Head for the front. Look around. If something is going on, figure whether it is advisable to attack right away. If yes, then Malaula! If no, then leave immediately and seek a better position. So cry Malaula only when by all standards of human judgement the attack is worth it. Schröder had certainly taken my words to heart, but he had not understood me properly.

> [In fact Leutnant Herbert Schröder was not killed, but only wounded. A former two-seater pilot with FA(A)206, he later became a fighter pilot, joining Jasta 1 in January 1917. He had achieved five victories by the end of October and following a period as an instructor at AFP 1, was posted to Jasta 17 in late April 1918. He had not added to his score before being wounded.]

In addition to the pain over dead comrades came the gruelling pain in my body. Besides that, I was tortured by the thought of perhaps remaining a cripple for the rest of my life. All of this hampered my recovery. All of my insistence that I be allowed to return to the front was of no avail. The doctors did want to assume responsibility for my returning in my condition. In spite of the fact that the bullet had been removed from my left foot, it still hurt like mad. My right arm was not yet entirely healed from the wounding in November 1917 and was still suppurating. I was therefore sent from Lindau to Wiesbaden in order to receive further treatment there at a surgical clinic.

On the very day of my arrival in Wiesbaden I received a great surprise. While I was peacefully sitting in the bathtub there was an explosion. More violent detonations followed in the immediate vicinity. Was someone conducting blasting operations here? Or was an open German city really being visited again by enemy bombers as I had read in newspaper reports? Then I heard our flak [guns] barking and knew the answer.

I jumped out of the tub and rushed to the telephone. The [local] airfield answered. 'Send a car here immediately and have a machine made ready for take-off!' An hour later I took off. Of course, it was far too late. The enemy formation had immediately flown home. I had feared that it would honour some other cities in the neighbourhood with a visit and perhaps my hometown of Mainz. Shooting down an enemy flyer over Mainz would have provided me with a quite special sense of satisfaction. In any event, I wanted to do everything in my power to secure and protect my native town from harm.

From now on I had a car come by every morning around 4 am that took me from the clinic to the airfield. However, during the four weeks I spent in Wiesbaden there were no further raids. I waited each day in vain.

Since there was no other opportunity to still my thirst for action, I undertook something which one can only describe as a stupid boyish prank and which can only be excused because of my young age at the time. What I did, to the astonishment or horror of all those who happened to witness this dramatic episode, was fly beneath the bridge over the Rhine, the very same bridge upon which I had once performed my feats of climbing.

If I were a commander today and someone reported such a stunt by one of my subordinates, thus endangering both people's lives and material in a senseless and unnecessary fashion, I would probably have the guilty party locked up. Special tricks of this nature were in every respect reprehensible, especially in wartime. With the *Pour le Mérite* hanging round my neck and thirty-three confirmed aerial victories, was it really necessary for me to furnish such proof of my flying ability? The long period of rest did not sit well with me. I was bursting with the desire for some sort of action. I needed to accomplish something, only here I went about it in the wrong way.

In my free time I bathed a good deal, took trips on the Rhine, and got together with a couple of comrades I became acquainted with here. One of them was a naval officer, the other was Bongartz, a pilot who had also been awarded the *Pour le Mérite*. With one of his eyes shot out, he was like myself undergoing medical treatment.

> [A name Buckler does not mention, surprisingly, was that of his old pilot Kurt von Rudno-Rudzinsky, now leader of Jasta 60, who was shot down on 26 May and captured.
>
> Heinrich Bongartz, from Gelsenkirchen, Westphalia, was a former school teacher who first saw service with the 16th Infantry Regiment, then the 13th Regiment. Wounded at Verdun he joined the air service and after a period on two-seaters, went to Jasta 36 as a fighter pilot, a unit he later commanded. His score rose to an eventual thirty-three – strangely the same score as Buckler at the time of their meeting – but he was shot down by an SE5 of 74 Squadron RAF on 29 April 1918. He had won his Blue Max just short of three weeks after Buckler had received his. Surviving the war and fighting against post-war revolutionaries, his military career already under threat with the loss of his left eye, Bongartz received a serious leg wound in the fighting. Continuing in aviation circles post-war, he was injured in a flying accident in 1921, but again returned to flying later. He died in January 1946.]

Staffel commander

In August 1918 I returned to the Staffel. With von Esebeck's death it had been orphaned and still had not received a replacement commander. Strasser and my old comrades greeted me as warmly as ever. Only I missed Rudno bitterly. He had been transferred to another Jagdstaffel as its commander. Otherwise everything was just as I had left it, except that the three trailers had been freshly painted.

> [Jasta 17 were now based at Vivaise, north of Lâon, operating on the 9th Army front. It had moved here on 25 July. It would remain at this airfield until 25 September, although from the 17th it was under 7th Army control.]

When I awoke on the first morning inside my trailer I heard a strange scouring sound back and forth on the wall. Through the window I could see that the painters were back at work. But why? The trailers had just been newly painted. I leapt outside and saw to my surprise that on each trailer an inscription boasted: Circus Buckler. What was the meaning of this? The Staffel had been called that in the vernacular for some time now, so why was this nickname now being applied as though it were 'official'? I thought it was a joke.

I could not get anything out of the painters. They just stood to attention, so I attributed it to their respect for the *Pour le Mérite* that through me had made its appearance in the Staffel. In the officers' mess I was to discover the reason for the inscription and smart bearing. Overnight I had been appointed as the Staffelführer.

> [Buckler is not quite correct in saying there had been no leader of Jasta 17 (unless he was meaning a leader in the air) following the loss of von Esebeck. No front line fighter squadron would remain leaderless for very long. Two days after von Esebeck was killed, Oberleutnant Wilhelm Pritsch was posted in as a caretaker commander. Pritsch was a former Jasta 17 pilot, having arrived on 17 April 1918 but on 12 June he reverted to ordinary pilot upon the announcement that Leutnant Günther Schuster, almost one of the original Jasta 17 pilots, took control. Schuster had left Jasta 17 in September 1917, moving to Jasta 29. His victory score had risen to five, two with Jasta 17, three with Jasta 29. He gained his sixth victory on 15 July – a balloon – but had been wounded on 1 August, so it was this event that heralded the return of Buckler to Jasta 17. However, it is not clear if he was ever given command of the Jasta, but merely continued as 'leader in the air'. Nevertheless, it does not seem probable that Buckler would say he was Staffelführer if he had not been so

appointed, for in 1939 there would be enough people around to dispute this had it not been correct.

It is interesting to note again that the Jasta was so happy to see Buckler back. After his wounding on 3 May, it had not shot down a single Allied plane or balloon until Pritsch took over, gaining his first and only victory on 9 June. Leutnant Alfred Fleischer, who arrived on 12 April 1918, scored his first of six victories on 29 June, and Schuster had been the only scorer in July, with a balloon on the 15th. With another victory by Fleischer on 1 August, an American Nieuport 28 of the 27th Aero Squadron, these four victories had been the sum total of Jasta 17's efforts in virtually three months. However, the only two casualties had been those reported to Buckler while in hospital, von Esebeck and Schröder. Fleischer had been shot down near Balâtre on 6 June but had not been injured. This again emphasises that some Jastas' fortunes really did revolve around one 'ace'. By this time the Jasta had achieved some sixty-eight victories, so half had been secured by Buckler alone. The next highest scorers were Strasser with seven and Schuster (who'd left in September), with three.

And, despite Buckler saying that Georg Strasser had been among his comrades to welcome him back, Strasser had been posted away from the Jasta back on 19 May, going to FEA 3 as an instructor.

The pilots that were on strength upon Buckler's return were as follows:

Ltn Wilhelm Becker
Ltn Karl Bohny
Vfw Hans Donhauser
Ltn Alfred Fleischer
OffzStv Walter Horing
Oblt Wilhelm Pritsch
Ltn Ruppel
Ltn Seifert
Ltn Spindler
Uffz Fritz Wolff

So, not so many. Readers may be surprised how few pilots there were, but on occasion, Jastas operated as little more than flight size units, as compared to the RAF squadrons they faced.]

Chapter Eleven

The Last Malaula

The appointment, over which my comrades seemed to rejoice even more than I myself, did not alter the actual conditions in the Staffel itself. I had been their leader in the air all along, and the good von Esebeck had also continually followed my advice regarding all other questions of a military nature. The men in my Staffel could not offer me more respect that they had already done. The fact that I could move so freely amongst them, had so entirely lost my earlier inhibitions, and even when I was still not an officer could express myself so naturally and confidently, this I owe for the most part to your education, my dear Rudno.

Already, after a few days, I noticed that order and discipline had suffered in the Staffel. So I tightened the reins, but my old guard seemed to observe this with satisfaction. Everyone with the blood of a soldier gladly submits to orders, even strict ones as long as they are practical and just. The following incident showed me just how necessary it was to take decisive action.

Meisenbach, my batman, who incidentally was the father of five children, said one day: 'It's a good thing that the Herr Leutnant is back, otherwise we would have slowly starved to death.'

'How so?' I asked. 'Isn't the Staffel being issued with rations?'

'Sure, they're being issued, but….' he hesitated.

'But what?'

'The mess sergeants are cheating us.'

'Do you have proof?'

'No, but since the Herr Leutnant is back we have been getting more to eat.'

'Hmm.' This was a strange state of affairs. From the first day of my return I had sampled the men's food, as I had previously done. Without them noticing it, I had both of the accused watched over. There was nothing to implicate either, but I still remained distrustful. I knew that Meisenbach was too honest to have made such weighty accusations without reason.

Three days later when the mess sergeant and the orderly applied for leave I granted it, but on the following morning after the truck had departed at 4 o'clock with the soldiers going on leave, I followed them with my raiding party. I stopped the truck on an open stretch of road and had everybody climb out. Then the luggage was examined. The result of this search was devastating for the two members of the mess staff.

A few hours later they joined the infantry in the trenches. They had never been in contact with the enemy, so it was high time for them to become acquainted with the seriousness of the war. In this way I spared them both the aftermath of judicial proceedings and gave them the opportunity to make good their mistakes. They were both young fellows, and the two infantrymen for whom I exchanged them were old boys and proven soldiers. They had earned a more peaceful life and thanked me and the Staffel.

We can manage even without a soldiers' council

The superior strength of the opposing air forces grew from week to week. What could we do with our fourteen aeroplanes when matched against seventy to one hundred machines? In addition, our opponents were equipped with the best materials while we had to make do more and more with substitutes. Our resources even in terms of manpower were reduced. Of sixteen men sent to us [ground personnel], no fewer than ten of them had a criminal record. Amongst them were miserable, degenerate fellows. My 'old guard' helped me whip them into shape, which did not always go off smoothly. We even managed to teach these people a thing or two. This was cause for a little Malaula in the Staffel.

On 30 October 1918 I shot down my forty-second opponent and therewith attained my thirty-fifth confirmed victory.

> [The Jasta had moved from Vivaise on 25 September, moving to Chuffilly, between Rethel and Vouziers, west of the Aisne river. It remained here until moving to Malmy-Chémery, south of Mezières, on 9 October and then to St Medard, near Neufchâteau, on 3 November, all on the 3rd Army front. Since mid-May it had also been part of Rittmeister Heinz von Brederlow's Jagdgruppe 11, along with Jastas 48, 53 and 61.
>
> The list of Buckler's claims appear in the appendices. Although Buckler returned in early August, he did not score any further victories until October. The first of these came on the 5th, a Salmson 2A2 at 17.15 hours. This was probably a machine of Escadrille Sal.27. This French squadron lost two machines on the IV° Armée front, crewed by Maréchal-des-Logis Carlin and Soldat Catineau, and Maréchal-des-Logis Rey and Lieutenant d'Exea-Dourerc, who were all killed. Jasta 17 claimed two, one credited to Buckler and one to Karl Bohny. Earlier that day Jasta 17 downed a Bréguet to make it three for the day. The victorious pilot was Vizefeldwebel Donhauser.

> Hans Christian Friedrich Donhauser – usually known as Christian – had earlier been a two-seater pilot and after requesting to become a fighter pilot joined Jasta 17 in July 1918. Compared to the other pilots in the Jasta, he scored victories at an amazing rate. His first victory came on 20 August, his score rising to nine by the month's end. One more in September, plus three more unconfirmed and this 5 October claim was his eleventh. He would end the war with nineteen, which includes one victory he achieved on two-seaters (FA10), which indicates that some of his unconfirmed claims were later upgraded. He was awarded the Iron Cross 1st Class and the Golden Military Merit Cross. Commissioned just after the war he did not survive long, being killed in a crash in August 1919 at Schleissheim, near Munich.
>
> Buckler's next victory claim was on the 24th, reported as a Bréguet XIV B2 down at Méry, possibly a machine from Escadrille Br.257. The victory he talks of on 30 October is not known. He makes no comments on what, where or when, and as records so near the war's end were somewhat chaotic it is almost impossible to make any suggestions. The only claim noted for Jasta 17 was a balloon by Bohny, his eighth and final victory. On 8 November Buckler reported that he shot down a British RE8 but that it was unconfirmed. There is no recorded loss by the RAF.]

In November something began to simmer and there were growing signs of revolution. It began in the rear areas right amongst those who had for the most part been spared the horrors of war. Soon the weariness of war spread to the front, and there were more and more cases of breaches of discipline. My Staffel performed flawlessly until the bitter end and even today I am proud of them.

On 8 November when we were about to take off once more to meet the enemy, I noticed that I had forgotten my goggles. I had my men informed that they should take off and that I would catch up to them, then I headed back towards the mess. On the way from the airfield to the mess I ran across a disorderly column of men, most of whom were drunk. They blocked my path with a lot of howling and demanded that I get out of the car.

I saw my faithful mechanics rushing over from the airfield and informed the leader of the column that I would hold him responsible for everything that occurred in the next few minutes if he did not immediately clear a path for me. Since he did not succeed in doing so, the series of events I foresaw took their course. My mechanics fell upon those men and gave them a good beating to an extent that I was only to discover sometime later. Because I was in a hurry to catch up with my Staffel I continued on to the airfield and took off immediately.

We returned with three more aerial victories [this was possibly 3 November, Vfw Schuman claiming one, and Ltn Fleischer two] to our credit. With that, the number of victories claimed by Jasta 17 rose to 110. Eighty-nine aeroplanes and twenty-one observation balloons had been shot down [since formation].

The commander of the column which my mechanics had worked over was waiting for me in the officers' mess. Only now did I find out what a thorough job they did. Of course, the men from the column totally distorted the facts when they brought the matter before their commander. They were not entirely able to conceal the incident since some of them had had to be taken to the hospital. When I appraised the commander, a young Hauptmann, of the hair-raising lack of discipline amongst his men, the indignation of his part was no less than my own. We then had a long and serious discussion about the disturbing course of events. These sort of symptoms indicated how far the demoralization of the troops had progressed. We still had no presentiment of the revolution that was to break out in the homeland one day later. However, I was soon going to feel its effects.

* * *

'Herr Leutnant, we must elect a soldiers' council.' With these words Unteroffizier Hennicke – our capable armourer and a good, decent man – appeared before me in a fair state of puzzlement. In the meantime the outbreak of revolution had been communicated to us via wireless.

'Fine,' I said. 'There's nothing to prevent it, but just tell me one thing, my dear Hennicke. What is the meaning of this council and what sort of authority does it have?'

'Well,' he replied as he shrugged his shoulders in embarrassment. 'Well, what it actually means is… it's supposed to assist the Herr Leutnant in leading the Staffel.'

'Assist me?' I asked, shaking my head. 'What do you mean by that?'

'Well, that's hard to say. The Herr Leutnant is to continue leading the Staffel, but all orders issued must first be discussed and approved by the council.'

At that I burst out laughing. 'So we should hold a council of war in the sky! Do you think the enemy is going to wait until the order to attack is approved by the high council? No, my dear Hennicke, that is nonsense! Either I will continue to lead the Staffel alone as I do now or the council will lead it. Either one or the other. Go tell this to the men.' I looked at my clock. 'It is 8.40 and I want the Staffel to fall in at nine o'clock.'

'Yes sir, Herr Leutnant.'

At nine o'clock sharp the Feldwebel reported, 'The Staffel has fallen in.'

I spoke briefly with my men and gave them five minutes to think things over. After this time Unteroffizier Hennicke came back to me in the mess and announced with relief, 'The Herr Leutnant is to continue leading the Staffel. What the neighbouring Staffeln and units do is of no concern to us.'

'Malaula,' I replied, 'It's settled.'

* * *

On that day I led the united Staffel once more to the front. While doing so I shot down my forty-third opponent. It was no longer possible to obtain confirmation and after landing I found a telephone message waiting for me stating that I should report immediately to the Kommandeur der Flieger. On the way to Charleroi I was stopped four times by infantrymen wearing red armbands, who fell upon me like highwaymen. [Fortunately] the *Pour le Mérite* still exerted its influence and they did not dare touch me.

I arrived at Charleroi very late and the Kommandeur presented the assembled officers with a very gloomy picture of the entire situation. There was revolution at home, which had begun with the navy. The institution of a republic was proclaimed in Berlin. The front had not been penetrated but it had been undermined and worn down from within. There were 'red' agitators at work everywhere. We headed back feeling quite disturbed. Twenty-four hours later the decision was handed down that there was to be an armistice.

Thus approached 11 November 1918. Exactly two years previously the Staffel had been established. Weeks beforehand we had made all sorts of preparations to celebrate this anniversary in a suitable fashion but there was no mood for celebration on this day. The festivities rather resembled a funeral. We hummed the song: *Ich hat't einen Kameraden*. Did the comrades who had fallen believing in victory for the Fatherland not have a better lot than we who had to witness this humiliating end? The final vestiges of our good mood disappeared when the order came through that on the following day we were to return home – but without our aircraft. So this was not to be an honourable armistice. It was rather a matter of complete submission. We were simply to lay down our arms. Everything was supposed just to be delivered up to the enemy, including our aeroplanes and ammunition. All of us immediately agreed that we would never carry out this order.

On the following morning there was a counter-order. Our machines were to be delivered up in Saarbrücken. To whom? The red mob? Well, we would see about that. I ordered that all the machines be made ready for take-off and that all their guns be loaded. Anything else remaining that might be useful to the enemy was stowed in the three circus trailers. After this had been done, the trailers were driven to an open field, doused with petrol, and set on fire. Their contents exploded with a mighty roar. We watched this fireworks display from some distance. With it our last remaining bit of hope was blown skywards. We had no time left for complaining and philosophising, we were soldiers and followed orders.

While the engines of sixteen aircraft were clattering I had the Staffel assemble once more. Of their own accord, the officers formed the first and second ranks, thus the Staffel stood as one unit. Most had their heads bowed in absolute silence.

'You have all fulfilled your duty.' Thus began my farewell speech, more or less. 'Every one of you, and you have performed it faithfully up until this final moment in which you stand before me, as I speak to you for the last time as your Staffelführer. My comrades through thick and thin – we flew together against the enemy and fought in the air side-by-side. We vanquished many enemies and lost many dear and brave comrades. Just think of…' I mentioned the names of our dead and we thought of them in silence. Then I continued: 'How often have we helped one another, diving upon the enemy and driving him off. Each of us owes the other his life ten times over. We can hardly imagine an existence without one another. We belong to one another forever. Though years may pass, we will be there for one another in time of need. And if the Fatherland should need us again, we will all be prepared to serve once more as far is it lies within our power.

'And all you comrades in the Staffel – sergeants, corporals, and men – every one of you has faithfully served his post. As for the faithful mechanics, we could always rely on you. Our machines were like swords that you kept sharpened for battle. All of you industrious craftsmen, alert medical personnel, cooks looking after our physical well-being, and good orderlies can say that you have nothing to do with the traitors who are presently robbing our Fatherland of its defences and placing them at the mercy of our enemy. This is the same enemy that in the course of five years was unable to overwhelm our brave German army by feat of arms, despite its numerical superiority and in spite of the fact that it incited the whole world against us.

'We don't have anything in common with those who have left this great battle-proven army in the lurch. The battle for the Fatherland has brought us together, held us together, and welded us together. We have become one. We are returning now to our homeland as ordered – but undefeated by the enemy – and as a unit in close formation with the bonds of comradeship unsevered. I am leading you now for the last time. As your leader I want to thank you all for what you have done for the Fatherland. You rendered your services selflessly with only victory in mind. I thank you for your loyalty up to the very end.'

My men saw my tears as I spoke these words and I saw their own as they listened. We did not feel any shame before one another. Deeply moved, we felt the genuine comradeship which bound us together and which was stronger than any revolution. Perhaps upon the morrow we would all be scattered to the winds. Then came the old soldier's song, arising from every heart. '*'Ere we must part…*'

The flight crews said farewell to the other personnel, who were to be transported home by railway. Then they climbed into their aircraft.

Malaula! – Malaula!

The Staffel flies home

We took off at equal intervals, flew a single circuit of honour around the field, and paid the front a farewell visit. We saw a poor little novice flying all alone. If the war had still been going on, poor fellow, your number would have been up! Nonetheless, our former foe considered it advisable to raise his tail as quickly as possible and clear off. I could not resist sending a couple of farewell bursts of fire after him, though I deliberately missed. That was the last cockade I saw in a hostile sky. Then followed a speedy flight home.

We had agreed that I would first land alone at Saarbrücken and if I found everything in order the others would follow. However, if I gave an emergency signal, then the others were to conduct a low-level attack on the airfield just as we had on trenches and tanks at the front. I had hardly landed when some pompous fellows rushed towards me with wild threatening gestures. I acted as though I had not seen them and continued to taxi so that they would have to run behind me. One of them bellowed: 'The machines are to remain here!'

I pointed with my finger at the aircraft of my Staffel roaring round the airfield and replied: 'Detain them if you can! By the way, I will decide who stays here and who doesn't.'

'The commandant will teach you what you have to do,' cried another with the repugnant face of a criminal. Before I could give this fellow an appropriate response, someone else wearing a red cravat said in an ingratiating manner: 'You will have to give in, Herr Leutnant. Times have changed.'

'Perhaps for you, but not for me!'

In the meantime some guy had clambered onto my machine and tried to switch off the engine. I tore his hand away and whilst doing so my leather jacket twisted and my *Pour le Mérite* became exposed. Even these fellows seemed to still have some respect for it.

Someone from the soldiers' council, recognisable by a stamped red armband, deigned to speak reasonably with me and consented that I should be allowed to decide which aircraft would remain in Saarbrücken and which would fly onwards. With that I gave the signal to land.

We were still standing together right in front of our aircraft as Red Guardsmen and civilians wearing red ribbons and ties stared at us with a mixture of hatred and contempt, when a second Staffel landed on the airfield. The first one who jumped out of his machine and rushed towards me was… Rudno! [Difficult – as mentioned earlier, Rudno had been taken prisoner on 26 May.]

We embraced one another. He too had received orders to deliver up his aircraft here. He cursed, raged, and threatened to shoot up the whole red mob, but in the end had to give in to the plight of our circumstances. Where else could we leave our machines? What else could we have done with them without any fuel? I decided that fourteen aircraft would remain and that their crew would travel home from here. Leutnant Fleischer and I were to fly to Mainz in my two aircraft – Mops and Lilly. Fleischer's home was in the vicinity of Mainz.

There followed a brief and difficult farewell. It was especially hard for me to say good-bye to Rudno and Strasser. I never saw either of them again. [Again, as mentioned earlier, Georg Strasser had become an instructor in May 1918.] Rudno, my dear Rudno, fell sick and died on the return trip to America and was lowered somewhere into the sea. Strasser, who could not give up on flying, first went to Fokker in Holland, and then became a pilot with the Junkers factory. He died in 1925 while testing a new machine. I recently found out that Höfig, my first teacher and a good friend, suffered a similar fate.

The bitter end

On 13 November Fleischer and I landed around 6 pm on the Big Sand near Mainz. We found the same picture as in Saarbrücken. Arrogant and insolent fellows were running around with revolvers and rifles and in spite of that could not secure any respect. We did not concern ourselves with them and stored our aircraft in one of the empty hangars. We still clung to the hope that not all was lost. Perhaps soon we would once more be able to fly our two machines against the enemy with a fresh Malaula. Unfortunately we did not take our parachutes along, as we did not want to be taken for thieves. On [our return next day] they had disappeared. The silk from parachutes was probably used to make shirts.

I issued Fleischer a railway ticket and accompanied him to the station. The red railway inspectors scornfully rejected the ticket at the gate. An officer's rank no longer meant anything to them. We had to go to the office of the commander. A man grabbed my arm and said: 'If you want something, kindly wait your turn.' At that point I lost my patience. If the commandant had not been a calm and reasonable person I would probably have been killed by the mob, but he immediately issued Fleischer a ticket. Only when Fleischer had departed did I go home.

The reunion with my mother was both tender and sad. Since I did not have a civilian coat and also had no money to buy one, I went out again the next day still in uniform. I was aware of the fact that it had become common practice to tear the shoulder tabs off officers and other ranks. At a tram stop stood two red soldiers who appeared to take a keen interest in me. I knew that I would immediately strike down anyone who dared to touch me, so in order to prevent an incident, I walked up to them and asked if they wanted something from me. They grinned and answered: 'No, Herr Leutnant.'

However, it soon became obvious that they were in fact up to something and this resulted in both of them being taken to the hospital some time later, which came about in the following fashion. I travelled to Wiesbaden and met up with some comrades at a concert in the spa hotel. For a couple of hours amidst the wonderful music we forgot all the misery, but as we went down the stairs – myself in uniform and the other two in civilian attire – the two guys I had met earlier were standing with a couple of sailors on the lowest step.

As he saw me coming, one of them shouted: 'Get rid of that thing!' He pointed at my *Pour le Mérite*. 'And tear off his shoulder tabs.' In the same instant an uppercut sent him flying onto the pavement. The second guy followed him in the same manner. The two sailors found it advisable to beat a hasty retreat. During the fourteen days I stayed in Mainz I was not bothered again. Perhaps word of the incident had spread. The only things these punks really respected was a solid fist.

* * *

Then the French came marching in, but I did not want to witness the event. I knew all too well that it would have had catastrophic results for me, as I would not have submitted to their orders. Deeply saddened at heart, I said farewell to my mother and to the city of Mainz. My sisters had married and were living in other towns. As I left the foot of the bridge over the Rhine on the right hand side, the left side was occupied by the French.

I travelled to Hannover, where my Staffel was being demobilised [at the base of FEA 5] and where I hoped to meet some of my comrades. Some soldiers still saluted while others dug their clenched fists into their pockets. During the journey I thought only of my hometown and my dear Rhineland that had now fallen under the yoke of a foreign power. According to newspaper reports, the entire region on the left bank of the Rhine, from the Wesel down to the Swiss border, was occupied by the French within a few hours. No one seemed to get worked up over it.

'Well, what of it?' I heard one worker in my compartment say. 'It's all the same. The main thing is that we all have something to eat now.' Unfortunately, that is what a lot of people thought. What I understood last of all was the fact that German men who had fought together for years against a numerically superior foe were now fighting and killing each other. A lot of officers who resisted having the tabs ripped off their [uniform] shoulders were simply gunned down by the red rabble.

Late in the evening I arrived in Hannover and took a room in a hotel. The whole night I brooded over what should become of me. I had learned two trades thoroughly: roofing and fighting a war. Perhaps in Mainz I could have returned to some of my old customers. I did not have enough money to settle down in a strange town as a master roofer. Quite frankly, I was not interested in hiring myself out as a journeyman. My wounds would not have prevented me from doing so. Judging from outward appearances, one could not tell how battered my body was. I was now twenty-three years old and try as I might I could not determine what I should do.

The next morning I went to the local barracks. I wanted to say farewell to my faithful troops. My men received me with a ‘Malaula’ and welcomed me with great warmth as though I had just returned to them at the front after being wounded. They displayed the same smart bearing as ever. I remained with them until lunchtime and they shared their meal with me.

Only then did I notice that there were other soldiers sitting around who did not belong to my Staffel. It was immediately noticeable because of their behaviour. They deliberately addressed me in an all too familiar fashion. This did not escape the notice of my men and suddenly Unteroffizier Hennicke – the same man who had approached me eight weeks previously due to the formation of a soldiers’ council – gave the command.

A cry of Malaula rang out and in the general brawl which broke out the outsiders were tossed out the door one after another. Jasta 17 remained victorious but soon it too was dispersed. I had to take leave of my men that very evening. There was nothing more for me to do here and my presence merely endangered the future of my comrades. There had been threats uttered to do away with me and to exterminate ‘the whole reactionary mob’.

On this day I heard for the last time as a soldier the battle cry of my Staffel, but in the life which now began, Malaula was often a signal for me in bitter times to pull myself together and take up the fight.

Malaula!

The End

Après La Guerre

By Norman Franks

Julius Buckler did not indeed return to his former profession of roofer. It is not difficult to understand that as a successful fighter ace and holder of his country's highest decorations, and being a commissioned officer, the title of roofer, or even master roofer, would not have sat easily upon his young shoulders.

At some stage he was demobilised from the army and found work in the motor-car industry, becoming a motor vehicle specialist. However, he was far from done with aviation and in 1925 he was a flight instructor at the DVS (Deutsche Verkehrsfliegerschule – civil aviation flight school) at Staaken, under Alfred Keller. At one stage here he organised aerobatic flights on a special Flugtag – or Day of Flight.

In December 1928 we find him as a director of Kopp and Co, a road construction firm in Berlin, which in turn led to work in the asphalt business, making airfield runways.

With the unrest in Germany at the start of the 1930s, and the later rise of Hitler's Nazi party, Buckler joined the SA – Fliegersturm. This, later called the SS-Fliegersturm, became a flying unit of the general SS. Formed in Munich in November 1931, it was later absorbed by the DLV – Deutscher Luftsportverband – German Aerial Sport Association, in September 1933. That same year Buckler received a new pilot's licence and the following year became a DLV captain.

By 1937 he was a NSFK (National Socialist Flying Corps) unit leader and began sport flying which also entailed flights across Germany as well as entertaining crowds at flying displays. One such *Deutschlandflug* – flight across Germany competition – took place between 20 and 27 June 1937 in a Focke-Wulf 44, with Buckler coming home in thirty-seventh place. However, the next year, between 22 and 29 June, he came tenth, again in a FW44, flying for Unit P9 NSFK, Gruppe 4/26 Berlin.

With the coming of World War Two he became a special duties officer at the Jagdfliegerschule (Fighter Pilot School) at Werneuchen and in May 1943 was again at Staaken, in the commander's office, as an instructor. At the beginning of 1944 he was Headquarters Commander, Airfield Command, 42/III, and after the war was once again involved in road construction, with the Asphalt & Strassenbau, GmbH.

Ten years after the end of WW2 Buckler once again renewed his pilot's licence, this time being tested with Peter Schulte in Bonn. That October he was the founder of the Godesberg Sport Flying Club, and was also its first chairman. Over the next few years he once again participated in the *Deutschlandflug*, 1956, 1957 and 1958, and in 1959 he took part in the *Europaflug* – flight across Europe. His last flight came on 13 February 1960, in his Tiger Moth, which he had named 'Malaula'.

He married Erica, Baroness von Braun (1908-1986) and had a son Michael. Julius Buckler died at Bad Godesberg, just south of Bonn, on 23 May 1960, aged sixty-six, and is buried in the Central Cemetery, Field XII, No.177/178.

Appendix A

Julius Buckler's Combat Claims and Victories

1916					
1	17 Dec	Caudron	Fort Douaumont, Verdun	1620	Esc C74?
1917					
–	11 Feb	Balloon?	Unconfirmed		
2	14 Feb	Caudron	W of Facq Wood	–	–
3	15 Feb	Caudron	Pont-à-Mousson	–	EscB107?
–	21 Mar	Nieuport XVII	Unconfirmed		
4	15 Apr	Spad VII (No.117)	Prouvais	am	Esc Spa 3
5	16 Apr	Nieuport	Berry-au-Bac		
6	26 Apr	Balloon	Bois de Genicourt	0920	26 Cié
–	6 May	Spad VII	Unconfirmed Pont-à-Vert	Esc N69?	
7	12 May	Nieuport XXIV (3674)	La Malmaison	1840	Esc N75
8	11 Jul	Sop Triplane (N5476)	SE Zillebeke	0850	10 Naval
9	13 Jul	FE2d	Stuivenkenskerke	1320	
10	14 Jul	M'syde G102 (A6266)	Leffinghe	1750	27 Sqn
11	17 Jul	Sopwith Pup (B1713)	S of Keyem	0730	54 Sqn
12	9 Aug	Sop Camel (B3870)	SE of Nieuport	0745	9 Naval
13	11 Aug	RE8 (A4645)	W of Spermalie	1415	52 Sqn
14	29 Sep	AWFK8 (B277)	Fleurbaix	1805	10 Sqn
15	30 Sep	Sopwith Camel (B2398)	SW Lens-Arras	1155	70 Sqn

1917					
16	11 Oct	RE8 (A4330)	Roclincourt	0945	5 Sqn
17	11 Oct	Sopwith Camel (B6314)	Armentières	1725	28 Sqn
18	17 Oct	BF2b (A7209)	E of Roucourt	1120	11 Sqn
19	24 Oct	RE8 (B5896)	S of Méricourt	1620	16 Sqn
20	28 Oct	RE8 (A4426)	N of Mont St Eloi	1705	16 Sqn
21	29 Oct	Balloon	Neuville	0914	20-1-1
22	29 Oct	Nieuport XXVII (B3630)	E of Houthem	1210	1 Sqn
23	31 Oct	AWFK8 (B319)	N of La Bassée	1130	10 Sqn
24	31 Oct	Balloon	Laventie	1620	42-4-1
25	12 Nov	RE8	Oostkerke	1545	6 Sqn
26	15 Nov	RE8 (A4652)	Ypres	0845	21 Sqn
27	18 Nov	Balloon	Ypres	0910	36-17-2
28	18 Nov	Balloon	Dickebusch	0925	
29	18 Nov	RE8 (A3669)	Bixschoote	1415	9 Sqn
30	29 Nov	Balloon	Bapaume	1205	31-18-3
1918					
31	16 Apr	Bréguet XIV	Vaux, Belgium	1635	Sal 225
32	21 Apr	Bréguet XIV	Mareuil	1230	
33	3 May	Balloon	Tricot	2100	67 Cié
34	5 Oct	Salmson 2A2		1715	Sal 27
35	24 Oct	Bréguet XIV	Méry		Br 257?
36	30 Oct	EA			
–	8 Nov	RE8	Unconfirmed		

Appendix B

Buckler's Combat Successes

By Norman Franks

In his memoirs, Buckler unfortunately describes only a few victories in any sort of detail, while many others receive no mention at all. This appendix will help fill in some of the blanks and provide the reader with a fuller understanding of the wartime career of this leading German fighter ace.

Buckler does mention some of his early claims, but only writes about a couple after May 1917, and those few prior to his major wounding at the end of November. His eighth victory was over a Sopwith Triplane of the Royal Naval Air Service on 11 July. The action was fought around 08.50 hours south-east of Zillebeke during a fight with several Triplanes. There is no firm indication on which side of the lines it fell but as only one Triplane is recorded as lost, a 10 Naval Squadron machine, with its pilot taken prisoner during the evening, one assumes Buckler's victim got down on the Allied side, but was still credited to him.

On the morning of the 11th, 1 Naval Squadron had nine Triplanes out on an Offensive Patrol between 07.55 and 10.00 hours. They encountered six enemy fighters but these all dived away on spotting the Sopwiths although one was engaged indecisively by Flight Sub-lieutenant H V Rowley flying N5476. Herbert Victor Rowley came from Crich, in Derbyshire and had joined the RNAS in April 1916. He arrived at 1 Squadron in February 1917 and gained his first victory in April. He obviously made no claim for his action on 11 July although before that month was out he had claimed two more kills. With Triplanes and later Camels, Rowley achieved nine victories by April 1918. He saw no further operational service but during WW2 he served in the Far East with the RAF rising to the rank or air commodore. References to FSL C R Pegler of 10 Naval being Buckler's victim are incorrect as he fell on 12 July, a victim of Jasta 24s. Obviously Buckler had some indication that he had downed the Triplane but it was probably no more than Rowley diving headlong across the lines, perhaps low on fuel or feeling that his German antagonist was 'a bit good' and deciding that discretion was the better part of valour!

This shows the fallibility of claims, and that, despite what some historians claim, Allied aircraft that went down inside their own lines were often claimed as victories, and even credited as such, where there is no evidence that the aircraft was even hit. It all depended on who saw what and who believed whom. Of course, as mentioned earlier, there was always the chance, sometimes a good chance, that the Allied airman or airmen did in fact fall, were killed, or landed seriously or mortally wounded, with their aircraft either shelled to fragments or un-retrievable. But there are more than enough instances of aircraft claimed as shot down, like Buckler's eighth, that returned virtually undamaged and with the pilot both intact and unlikely to be even slightly aware that he had been credited as a 'victory'.

Victory number nine, which Buckler claimed on 13 July, is similarly a question mark. In this case we do know that he reported that the British machine – an FE2d – went down inside Allied lines, but there are no reports of any FE2 'pushers' lost this day. Buckler timed the victory at 13.20 over Stuivenkenskerke – right on the lines, north of Dixmude – but who the crew was or what their story might be remains unknown.

The 'BE2' claim on the 14th has been explained earlier – the Martinsyde G100 of 27 Squadron, whose pilot jumped from his burning machine. Likewise the Sopwith Pup Buckler shot down on the 17th has been referred to, especially by the report of the captured pilot, Second Lieutenant C T Felton.

His next claim, on 9 August, although going down on the Allied side, can be identified. Buckler was in a fight south-east of Nieuport early that morning and at 07.45 reported the downing of a Sopwith Camel (B3870). This was a machine of 9 Naval Squadron whose pilot, Flight Sub-lieutenant M G Woodhouse, died. 9 Naval were on an Offensive Patrol and ran into Jasta 17. Buckler's machine-gun bullets set the Camel on fire, sending the eighteen-year-old Mosley Gordon Woodhouse to his death. The youngster came from Little Baddow, Essex, born on 26 October 1898, and he had joined the RNAS in 1916, going to 9 Naval on 11 June 1917, so he had been a few days short of two months with this unit.

Buckler's next success, on 29 September, by which time Jasta 17 had moved south to the Lille area, is a trifle confusing. Jasta records indicate a 'Sopwith', while another reference says it was a DH5. It should be mentioned here that German pilots were no great shakes at identifying opponents, or at least, did not feel it sufficiently important to do so, as long as the hostile machine carried British or French roundels on their wings. With the variation of aircraft they could encounter, several of them being a product of the Sopwith Company, quite often a pilot would merely refer to the aircraft he had engaged as a 'Sopwith' especially if it was a fighter such as a Pup, Camel, Triplane, SE5, DH5, even a Spad, in British service. Also, any new types to the front, where a name was totally unknown, also could be referred to as simply a Sopwith.

There are only three recorded losses on this day: a Bristol Fighter of 48 Squadron in the early afternoon, so that's out; an FE2b night bomber, in the early evening, so no joy there; and an AWFK8 from 10 Squadron at 18.00 hours. The latter seems favourite. 10 Squadron's AWFK8 – known affectionately as a 'Big-Ack' (the 'Ack' referring to the A of Armstrong in the phonetic code) – B277 was on an artillery observation mission near Richebourg and was seen to be engaged by five hostile scouts and forced to land west of the lines – Allied territory. Buckler claimed his victim went down at Fleurbaix, south-west of Armentières.

Both British crew members were wounded in the action, but the pilot, Lieutenant E L Burrell, managed to get his stricken machine down, although his observer, Second Lieutenant E A Barnard, died. Burrell, from Alton, Hampshire had joined the RFC in May 1917 and once trained as a pilot was sent to France and joined 10 Squadron on 29 July. He never fully recovered from his injuries and had to relinquish his commission in July 1918 due to ill-health. He died in January 1949.

Edward Arnold Barnard, from Cheltenham, Gloucester was twenty-one years of age. He had previously served in the Royal Naval Division, and then the Royal Field Artillery as a second lieutenant. Men from the artillery often volunteered for artillery-observation work, and seconded to the RFC due to their expertise in registering the fall of shot, and he had done so in June. He is buried at Chocques, France.

The following day Buckler shot down another Sopwith Camel. It has been suggested it came from 70 Squadron (B2398), but Buckler having claimed his victim south-west of Lens at 11.55 puts this in doubt. 70 Squadron had flown out on an Offensive Patrol at 11.00 and met a number of Albatros Scouts south-east of the well-known landmark – Houthulst Forest, south of Dixmude. They lost one machine, piloted by Lieutenant C Dalkeith-Scott, who was killed. A native of Vancouver, British Columbia, but with connections in Bath, England, Charles Dalkeith-Scott had been with the 16th Canadian Infantry and then the 5th Battalion, 1st Ontario Regiment. Transferring to the RFC in June 1917, he arrived at 70 Squadron on 15 September, and had lasted just two weeks. Aged twenty-eight, his grave was never found and his name is amongst the missing airmen recorded on the Arras Air Force Memorial. However, Houthulst Forest must be too far north to be considered as Buckler's opponent, it being in the area where he and Jasta 17 had been operating till 28 August. Now they were much further south, on the Lille front.

There are no other Camel losses this day, and two Sopwith Pups shot down from 66 Squadron over Gheluwe, near Menin, around mid-day, were the victims of Jasta 18, and in any event, still well south of Houthulst and north-east of Lens. There is no indication of which side of the lines Buckler saw his victim go down, but it must be assumed it was into the British side, so again we are left with a question mark.

Buckler's next claim was made on 11 October, or to be exact, there were two claims. The first was an RE8 observation machine at 09.45 that he despatched over Roclincourt. This appears to be an aircraft from 5 Squadron on an artillery patrol. From the British side it was observed to be engaged by three German fighters and forced to land south of Farbus, both places being north of Arras. Both crew members were mortally wounded in the encounter, the pilot, Lieutenant F C E Clarke dying later this day, his observer, Lieutenant P Mighell only surviving till the next day. Coming down on the British side of the lines, both men were buried at Duisans Military Cemetery, at Etrum.

Francis Charles Erlin Clarke was twenty-one and came from Larkhill, Worcester. After service with the 5th Warwickshire Regiment he moved to the RFC in March 1917. He was posted to his squadron on 26 September, so had survived for just two weeks. Philip Mighell, whose parents had a farm at Beddington, Surrey, was twenty-four years old and had joined the RFC in August 1917 from the East Surrey Regiment, and sent to 5 Squadron on 2 October. He died ten days later.

Later on the 11th, Buckler engaged and shot down another Camel (B6314) near Armentières, at 17.25. This time there is no doubt about the identity, as it came down in German lines and the pilot was captured. This was Second Lieutenant W H Winter of 28 Squadron. The squadron was new to France, having arrived on 8 October and landing at St Omer, where the majority of squadrons, aircraft, and pilots landed prior to moving to or being posted to airfields on the British front. 28 Squadron moved on from here two days later to Droglandt, between Cassel and Poperinghe, west of Ypres. Operational within a day or so, the squadron would be ordered to do little else except line patrols until they became familiar with the landscape and landmarks. On the 11th they were flying a practise formation flight with no hostile intent, taking off at 15.05 hours that afternoon. Obviously Winter felt confident and was perhaps what might later be styled as a 'press-on' type, for he strayed east of the front lines and fell victim to Buckler. Upon his return from prison camp at the end of the war, Bill Winter recorded:

> 'I was in formation when main [fuel] tank failed. I left formation, but owing to not knowing line went too far south and went over enemy lines; met enemy machine and in the encounter went well over the lines. Coming back at low altitude, 6,000 feet, was hit by AA guns from Lille. Not wounded.'

William Hedley Winter came from Herne Hill, SE London, and was on what he described as a 'viewing the lines' flight. Each prisoner of war who returned after the war had to write a report on how he was taken captive. These almost innocuous reports may well have been daunting to returning airmen, not knowing how their capture would be reviewed or if any repercussions would ensue. Of course, nothing untoward happened and all received a printed letter from the King some time later, exonerating them from any blame. Nevertheless, faced with this form within hours of landing back in England, usually by ship, there must have been a number of thoughts going through these men's minds.

Most of the comments made by these returning men were quite short and to the point, while others sometimes felt a longer tale of woe was necessary. Almost all make interesting reading, and it is strange that there was a space on the form for them to insert the serial number of their aircraft in which they were lost. Even more surprising is the fact that most could remember it and wrote it down! There are some that are more interesting than others, especially those whose aircraft might, through no fault of the pilot, be captured intact, but in their report they say that they had succeeded in burning the said machine. Post-war photographic evidence has turned up several pictures among German pilots where the new prisoner is standing next to not only the victor in the combat, but the aircraft behind them – far from burnt. These men were still only little more than boys and young men so they can be forgiven for trying to cover up something they might prefer to forget, and it is also natural for them to try and put themselves into as good a light as possible. So Winter says his petrol tank failed and he got lost, it might well be true, but the squadron had been watching and they certainly felt he had strayed, pure and simple. Had he come home with a kill he would have been quite a hero in everyone's eyes, but instead, a German fighter ace got him. That again might be a good enough reason to report being hit by AA fire, rather than be bested by an enemy pilot. It was, however, 28 Squadron's first loss in France. In any event, Buckler achieved his seventeenth victory and his first two-in-one-day.

Six days later, on 17 October, Buckler scored again, this time a Bristol Fighter (A7209) of 11 Squadron. This aircraft, despite its poor beginnings in April 1917 due to the incorrect tactics being employed, had by this time turned into a formidable two-seater fighter, with the pilot having a fixed forward-firing machine gun and his observer having a clear view of fire in a 180 degree arc with the rear one, sometimes two, Lewis guns. It was almost like a mini-Jasta tactic, where the pilot could concentrate on his attack knowing that his back was covered by his observer/gunner. The BF2b was used as a fighter, a fighter-bomber, an escort fighter and, as on this day, a photographic machine.

Jasta 17 engaged the Bristols over the Sensée Canal at 10 o'clock British time, and A7209 was hit and seen to dive vertically. Its pilot, Second Lieutenant S E Stanley had been mortally wounded, and was unconscious. His observer, Second Lieutenant E L Fosse managed to get them down, the machine having a spare control column for use in just such emergencies. Buckler reported his victim had come down east of Récourt, some ten kilometres south of Douai.

Sidney Edger Stanley, who was nineteen years old, and had enlisted from a Clapham Common, SW London address, was born on 10 June 1898. His parents, George and Ellen, lived at Ashford, Middlesex. Commissioned into the General List, he had joined the RFC in March 1917, trained as a pilot, then was sent to 11 Squadron on 5 September, a scant six weeks earlier. He is buried at London Cemetery, Neuville-Vitesse, south of Arras, France.

Edger Lewis Fosse, in the back cockpit, had also been wounded, but survived as a prisoner. He too made a report upon his return to England in May 1918, the month in which he was repatriated:

> 'During a reconnaissance over enemy territory, owing to engine trouble [we] became detached from the patrol. Attacked by three enemy planes. I received a bullet in the chest, [but] I managed to [re]gain control and brought machine to earth, crashed badly, fracturing my arm in doing so. Lieutenant Stanley received a burst of bullets in the abdomen and died in the air.'

Buckler's next two victories were both RE8s and both from 16 Squadron. The first he shot down on 24 October (B5896), whilst the crew were busy with artillery observation duty south of Méricourt on the south-east outskirts of Lens, in mid-afternoon. Both pilot and observer perished, the RE8 going down in flames. The RE8 was often referred to as 'the flying coffin'. Buckler's claim was timed at 16.20.

Lieutenant Augustus Orlando Balaam – the pilot – came from Goodmayes, Essex. He was twenty-five years old and married. After serving with the 5th Battalion of the Suffolk Regiment, he transferred to the RFC in May 1917, and joined 16 Squadron on 4 August. He is buried in Aubigny Communal Cemetery.

His observer, Lieutenant Donald St Patrick Prince-Smith, had been seconded to the RFC from the Royal Dublin Fusiliers. He came from Kilcool, County Wicklow, Eire and also lies in Aubigny Cemetery.

The other RE8 (A4426) fell to Buckler four days later, on the 28th, north of Mont St Eloi, to the south-west of Lens. Again both men were killed, going down shortly after 5 pm, and crashing at Carency, which is north of Mont St Eloi, and burning. They had taken off at 15.10 for an artillery observation sortie to Lens. Mont St Eloi was a well-known landmark for pilots on this section of the front, an abandoned monastery which had two ruined towers. British pilots on nearby airfields used to chance their arms by flying through them! Having fallen inside British lines it became apparent that the observer had fired at least two drums from his Lewis gun before being hit in the head, and killed instantly. The unfortunate pilot took longer to die for it seems that a severed wire had wrapped itself about his neck as the machine went down and he was slowly strangled to death. He had managed to get down to 200 feet before the RE8 suddenly plummeted to the ground.

The RE8 pilot had been Lieutenant Edward Hugh Keir from Lancaster, aged twenty. He was born in Huddersfield and became a second lieutenant in December 1914 from the Lancaster Royal Grammar School's OTC. He joined the Royal Lancashire Regiment (3rd KORLR) from where he moved to the RFC in March 1917. Becoming a pilot he was sent to 16 Squadron on 4 August. He is also buried in Aubigny Cemetery.

Captain Cyril Walter Carleton Wasey, his observer, came from Marlborough, Wiltshire, born in 1893. Educated at Eton, 1907-11, he went to Sandhurst and then became a second lieutenant with the Royal Warwickshire Regiment in March 1913. He went to France with the Warwicks in August 1914 and his gallantry in action brought him the French *Croix de Guerre*, followed by his being made a *Chevalier de la Légion d'Honneur*, as well as being Mentioned in Despatches. He had transferred to the RFC during the summer of 1917, joining 16 Squadron in September. The award of the Military Cross came next, but this was gazetted after his death, on 1 January 1918. Wasey is also buried in Aubigny Cemetery.

The day following this victory, Buckler shot down a balloon at Neuville at 09.14. Its unit was the 20th Section, 1st Balloon Company, 1st Balloon Wing, and its two observers both survived the attack and their parachute jumps – Captain J L Fry and Lieutenant J M O'Donnell. The report from the 20th Section recorded that the balloon (FM 118/D) had gone up early that morning but between 08.00 and 08.20 no artillery fire could be directed due to ground haze, and then came the attack and the balloon fell in flames.

Fry had won the Military Cross with the Royal Field Artillery, and he had arrived in France in December 1914. James Henry O'Connell had celebrated his thirty-first birthday ten days previously. A married man from Putney, SW London, he had been a stockbroker at the London Stock Exchange between 1902 and 1914. He had been an officer with the 8th Battalion of the Royal West Surrey Regiment, before transferring to the balloon service in October 1916, going to France in December to join the 8th Balloon Section and later the 1st Balloon Company as balloon commander in October 1917. Surviving the encounter with Buckler, he went on to be Mentioned in Despatches twice in 1918 (May and June) and finally received the Distinguished Flying Cross, which was gazetted on 2 November. The citation read:

> *This officer has been ballooning continuously for two years, and his flying time amounts to about 600 hours. On several occasions his balloon has been subjected to severe shell fire, but he has invariably carried on his observation work, calm and collected, thereby setting a fine example to other*

observers, notably on a recent occasion when his balloon, under heavy fire from a long-range gun, was eventually so badly hit that it commenced to fall. Lieutenant O'Connell continued to give observations until he was forced to descend in a parachute.

Thus James O'Connell made at least two parachute jumps. He survived the war and left the RAF in April 1919.

Almost three hours later Buckler shot down a Nieuport XXVII of 1 Squadron (B3630), east of Houthem. The pilot was not as lucky as the balloon crew had been, Second Lieutenant A W MacLaughlin being killed. Alexander Wilson MacLaughlin was twenty-three, the son of the Reverend David and Mrs Annie MacLaughlin of Druminnis Manse, County Armagh. He has no known grave but his name is on the RAF Memorial at Arras. He had been on an Offensive Patrol which was engaged with seven hostile aircraft and was seen to dive with these on his tail at 11.35 (British time).

On 30 October the Battle of Passchendaele began. Whether Buckler was involved he does not say, but he was in action on the 31st claiming his third double on one day. First was another 10 Squadron AWFK8 (B319) which fell in the front line area north of La Bassée at 11.30. Lieutenants W Davidson and W Crowther were on a photo-op, which began at 09.30, and they were seen to be attacked at 10.40 and go down on fire. The flames were extinguished at 1,500 feet but the Big-Ack crashed and was destroyed.

William Davidson came from Forest Gate, Essex, and was twenty-nine years old. He had joined the RFC in September 1916, and had been posted to 10 Squadron in May 1917. His body was never found so his name appears on the Arras Memorial. William Crowther was a Canadian, from Welland, Ontario. He was with the 8th Reserve Battalion, 2nd Ontario Regiment, Canadian Infantry, but moved to the RFC in March 1917, joining 10 Squadron in July. For reasons we need not go into here, he was severely reprimanded by a court martial in September, but continued to fly. He was twenty-one years old and his name is also on the Arras Memorial to the missing.

Buckler scored again in the afternoon, another balloon, this one at Laventie, at 16.20, from the 42nd Section, 4th Company, 1st Wing. The records of the 42nd Section tell us that this was the second ascent this day by Major J R Bedwell. The first was at 11.53, but finding the visibility poor he came down again at 12.01. At 13.33 he tried again, in company with 2nd Air Mechanic Stanley, and this time with better weather they got to 2,900 feet in their FM 91/D. At 15.18 they were attacked and set on fire by a German fighter and both men took to their parachutes. Buckler timed his attack at 16.20 (German time).

James Robert Bedwell was born on 11 January 1888, so was twenty-nine when he 'met' Julius Buckler. A married man from Stroud Green, London N4, he had been a clerk at the London Stock Exchange in the last year of peace. An officer with the Royal Garrison Artillery, Territorial Force, he went to France in January 1917 to join the 20th KBS, and in May went to the 2nd Balloon Company and later still the 4th Balloon Company. He was Mentioned in Despatches and rose to colonel. He died in March 1949.

Buckler's twenty-fifth victory came on 12 November, at 15.45, and was yet another RE8, this one from 6 Squadron, although being another machine that was seen to go down into the British lines, was 'apparently' deemed as a loss by German observers. However, there is no loss recorded, although the observer in the machine, 2nd Air Mechanic G Wyatt, acting as air gunner, had been wounded in the combat. He and his pilot (not known) were flying a photo-op when engaged by enemy fighters near Oostkerke at 14.45 (British time)

Three days later – the 15th – another RE8 (A4652) was claimed, this one from 21 Squadron, on an artillery observation mission near Ypres. People on the ground within the salient saw the two-seater attacked by fighters and go down, but it came to earth inside British lines with a mortally wounded pilot at the controls. It was not a good landing and the observer was fatally injured in the crash.

The wounded pilot was George John Bakewell, from Warwick. He was twenty-seven and left a wife, Elsie Lillian. Initially with the Warwick Yeomanry, he became an officer with the 6th Battalion of the Border Regiment and had joined the RFC in May 1917. He died the next day, and is buried in Dozinghem Military Cemetery, Belgium.

William Augustus Barnett hailed from Brixton, South London and had been commissioned into the RFC via the General List in July 1917. He had joined 21 Squadron on 21 July, so had survived nearly four months of active duty. He is buried in Ypres, Duhallow ADS, Belgium.

* * *

The two balloons and the RE8 Buckler shot down on 18 November have already been mentioned by him in an earlier chapter. The RE8 of 9 Squadron had been crewed by Second Lieutenants W J H Courtis and E T Taylor. They had been on an artillery observation sortie that began at 10.20 am, and came down near Langemarck on the Allied side, and while both men scrambled away unharmed, their machine – A3669 – was shelled. Buckler timed this victory at 14.15 (German time) near Bixschoote, which is only a few kilometres from Langemarck, where today there is a large German cemetery.

The balloon Buckler shot down on 29 November 1917 over Bapaume just after mid-day, 31st Section, 18th Company, 3rd Wing, was crewed by Lieutenants Weekes and Gordon (or Goodwin). The only name that I have found that might correspond with the first-named is that of Owen Henry Weekes, from Monkstown, County Dublin, who was born in May 1880. A former clerk with the Guinness Brewing Company in Dublin between 1910-15, he became a balloon officer in April 1916 and by January 1917 he was with 1 KBS. In December 1917 he was with the 7th Balloon Wing.

* * *

These victories up to 29 November brought Buckler's score of confirmed successes to thirty. High victory scores for fighter pilots in the German Air Service generally brought forth the coveted *Orden Pour le Mérite*. In the early days as fighter pilots began to score victories, eight seemed the appropriate total to become eligible for this high decoration, and the first two pilots to be awarded this medal, known as the 'Blue Max,' were Oswald Boelcke and Max Immelmann. They both received the accolade on the same date, 12 January 1916. It was the date, coincidentally that both Boelcke and Immelmann scored their eighth victories, both men flying with FA62 in Fokker Eindecker fighters.

The next air fighter to be so honoured was Hans-Joachim Buddecke, on 14 April 1916. It has now been established that officially he had only had seven victories confirmed, but in addition he had six others unconfirmed and another lost to arbitration between him and another pilot. He was also the first to receive the Blue Max on another front. His first two had been scored whilst with FA23 in France, but then he had moved to Turkey (with the Gallipoli battles raging) flying with FA6. His aeroplanes were the Fokker Eindecker and the Halberstadt DII and DV biplanes.

Following Buddecke were two more Western Front Eindecker pilots, Kurt Wintgens on 1 July, following his eighth victory on 30 June, and Max von Mulzer on 8 July, the date of his eighth victory in France. Before 1916 ended, eight more fighter pilots had been decorated with the *Pour le Mérite*, all having achieved the magic eight victories. However, it now seemed to the High Command that achieving eight kills was beginning to be a good deal easier than it had earlier in the year and suddenly they 'changed the goalposts', doubling the required total to sixteen.

The first one to be affected by the change was none other than Manfred von Richthofen. It is true to say that these pilots were all influenced to some degree by the awards and honours that could be won, and no doubt it added an extra impetus to bring down opponents in air fights. Von Richthofen had achieved his eight victories on 9 November, but by the time his name was submitted for consideration for the Blue Max, the number had been changed. One can imagine he was a trifle put out by this new benchmark. By the end of 1916 he had scored fifteen – just one short of the required total, and he would not be human if he didn't wonder if the total might yet be changed again. So near and yet so far?

In fact, so keen was he to get to sixteen, that his fifteenth was no victory at all. He fought an action with some DH2 pushers of 29 Squadron and had sent one spinning down over British territory, the result – he thought – of his fire. However, we now know that the British pilot was Sergeant James McCudden, later holder of the VC DSO and MC, who would go on to achieve over fifty victories before his tragic death in a flying accident in July 1918. True, von Richthofen had seen the DH2 spin down from 10,000 to 1,000 metres, but McCudden had had his gun jammed, and knew there was no future in fighting without it, so kicked his machine into a spin to get down and away. Then, at low level he righted his craft and headed for home.

No doubt von Richthofen was keen to get this victory under his belt and the adjutant of Jasta 2 would have been telephoning observers in the trenches to see if they had observed a *Gitterrumpf* going down over Ficheux in the late afternoon. They would have replied that they did, but in point of fact it only looked as if it might have crashed. That's all it took and number fifteen was soon confirmed. Number sixteen came on 4 January, and eight days later he received the Blue Max. The Baron was given command of Jasta 11 on the 10th, just prior to the award being approved.

Not long afterwards the victory score required rose again, this time to twenty. The first recipient of the Blue Max then was Werner Voss on 8 April 1917, by which time the young fighter pilot who had flown with von Richthofen in Jasta 2, had a score of twenty-four. Then Otto Bernert of Jasta 4 and Jasta 2, got his on 24 April, the day he downed no less than five British machines in one twenty-minute action, to bring his total also to twenty-four. A feat which was never beaten in WW1.

Several more pilots achieved the required number of kills, especially during and following the tremendous losses inflicted on the RFC by the new German Jastas during April 1917 or, Bloody April as it became known.

By the end of 1917 the figure seems unclear. Certainly no fewer than twenty victories were needed, but by the time the award was approved by the Kaiser, scores had often risen. In the case of Buckler, his score had risen to thirty by the time he received the high honour, which no doubt was due in part to his recent NCO status. He also missed out on the normal intermediate decoration that usually precedes the Blue Max, the *Knight's Cross with Swords of the Royal Hohenzollern House Order*.

One decoration that Buckler would not have minded missing, was the Wound Badge in Gold, which signified five or more woundings. In German soldiers' parlance, as Neal O'Connor once noted, Buckler was a real *Kugelfänger* – 'bullet catcher'.

He had been wounded during his army service, in September 1914 during the fighting at the Marne. Whilst flying he was wounded in May 1917, then lightly on 17 July, again on 12 August and severely on 30 November – and he hadn't finished yet!

Index of Personalities